Dear Rhonda,

Best of luck in all
things.

From all of us

A TREASURY OF THE GREAT CHILDREN'S BOOK ILLUSTRATORS

A TREASURY OF THE GREAT CHILDREN'S BOOK ILLUSTRATORS

Susan E. Meyer

Abradale Press

Harry N. Abrams, Inc., Publishers

New York

TO THE MEMORY OF MY FATHER

ERNEST L. MEYER

PAGE 1: From *Through the Looking Glass*, illustrated by
John Tenniel. PAGE 2: From *The Sleeping Beauty and Other Fairy
Tales*, illustrated by Edmund Dulac. TITLE PAGE:
From "The Owl and the Pussycat" by Edward Lear. ABOVE:
From *East of the Sun and West of the Moon*, illustrated
by Kay Nielsen.

Editor: Edith M. Pavese
Designer: Patrick Cunningham
Rights and Reproductions: Eric Himmel

Library of Congress Cataloging-in-Publication Data

Meyer, Susan E.
A treasury of the great children's book illustrators.

Bibliography: p. 267
Includes index.
1. Illustrated books, Children's—Themes, motives.
2. Illustrators—Biography.   I. Title.
[NC965.M49   1987]   741.64′2′0922   [B]   87-1334
ISBN 0-8109-8081-9

Contents

From "The Three Princesses in the Blue Mountain"
in *East of the Sun and West of the Moon*, illustrated by Kay Nielsen.

Preface

From *The Language of Flowers*
by Kate Greenaway.

IT MAY SEEM PRESUMPTUOUS to have dared a book bearing the imposing title, "great children's book illustrators." What, after all, defines a "*great* illustrator," let alone "a great illustrator of *children's books*?"

By qualifying the title, therefore, I confess to my own bias on the subject. "Great" is primarily subjective. I could, of course, define my criteria for "great" by objectively pointing out the significance of each artist selected, but my interest in the subject has never been dispassionate, so I prefer to confirm my bias rather than defend it. Essentially, these illustrators are my favorites, and they have been since childhood. If children were the arbiters, rather than scholars of children's literature, I suspect their choice would not be too different from my own. But even children would be compelled to limit their selection, because every story must have—as they all know—a beginning, middle, and end.

So I have limited the selection of illustrators to a manageable number in an attempt to avoid the frustrations of superficiality inherent in a "comprehensive" anthology. By selecting only thirteen illustrators, each of whom represents some aspect of the total picture, I was able to focus at some length on more than a detailing of their lives and contributions. In so doing, I attempted to connect my subjects to a larger phenomenon, and also to probe some of the driving forces that propelled each to his or her calling.

As we shall see, even the term "children's book illustrator" is misleading. Although I have selected to reproduce here only pictures for children, these were by no means the *only* kinds of pictures these artists created. Many illustrators were even more active in providing pictures for magazines read by adults—although the artists hardly seemed to change hats when they happened to direct their images to children—and many went on to other activities entirely. I have, however, limited this study only to the work they did for children's books, devoting little attention to other aspects of their full careers.

I have also selected what may be regarded as the *classic* illustrators and primarily, though not exclusively, to those who worked until World War One, leaving the subject of living, contemporary children's illustration to a whole body of specialists who rarely seem to agree on anything. Finally, I've limited my selection to illustrators of the English language only, a subject so vast in itself that even this restriction hardly seems narrow.

But it would be sheer nonsense for me to suggest that these are the *only* great classic illustrators of the English language. In fact, for every individual included in this volume, I have certainly omitted a good half-dozen others whose presence might have been equal in stature to those presented here. But I like to think that the illustrators represented here offer something universal that applies to the others who may be absent. Each displays the triumph of the imagination, the blend of reality and magic that transforms the written word into something seen and experienced. These are the wizards of the brush whose images continue to beguile children today as they did years ago. These illustrators all knew something that children know, and sharing this secret is their ultimate gift.

Susan E. Meyer
New York City, 1983

Introduction

The White Rabbit from *Alice's Adventures in Wonderland*, illustrated by John Tenniel.

THE ILLUSTRATORS PRESENTED here were all born in the nineteenth century, Edward Lear at one end in 1812 and Kay Nielsen at the other in 1886. This is not a coincidence, nor is it a contrived editorial device. It happens that the nineteenth century delivered to the nursery the first children's publications as we know them today, charming books of wonder designed simply to entertain. This odd collection of illustrators represents a phenomenon of sorts, therefore — talented men and women who may or may not have known one another, but who lived in a time when their magical creations achieved an unprecedented success. They could not have accomplished this feat in isolation, of course. The artists worked in an environment that encouraged their efforts, making it possible for them to cast their spell over the nursery. With the nineteenth century, all the pieces fell into place, providing the artists with a large and receptive audience, marvelous stories to picture, and the

technical means to produce and disseminate their images. Indeed, England of the nineteenth century offered just the right setting and cast of characters to transform the children's book from the poor orphan it was into the lovely princess it became.

The Victorians

England of the nineteenth century is more accurately described as the Victorian era, conveying, as it seems, a point of view. In fact, neither the nineteenth century nor Victoria's reign should be regarded as a rigid method of dating the period. The era actually began before the ascension of the Queen in 1837 and terminated more precisely around World War One, over a decade after her demise. John Tenniel, for example, who represented the quintessential Victorian artist, was born seventeen years before Victoria's assumption of the throne and died thirteen years after her departure. As a cohesive artistic style, the term "Victorian" is

There was an Old Man on whose nose,
Most birds of the air could repose;
*   But they all flew away*
*   At the closing of day,*
Which relieved that Old Man and his nose.

Edward Lear

also a misnomer. Edward Lear's "style" is altogether unlike that of Walter Crane, yet both are truly Victorian. If the label "Victorian" is to have any meaning whatsoever, therefore, it must embrace just this element of contradiction. The paradox of the Victorian era is that it was a stable, relatively peaceful period on the surface, with great rumblings of change and discontent below. Rectitude and vice, reaction and reform, worldliness and provincialism were contradictions marching simultaneously and consistently through the era, often at different rates, but always constant.

The England Victoria inherited when she ascended the throne in 1837 was still largely agrarian, its government ruled by a wealthy elite. By the end of her reign, England had become fully industrialized, was governed by a modern parliamentary system, and had the stamp of its culture marked indelibly throughout the world. In 1801 the population of Britain was only ten million; at Victoria's

death it had reached forty million. The years in between shaped British society forever.

During the first half of the nineteenth century factories swept through the English countryside, transforming towns into industrial cities, villages into red brick suburbs. A number of enterprising individuals quickly emerged from English society to reap the rewards of this burgeoning industry, constituting a rapidly expanding and very self-satisfied middle class. The complacency of this new group of Victorians could not altogether conceal the ill-effects of progress, however. While industry may have been materially rewarding, it was by no means beneficent. Ugliness was everywhere; railroad tracks had fractured the picturesque farmlands; factories spewed smoke and soot; and the beggars crouched in alleys and doorways were reminders that progress was fickle in its rewards.

Against this setting of poverty, disease, and ugliness, the *nouveau riche* English family contin-

Out set Riding Hood, so obliging and
sweet,
And she met a great Wolf in the wood,
Who began most politely the maiden to
greet,
In as tender a voice as he could.

He asked to what house she was going,
and why;
Red Riding Hood answered him all:
He said, "Give my love to your Gran; I
will try
"At my earliest leisure to call."

From *Little Red Riding Hood* (1875) by Walter Crane.

Edward Lear by William Holman Hunt.

Sir John Tenniel.

ued to conduct its affairs with strict regard to moral principles. Victorianism was synonymous with respectability, stressing, as it did, qualities of thrift, duty, discipline, industry, and suppression of physical desires. On the other hand, opposing these traits was an equally compelling drive toward excess: ostentation and an exaggerated tendency toward sentimentality were also characteristic of the typical Victorian. After all, it was the prim, humorless Victorians who spawned Edward Lear and his nonsense.

In their cultural appetites, the Victorians displayed the same set of contradictions as they did in their moral deportment. While the homes they constructed and the furnishings they conspicuously acquired were in bad taste, the very same Victorians extolled the simple virtues of nature. While they sat stiffly in their plumped-up settees during the winter, they marched in an endless parade to the most primitive parts of the world during the summer, in order to admire the unspoiled glaciers at Chamonix, perhaps, or to appreciate the architecture and landscapes of Switzerland, Holland, Italy, and France. While they devoured the most dreadful contemporary railway novels, they also cultivated a keen interest in the classics, natural history, and fine music. For a nation that believed all other contemporary cultures were barbaric in the face of English progress, they looked back to the splendor of the French rococo for their aesthetic inspirations, and proudly displayed the revival of these opulent styles for the entire world to behold at London's Crystal Palace in 1851.

When Edward Lear set pen to paper, in the 1830s, English was already the *lingua franca* of civilization and London might just as well have been the center of the universe. Artistic or literary talent was drawn to the English capital at the same time the empire was spreading its influence over Africa, India, and the Far East. A rich, literate middle class, hungry for knowledge and novelty, eagerly consumed whatever the publishers issued. Never before had the opportunities been so great.

The Children

The contradictions evident in all aspects of Victorian society applied in full force to the upbringing of children as well. A responsible Victorian parent was bound to enforce in the child the simple values that laid the formation of character, asserting the virtues of a God-fearing life. Wickedness went punished and goodness rewarded. The moral tale in children's literature in England had existed since the Middle Ages, and did not altogether disappear even during the nineteenth century. But something new was added: stories were written and illustrated specifically *for* children and were meant to be attractive and interesting, not simply to instruct or keep them quiet, but also to *entertain* them.

It has been said that childhood is a middle-class invention of the nineteenth century. Although somewhat exaggerated, the statement has a certain validity. That the idea of childhood did not exist until the nineteenth century does not mean, of course, that children were neglected or disliked until then. What the nineteenth century institutionalized was the awareness of childhood as a period distinct from adulthood—with appreciable measures of differences between age groups of children —and embraced the marvelous notion that childhood was even meant to be happy!

Victorian families tended to be large (the high mortality rate prevented any risk of over-population), and children represented a welcome addition to Victorian domesticity. Even with their stress on austere Christian values, these parents loved to pamper their youngsters, clothing them in the very finest fashions, wheeling them about in shining prams, romping with them during seaside holidays, entertaining them with charming little picture books and ingenious toys. Naturally, youngsters were carefully monitored by a retinue of governesses, and boys were soon sent off to boarding schools to ensure the proper development of

From *Under the Window* by Kate Greenaway.

character, but young children were happily hauled down from the nursery to greet visitors in the parlor and they provided delightful diversion to parents during leisure hours, times now made possible by luxury.

Children were no longer simply recipients of moral instruction, therefore. Now they were enchanting playthings, and giving them pleasure was a guiding principle of parenthood. Little girls, especially, were cause for rapture. Despite present-day suspicions to the contrary, there was nothing prurient about a gentleman's passion for pre-pubescent girls. Such affection was common. The respected critic, John Ruskin, delighted in virginal purity, an indulgence that propelled him to admire Kate Greenaway's innocent maidens dancing merrily before his adoring eyes. At Oxford, Ruskin's colleague, the deacon Charles Dodgson—better known as Lewis Carroll—recorded the beauty of young maidens with the lens of his camera, and his infatuation for Alice Liddell—the Alice of Wonderland—is well known. Alice's description of her meetings with Dodgson is interesting not only because it provides a sense of their own relationship, but also it describes what may have been a fairly typical scene in the Victorian nursery:

We used to go to his rooms . . . escorted by our nurse. When we got there, we used to sit on the big sofa on each side of him, while he told us stories, illustrating them by pencil or ink drawings as he went along. When we were thoroughly happy and amused at his stories, he used to pose us, and expose the plates before the right mood had passed. He seemed to have an endless store of these fantastical tales, which he made up as he told them, drawing busily on a large sheet of paper.

Until the nineteenth century the young reader had never been clearly defined, certainly not classified by age. They were simply "children," which covered the spectrum from toddler to adult. Now a vast array of books was issued to meet a diverse and plentiful audience composed of infants, boys and girls, and even adolescents: picture books containing nursery rhymes or fairy tales, alphabet books and poetry, nonsense limericks, adventure stories and fables, all designed to make children laugh or cry, tremble or dance for joy. Turning the pages of these books, children were beguiled by the magical images before them, never thinking for one moment that once upon a time an artist had actually created them under the north light of his studio window, far, far away.

The Stories

The nineteenth century did not invent "the children's story" any more than it actually invented childhood itself, but in that century stories designed specifically for children became respectable, even admirable. In fact, several of the most enduring illustrators in this volume made their mark by illustrating so-called "classics" of children's literature, stories that have been around, it seems, since the beginning of time. Without substantially altering any of the words (and surely never the plot or meaning), the illustrators cast their particular vision on time-honored fairy tales, nursery rhymes, and fables. What distinguished these artists, therefore, was how they truthfully visualized these old tales, presenting the stories as if told for the very first time.

Aesop's Fables had been in English print since William Caxton's translation from the French ap-

"The Owl and the Birds," original watercolor illustration for *Aesop's Fables* (1912), by Arthur Rackham.

peared in 1484. By the late sixteenth century there were numerous versions of *Aesop* making the rounds of the schools (where they served as a means of teaching English, Latin, and morals) and shared among the fashionable society, where they

From *Winnie-the-Pooh*,
illustrated by E.H. Shepard.

The Mock Turtle and the Gryphon
from *Alice's Adventures in Wonderland*,
illustrated by John Tenniel.

served as entertainment. Actually, *Aesop* was only one collection of animal fables. The tradition of the bestiary dates back to the fifth century. In England bestiaries combined a study of natural history with spiritual instruction, and were actually the earliest example of illustrated books. For centuries, therefore, animal life has delighted the imagination of artists as well as story-tellers. Animals assigned to do the talking for humans is a device used by illustrators to this very day. In this volume, for example, many of the illustrators have come to be associated with very specific creatures who talk: the owl and the pussycat (Lear), the Mock Turtle (Tenniel), Beauty and the Beast (Crane), the cat with the fiddle (Caldecott), Peter Rabbit (Potter),

Winnie-the-Pooh (Shepard), Toad, Rat, and Mole (Rackham), and the Cowardly Lion (Denslow).

The fairy tale found its way into print during the seventeenth century, arriving in England from the French court of Louis XIV, where stories told by peasants were a favorite pastime of the aristocracy. These tales were collected and put into writing by such fashionable ladies as the Countess d'Aulnoy, Madame de Villeneuve, and Madame Le Prince de Beaumont. The greatest of these writers, however, was Charles Perrault, who collected a group of

The Cowardly Lion from
The Wonderful Wizard of Oz,
illustrated by W.W. Denslow.

From *Hey Diddle Diddle* by Randolph Caldecott.

tales and published them in 1697. Called *Histoire ou Contes du temps passé; avec des Moralités*, the book included such familiar stories as Sleeping Beauty, Red Riding Hood, Blue Beard, Puss-in-Boots, Diamonds and Toads, Cinderella, Hop o' my Thumb. On the frontis of Perrault's book appeared a picture of an old woman telling her tale to three children while she spins her yarn, a scene bearing the famous inscription, *Contes de ma Mère L'Oye* (*Tales of Mother Goose*). Never before appearing in English, the tales were translated thirty years later by Robert Samber and published in England.

As the Mother Goose stories were enjoying a certain popularity in England, they were also supplemented, from similarly fashionable sources, by the *Arabian Nights*, stories introducing Aladdin and Sinbad and which soon swept over western Europe like magic carpets.

The earliest known edition of Charles Perrault's fairy tales, *Contes de ma Mere L'Oye*, 1695.

Not all fairy tales were imported. Some were indigenous to English society, tales based on legendary heroes. Long before the nineteenth-century illustrators set their pens to describe them, the folk heroes of England had fascinated children in the nursery: Robin Hood, Tom Thumb, and countless Jacks became central to the English folk tales. (Considering the *fin de siècle* craze for fairies, it is curious that these eternal creatures seem entirely absent from the earliest English tales, making their first appearances only during the Elizabethan era!)

Nursery rhymes have a more elusive origin. As singing games played by groups of children, nursery rhymes are every bit as old as fairy tales, changing in form from one region to the next, from one generation to the next. But no Perrault collected these rhymes; they were never codified. The jingles, having so little meaning and often no rhyme either, were better left in the nursery where they belonged. Indeed, nursery rhymes were not set down on paper until books for children became items of commerce during the nineteenth century. Only then did cows leaping over the moon, Banbury cock-horses, bridges falling down, mice running hickory dickory dock, or songs of sixpence assume any significance in the realm of children's literature. And how could any nineteenth-century artist resist the images suggested by these little verses?

Until the nineteenth century all this foolishness was condemned as trash. Lacking in moral value, all light reading (as fairy tales were regarded) was discouraged. The rational world described by Rousseau and Locke—thought which dominated much of children's literature until the first years of the nineteenth century—had no room for fairies.

The admission of fairy tales into the nursery was

gradual, hastened by a number of publications that appeared during the first half of the nineteenth century. An important collection was published in 1804, a veritable omnibus of fairy tales edited by Benjamin Tabart called *Collection of Popular Stories for the Nursery: Newly Translated and Revised from the French, Italian, and Old French Writers*. Between 1823 and 1826 another major collection appeared, this time from Germany. For a number of years Jakob and Wilhelm Grimm had been collecting the popular tales of Germany, copying them down exactly as they were narrated by the German peasants. The translation of these contained much that would charm English children in years to come: *Hansel and Gretel, Brother and Sister, Little Red Riding Hood, Snow White, Rose-Red*. That the two-volume edition of *German Popular Stories* was translated almost immediately after its original publication in Germany, and that the book was illustrated by one of England's most popular artists —George Cruikshank—testified to a changing attitude toward folk stories.

The fairy tale took another step toward the nursery in 1840 when a distinguished gentleman named Sir Henry Cole looked around for suitable reading for his own young family and found little to please him. "My young children being rather numerous," he explained, "their wants induced me to publish." Under the pseudonym Felix Summerly, he devised *The Home Treasury*, a series of books—including such titles as *Jack the Giant Killer, Jack and the Beanstalk, The Sleeping Beauty, Little Red Riding Hood, Cinderella*, and *Beauty and the Beast* —each illustrated by a respectable artist of the day.

During the decade of the 1840s several other collections of fairy tales were issued as well, the

most notable of which came from Denmark in 1846, forty tales re-told by Hans Christian Andersen. That, incidentally, was the very same year in which Edward Lear published his own *Book of Nonsense*. By then, both nonsense—a peculiarly British phenomenon—and fantasy—an international phenomenon—had finally gained positions of respectability.

There was an Old Man of Coblenz,
The length of whose legs was immense;
He went with one prance
From Turkey to France,
That surprising Old Man of Coblenz

Edward Lear

By the time Walter Crane illustrated his first book for children in the 1860s, stories that aroused the child's imagination were not only acceptable, but downright necessary. "The best of designing for children," he asserted, "is that the imagination and fancy may be let loose and roam freely." For the illustrator, this was a responsibility not to be taken lightly, and Crane applied his skills to educating the reader through books, convinced that the eye was the "chief organ for the reception of ideas." He designed several alphabet books— whose function had been purely didactic ever since the early eighteenth century—and he raised them to a high artistic level as he taught children to read through visual stimulation.

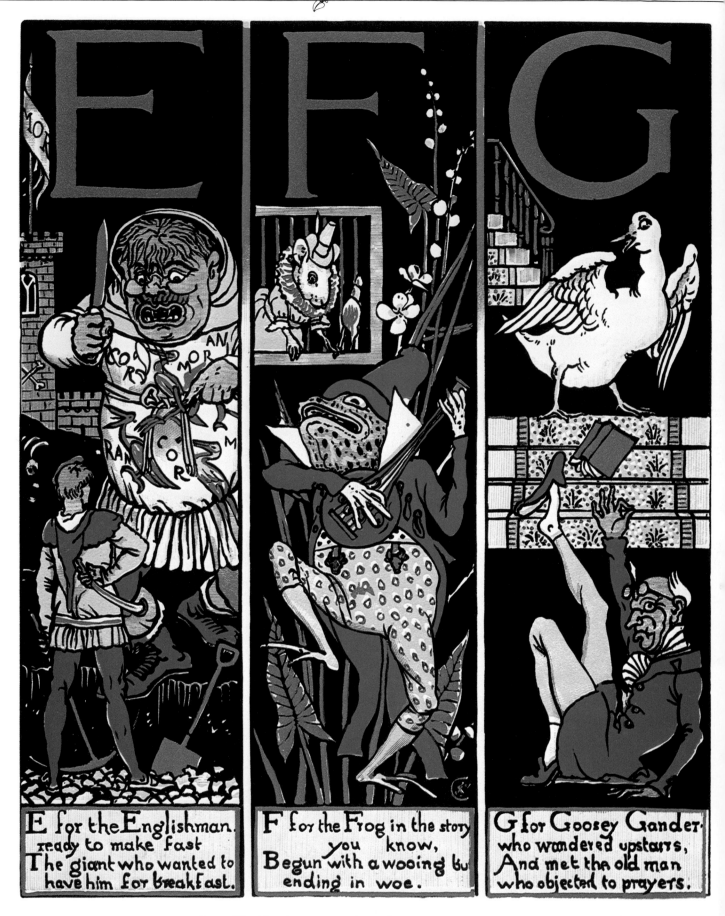

E for the Englishman ready to make fast The giant who wanted to have him for breakfast.

F for the Frog in the story you know, Begun with a wooing but ending in woe.

G for Goosey Gander who wandered upstairs, And met the old man who objected to prayers.

From *The Absurd ABC* (1874) by Walter Crane.

H for poor Humpty who
after his fall.
Felt obliged to resign his
seat on the wall.

I for the Inn where they
wouldn't give beer,
To one with too much
and no money. I fear.

J does for poor Jack and
also for Jill.
Who had so disastrous
a tumble down hill.

Now that it was an accepted fact that children's books were an essential part of a child's upbringing and that the imagination was a means of entry into the child's intelligence, a full range of books would soon be permissible—modern tales as well as ancient ones—to delight children of all ages. The artist's brush, his magic wand, became the instrument of that enchantment.

The Reformers

In following the example set by their beloved Queen, middle class Victorians made every attempt to uphold high standards of moral deportment and to carefully monitor the workings of their spiritual life. The incessant search for improvement and the emphasis on moral principle eventually made it impossible to ignore the inequities introduced by the industrial age, and throughout much of the nineteenth century a number of personalities stepped forward to reform the system. Reform was not limited to the domain of politics or religion. The work of the artist—every bit as much as that of the statesman or clergyman—possessed a moral purpose. Art, too, had an obligation to improve society, to cure corruption, to promote virtue over evil. The tick-tock swing —from reaction to reform, from nostalgia to radicalism, from romance to realism—beats its rhythm in art throughout the Victorian era. In different degrees, the illustrators of the nineteenth century were all touched by these extremes and some assumed positions of leadership in advancing the cause of reform.

The Royal Academy Schools in London provided the most prestigious training ground for English artists. The Royal charter granted to the institution in 1768 guaranteed that the school would turn out artists of the highest standing. Its seemingly endless course of study included three years of drawing and anatomy, followed by a Preliminary School of Painting, followed by a course at the Upper School of Painting where the student was finally permitted to work from a live model: a total of ten years. By the mid-nineteenth century, the school had evolved into an unbearably academic institution, and younger artists grew restless in the stagnant atmosphere of the crowded classrooms.

In 1848 seven intense art students formed a secret brotherhood (modeled after the German Nazarene) called the Brotherhood of the Pre-Raphaelites: W. Holman Hunt, John Millais, Dante Gabriel Rossetti, Thomas Woolner, F.G. Stephens, James Collinson, and William Rossetti. Although the Brotherhood was disbanded within four years, the members had a great influence on the development of nineteenth-century art in England. According to Millais, the Pre-Raphaelites had "but one idea—to present on canvas what they saw in Nature." They looked to the work of the early Italian masters as examples of what was "direct and serious and heartfelt," whereas everything created after the time of Raphael was considered merely artifice. The Pre-Raphaelites protested the ravages of modern industry, urging a return to simplicity, sincerity, and a respect for nature. Only by studying nature closely, accepting and depicting everything seen, selecting and rejecting nothing, could the artist obtain versimilitude of fact. The test of truth was accuracy of detail.

By turning their backs on the traditional precepts of the Royal Academy, the Pre-Raphaelites offended the art establishment, and the reviewers sneered at their canvases exhibited in 1851. To their good fortune, John Ruskin, the famous critic and writer, came to their rescue. He wrote two letters to *The Times* in defense of the Pre-Raphaelites, maintaining the work to be "in finish of drawing and splendour of color, the best in the Royal Academy."

The endorsement of John Ruskin carried considerable weight. Renowned throughout Britain for his books and lectures on aesthetics and social criticism, the brilliant Ruskin was unquestionably the most widely read writer in the English language at the time. His career spans nearly the entire century and touched the lives of nearly every artist and writer of his day. Ruskin's power to influence taste was enormous. With authority that was reassuring to a public unsure of its own mind, Ruskin appealed equally to cultivated aristocrats —who regarded him as their peer—and to middle-class merchants and industrialists who looked to his approval before acquiring objects of art. An artist's career could be ensured by his endorsement, or destroyed by his condemnation. Complaining about this tyranny of taste, a contemporary artist had this to say about Ruskin:

I paints and paints
  Hear no complaints.
  And sells before I'm dry;
Till savage Ruskin
Sticks his tusk in
  And nobody will buy.

In endorsing the Pre-Raphaelites, Ruskin was altogether sincere. Ruskin had advocated the close study of nature in his books, drawing classes, and

Isabella and the Pot of Basil (1866)
by William Holman Hunt.

From *The House of Fame* (1896), woodcut by Edward Burne-Jones.

lectures at Oxford, and he shared with the Pre-Raphaelites an enthusiasm for Gothic forms, finding the Medieval designs to be straightforward and honest. Ruskin, too, was appalled by the bleakness of industrialized England that "today grinds children to dust between millstones, and tears them to pieces on engine wheels." The machine, he asserted, had imposed standards of perfection which could only result in the total enslavement of man. If man is to be liberated, he must be allowed to think instead of copy.

At the time Ruskin wrote his letter about the Pre-Raphaelites to *The Times*, Edward Burne-Jones and William Morris were undergraduates at Oxford. Years later Burne-Jones joined Hunt, Rossetti, and Millais as an outstanding representative of Pre-Raphaelite thinking, although he was never a formal member of their group; and he worked with his life-long friend William Morris to carry out Ruskin's ideals. Through Burne-Jones and Morris the influence of the Pre-Raphaelites reached into the decorative arts, where an attack on commercialism and poor taste was even more necessary than in painting.

The Pre-Raphaelites and their friends became popular quite rapidly, partly because of Ruskin's endorsement, partly because their purpose was simple enough for public opinion to understand and accept it. What all these gentlemen had in common, in spite of their differences in age and temperament, was their conviction that the honesty of hand craftsmanship would correct the evils of industrialization. If Ruskin's influence was channeled mainly through his writings, the Pre-Raphaelites through their paintings, William Morris put the theories into practice with social action.

Morris was at the center of the design reform movement (termed the Arts and Crafts Movement, after the exhibition society of that name established in 1880), and he came into contact with every contemporary artist, designer, and architect sympathetic with the ideals of "honest" design and craftsmanship.

John Ruskin.

Because art was seen as a moral force, Ruskin and Morris despised what they viewed as the dangerous philosophy of that irresponsible American painter, James McNeill Whistler, who declared that art should stand apart from "all clap-trap." They deplored Whistler's lack of traditional craftsmanship, insisting that artists and craftsmen had an obligation to reform a corrupt society. Ruskin and Morris both saw in the Medieval guild system a model for achieving this higher ideal. Ruskin formed the Guild of St. George in 1871 to provide a framework for the individual craftsman to achieve true freedom of expression. Ruskin's plan proved unworkable and failed shortly after its formation, but several other guilds formed later, and the Art Workers Guild, founded in 1884, eventually attracted all the artists, architects, designers, and craftsmen of any importance—including William

Morris, Walter Crane, and Arthur Rackham—and provided a forum for expressing the ideals of the craft revival movement.

Morris' influence on the decorative arts of the time cannot be overestimated. With his firm, Morris and Co., dedicated to manufacturing functional and simply constructed furnishings for the home, with his Kelmscott Press, established to create fine books as objects of beauty, with his lectures and writing, and with his charismatic personality, Morris inspired artists, architects, designers, and craftsmen on both sides of the Atlantic. Among his many followers, Walter Crane emerged as one of the most ardent promoters of the cause in England, and W.W. Denslow was active in promoting the Arts and Crafts movement in America. Morris had touched the core of the illustrator's relationship to his craft, and no contemporary artist could remain altogether unaffected by the urgency of his cause.

The Printers

Industrialization may have had certain unfortunate effects on society, but it also created an environment ideal for the commercial illustrator. After all, the health of publishing requires precisely the same set of ingredients as that of any other industry: a sufficient market, an effective means of distribution, and sufficiently advanced technology to implement the product with speed and economy. The illustrators of the nineteenth century were beneficiaries of an industry in which all three ingredients were in place. The general well-being of a growing middle class provided a literate and prosperous market for books. The expansion of the railroad and shipping made it feasible to distribute

books throughout the British Isles, across the Channel, and to America. Finally, the technology of color printing advanced in the second half of the nineteenth century at a time when the standards of book production were badly in need of improvement. In spite of the industrial revolution, however, the very basis of this thriving industry required the growth of a great craft relying largely on manual skills.

A wood-engraving press room.

Until the middle of the nineteenth century pictorial books were printed in black and white only. The most widely used method of reproducing these publications was by means of wood engraving, a process developed by an Englishman named Thomas Bewick who died shortly before Victoria came to the throne. The wood-engraving process was painstaking. From the torso of a boxwood tree a block would be sliced, its endgrain surface highly polished, then spread with Chinese white to accept pencil or pen marks. After the design was indicated on this whitened surface, the engraver would carefully cut away the image, using a graver, tint-tool, gouge, and chisel. The process was so slow that an experienced engraver might require ten to twelve hours simply to prepare a block 4 × 5 inches in size. Although the density and texture of boxwood is ideal for engraving, the torso of its trunk is slender—never larger in diameter than twelve inches. By the time the boxwood slices of about one inch thick were seasoned, scraped, sanded, and squared into rectangular shapes, the blocks could never be larger than a few inches square. Even a six-inch block would be exceptional. Therefore, a large illustration might require a composite of several individual blocks bolted together. (As many as thirty-six such blocks, for example, might be used to accommodate an illustration of 16 × 22 inches!) When deadlines demanded the rapid delivery of a large illustration, the blocks would be distributed among several engravers and joined later.

Proofing was also an exacting job. The block was coated with special ink applied by dabbing and wiping to obtain the depth of ink required. By laying down the paper on the inked block, rubbing the back with a metal burnisher, spoon handle, or paper knife, the engraver could make impressions for approval by the artist. (Corrections were made by inserting plugs and re-engraving the surface of the block.)

The technique of engraving was a novelty to many artists, such as the Pre-Raphaelites, who experimented with the rich textures of wood, and several illustrators elected to serve as apprentices to engravers in order to acquire the techniques of drawing on wood for better reproduction. To accommodate the growing volume of printing, a number of wood-engraving firms were established in London. (In 1817 fourteen London firms were listed; in 1852, forty-seven; and in 1872 a hundred and twenty-eight.) Only a few of these firms were capable of meeting the most exacting demands of the artists they served. The most outstanding of these were the Brothers Dalziel, Joseph Swain, Orrin Smith, and W.J. Linton.

The growing interest in illustrated books naturally stimulated engravers to print in more than one color. Of all the most eminent technicians in this development none was more instrumental in transforming the children's book than Edmund Evans. Beginning his experiments with color in the 1850s, he simplified the process by creatively mixing pigments, using three oil-based inks to obtain effects that might require from four to twenty colors in the hands of another printer. Evans' business prospered when he started to print "yellow backs," bright three-color covers for books distributed to the railway bookstalls, but his reputation ultimately rested on the high quality gift books which bore his name—as engraver and printer—on the title pages.

In addition to his skills as a businessman, engraver, and printer, Evans also had a gift for detecting talent. He had long tendered the idea of printing children's books, in which he would commission an artist, engrave and print the books, and contract with a publisher for their distribution. Such a prospect was feasible only if he could work with an artist to design a complete book, print it in full color, and sell it at a reasonable price. In 1865, he found the illustrator he wanted, a young man named Walter Crane, and thus began an enterprise that flourished for the following two decades.

The success of all his illustrators—Crane, Randolph Caldecott, and Kate Greenaway—derives in no small part from Evans' ability to translate the subtleties of color and line from the original to the

Walter Crane.

Randolph Caldecott.

Kate Greenaway.

printed book. The techniques of engraving in color involved an even closer partnership of artist and engraver than that required for printing in black and white. For a single color, the engraving process ended when a single block was engraved, but for colored illustrations, it was necessary to create additional plates to print the additional colors. Several prints of the first block—called the key block—were made onto other boxwood blocks. Following the original watercolor as a guide, Evans engraved the other plates, striving to obtain not only the same colors, but the gradations of tones and the textures of the original. It was his skill as an engraver that enabled him to achieve remarkably diverse effects from only a limited number of tools and inks.

Invented in 1835 and commonly employed in the 1860s, photography used as a printer's tool significantly altered the engraving procedure. No longer was it necessary for the engraver to copy the first drawing on the key block. The artist's drawing could be photographed (enlarged or reduced, in fact) and the negative printed onto boxwood coated with a photographic emulsion. In this way, the image was transferred precisely and the printer was able to return the original to the artist.

Photography eventually transformed the printing process entirely, eliminating the need for an engraver altogether. Evans' firm declined as a result: "Engraving has had its day," he wrote in his memoirs. "I used to employ two rooms of engraving assistants at one time, now they [his sons] can scarcely keep the engravers employed." By the time he died in 1905, the heyday of commercial wood engraving was over, replaced instead by lithography.

She went to the tailor's
    To buy him a coat,
But when she came back,
    He was riding a goat.

She went to the cobbler's
    To buy him some shoes,
But when she came back,
    He was reading the news.

From *Mother Hubbard and Her Dog* (1874) by Walter Crane.

With a series of cross-hatched or parallel lines, the wood engraving rendered a semblance of modeling. To be more truly realistic, however, a better method was required to break up continuous tones into separate elements in order to simulate the middle (or half) tones between black and white. The so-called "half-tone process" of photo-engraving provided this solution. With this method, the art was photographed by a large camera through a sheet of glass on which a series of cross lines had been finely and expertly drawn. This photograph would result in a screen negative, the lines of the glass breaking up the tones of the original art into a series of dots, larger or smaller, densely or sparsely populated, depending on the nature of the tones in the original subject. These dots could then be etched into the plate chemically so that the image would be translated onto the final printing surface mechanically in the form suitable for reproduction.

Early halftone printing was abominable, but by the end of the nineteenth century advancements made possible a range of expressive possibilities that even Evans could not have offered. The improved techniques of color photography and printing promised nearly exact copies of the original colored pictures. It's true, the promise was not generally delivered, and deplorable results were commonly issued from printing firms at the turn of the century, but at its best, the new color printing methods resulted in the handsome gift books so widely circulated in England and America until the 1920s.

The firm of Carl Hentshel was the most successful of these English printers, having developed a process called Colourtype. The process involved the making of three negatives, each taken through a different colored filter, from which plates could be printed in yellow, red, and blue halftone. These were then superimposed onto a key plate made from a black-and-white negative, a step that required great care in positioning the plates exactly. Practical and economical, its main disadvantage was the need for a heavy, glazed art paper to take the inks, which meant that the illustrations could not be bound in with the book paper, but had to be "tipped in" by hand. Although this added to the cost of production, the hand-tipped pages enhanced the aesthetic effect and encouraged the creation of decorative borders to surround the color productions. For Arthur Rackham, this process meant that he could add watercolors more freely to his pen-and-ink line work, and for Edmund Dulac, Colourtype permitted a full use of watercolor applied over his pencil drawings.

In America printing technology lagged in time behind the English advancements. Until the 1880s all printing was accomplished by means of the wood-engraving process, but American craftsmanship was not on a par with the English. W.J. Linton, the distinguished English engraver to whom Walter Crane had been apprenticed, even went to live in America on a self-appointed mission to upgrade the standards of American production. He did not succeed. Techniques of wood engraving did manage to improve somewhat with the emigration of European craftsmen at the turn of the century, but no equivalent to Edmund Evans emerged in America to produce an attractive and economical picture book in color for children. In 1881 Howard Pyle illustrated two small books in color, but the results were so

Arthur Rackham.

Edmund Dulac.

disappointing that in the future he prepared books for reproduction in black-and-white line only. In periodicals Pyle's oil paintings were reproduced in color, but one has only to compare the printed results with those of the originals to assess how faulty the printed versions were. W. W. Denslow's illustrations—flat applications of color and line —made the best of American wood engraving in color by the imaginative methods he employed to enhance the effects of an otherwise limited process.

The Publishers

Although they had been around since the fifteenth century, books published for children were limited to those whose function was purely didactic. There had been the chapmen, of course, street merchants who traveled through the countryside and stood on London street corners, hawking all forms of household merchandise, including penny publications "for the young." Containing little more than crude woodcuts, these "chapbooks," as they were called, were hardly items to be treasured in the nursery, but their popularity suggested the future for books designed to entertain young readers. The actual beginning of the children's book trade occurred in 1744, the year in which a gentleman named John Newbery published his first children's book. By successfully augmenting his family book-selling business to include a program of publishing books (twenty or thirty of which were prepared specifically for children), Newbery demonstrated that here was a business with untold possibilities. He discovered what publishers soon accepted as a maxim: an appetite for books could be aroused and sustained with a diet of reading material produced on a steady basis for consumption. Children's

"The Crooked Man," original watercolor illustration
for *Mother Goose* (1913), by Arthur Rackham.

"After these, maidens on white horses, with heads unveiled, bearing in their hands baskets of precious stones," from *Arabian Nights*, illustrated by Edmund Dulac.

books were soon to be turned out in quantities as items of commerce. When the business of publishing was separated from the business of book selling in the nineteenth century, it assumed a form not very different from what we know as publishing today.

Considering the enterprising spirit of the forefathers in the publishing industry, it may be surprising to learn that so many of the business practices adopted more than a century ago are still in operation today. This may be explained by the fact that publishing companies began and continued essentially as small family businesses. The traditions as they passed down the line of succession from fathers to sons over the years discouraged any substantial change. The Warnes and the Routledges of England, the Harpers and Scribners of America were bound to adhere to the methods of operating established by their ancestors. This observation is not meant to negate the remarkable innovations introduced in the last century, however. The nineteenth-century publishers successfully exploited an age of popularization by providing books to reach a growing, literate middle-class market hungry for knowledge. With clever methods of distribution through bookshops, circulating libraries, and railway bookstalls, and using advanced methods of printing for production and efficient means of transportation for distribution, the publishers seized the opportunities offered by the industrial revolution.

Every illustrator in this volume benefited from this surge of activity in publishing. Not only books, but periodicals presented untold opportunities, providing an important client for ambitious illustrators. For the humorous illustrator no publication was more desirable than *Punch*, the weekly London periodical that featured the work of the best black-and-white illustrators of the day, including Sir John Tenniel, Randolph Caldecott, Arthur Rackham, and Ernest Shepard. In America, periodicals directed for children—such as *St. Nicholas* and *Harper's Young People*—represented an important source of business for Howard Pyle and his contemporaries.

The proliferation of magazine and book publishers (some firms published both) stimulated the growth of an enterprising business community dedicated to producing the most attractive publications at the lowest price. Money could be made or lost. Shrewd financial arrangements were of critical importance to the success or failure of each publication. For this reason, it was not always the publisher who engaged in speculation. Edmund Evans was a printer who recognized the profits to be made if he engaged the artist directly, engraved and printed books at his own expense, and contracted with a publisher for distribution only. Evans made the most of his idea. The sale of his toy books increased so rapidly that he was soon printing first editions of well over 50,000 copies. They were soon being bound in volumes of four or eight with paper covers and, after the first sixteen had been published, Evans printed a thousand copies of a deluxe edition containing them all, each numbered and signed. Other entrepreneurial personalities also invested their capital in projects they felt confident would succeed. The author Lewis Carroll published his *Alice's Adventures in Wonderland* at his own expense, a handsome sum that included the fees paid to his illustrator John Tenniel. Unable to find a publisher, Beatrix Potter published *Peter Rabbit* privately, in a small edition of 250, before

Beatrix Potter with her father and brother.

From *The Tale of Peter Rabbit* by Beatrix Potter.

Frederick Warne offered to publish the book in a more ambitious format. In America, the illustrator W.W. Denslow and author L. Frank Baum were prepared to invest their own money equally in the publication of *The Wizard of Oz* until a publisher came along and agreed to share the costs.

It was only in the latter part of the nineteenth century that the illustrator could anticipate any substantial earnings from the success of a book. Awarding royalties to an artist was not common practice until late in the century. John Tenniel was paid a flat fee by the author, and Evans did not share his profits with Walter Crane. Randolph Caldecott was willing to speculate *with* Evans, taking no advance fee, but sharing in the ensuing profits. With the promise of greater revenues, publishers competed for the most popular illustrators, offering far better financial terms. Mindful of his own loss of income, Walter Crane gave advice to the younger Caldecott about royalties. Caldecott must have benefited from Crane's advice. He succeeded in augmenting his royalties from 6¼ percent to 12½ percent of the list price. Even with the increased earnings, Caldecott resented that the publisher retained a disproportionate share of the earnings on his books.

When photography made it possible to transfer the artist's design to the plate without damage to the original art, the artist was able to put the original to new uses. Now business transactions between publisher and illustrator included the matter of the original art as well. N.C. Wyeth agreed to surrender the originals to Scribner's but Kate Greenaway insisted on retaining the art in order to control their future and to obtain additional income from their sale after publication.

"These people were all made of china," from *The Wonderful Wizard of Oz*, illustrated by W. W. Denslow.

With a market for originals, the art gallery also entered into financial arrangements. In London Leicester Galleries exhibited the original paintings and drawings by Arthur Rackham simultaneously with the publication of each Rackham book. To enhance the appeal of these originals, Rackham frequently improved upon the pen-and-inks by adding color to art reproduced in the book as black-and-white. So lucrative was this arrangement that Leicester Galleries went a step further with the young artist Edmund Dulac: the gallery paid a flat fee to Dulac for a number of original watercolors, including their copyright, and assumed full responsibility for publishing the book in consultation with the publisher Hodder & Stoughton.

The matter of copyright was a legal refinement that emerged in the nineteenth century as a necessary protection for the artist and publisher. Editions of books by Kate Greenaway and Beatrix Potter were pirated freely on the Continent and especially in America. Potter complained of this situation when she wrote, "the difficulties about 'copyrighting' an English book in America are now so very great that we are obliged to engrave and print *in* America all copies intended for American use." Not only books, but all sorts of paraphernalia appeared bearing images by Greenaway and Potter—plates, scarves, calendars, and toys—a prelude, it seems, to the present day in which the licensing of images has become the profitable domain of specialists. Greenaway was adamant on this subject. "I have made it a rule for a long time," she asserted, "not to part with the copyright of my drawings, for I have been so copied, my drawings reproduced and sold for advertisements and done in ways I hate." In America, the

land of golden opportunity, author and illustrator of *The Wizard of Oz* took advantage of ways to extend the success of their book. The musical version of *The Wizard of Oz* enjoyed an eight-year stint on Broadway after its opening in 1903, and two silent films of the story appeared long before the classic motion picture extravaganza, starring Judy Garland, opened in 1939.

W. W. Denslow self-portrait.

Original paintings, motion pictures, handkerchiefs, and coffee cups, all derived from a single source of inspiration: the book itself. Not until the nineteenth century was a child's book considered a cherished possession of the nursery, delightful to read and lovely to behold. William Morris' ideal of the book as an object of beauty now represented an idea of enormous commercial potential for the publishers. Between 1900 and World War One, the so-called "gift book" became big business. Publishers offered their readers a choice: a deluxe limited edition—bound in calfskin, with tissue inserts,

and signed by the illustrator—or a lower-priced
"trade edition." Naturally, the limited edition sold
out instantly. After all, rarity signifies value, even
in a mass-produced item! After World War One,
the craze for deluxe gift books declined in England
but was adopted in America instead, brought to
fruition by George Macy. For his Limited Editions Club, Macy chose a text each month to be
printed on paper chosen specially by a typographer
selected for the book. Each was illustrated by a
well-known artist Macy felt would be sympathetic
to the text and exquisite production.

In less than one hundred years, publishing had
evolved from a collection of small enterprises to a
great business institution, an evolution that af-
fected every illustrator in this volume. The publisher had become the artist's most important
client, replacing all other traditional patrons as a
source of business. Neither the church nor the
court would ever again provide what was offered
by the barons of the printed image. The industrial
revolution had taken care of that.

The Americans

To listen to an Englishman in the nineteenth century,
one would think that America was nothing more
than a provincial backwater, a nation of barbarians
surrounded by primitive countryside. "I have just
seen a number of landscapes by a painter of some
repute," wrote John Ruskin in 1856 (he was the
authority on such matters, of course), "and the
ugliness of them is wonderful. I see that they are
true studies and that the ugliness of the country
must be unfathomable." When John Tenniel and
Lewis Carroll agreed that the first printing of
Alice's Adventures in Wonderland was simply too

W. W. Denslow.

Howard Pyle with his students in his Wilmington studio.

N. C. Wyeth.

dreadful to distribute in England, they didn't hesitate to sell the faulty sheets to an American publisher the following year, confident that the Americans wouldn't know the difference.

In fact, although they may have exaggerated their case, the Englishmen were not altogether mistaken about the sorrowful state of American culture. They may not like to have admitted that the American city at the end of the Civil War was certainly no less ugly than the infernal metropolis of Manchester or Birmingham in England, but there was also no equivalent of the cosmopolitan London to compensate for such unfortunate sites.

The nation that Ruskin, Tenniel, and Carroll perceived as uncivilized was altogether transformed after the Civil War. Between 1865 and 1917 the United States constructed its own publishing empire, and after World War One altogether usurped the position of cultural dominance held so long by the great English capital.

Expansion after the Civil War was sudden. If only seven hundred periodicals existed in 1865, for example, by 1900 nearly five thousand had come into being. The explosion of books and periodicals produced was a direct result of America's growing demand for reading matter as illiteracy was reduced by the introduction of public education. Public libraries—another great American institution that expanded substantially after the Civil War as a result of legislation and private philanthropy—provided ready access to reading matter. In 1876, for example, the United States Commission of Education published the first general statistics on libraries: 12,000,000 volumes were contained in 2,500 libraries. By 1896, this number had increased to 33,000,000 in 4,000 libraries.

Just as the market had developed, so had the means of distribution. The growing network of railroads provided an economical and rapid method of carriage across the nation. A new postal law in 1885 reduced the rate of second-class matter to a cent a pound and a rural free delivery system was instituted in 1897, giving rise to a brisk mail order business.

All these impressive numbers represented an enormous market, not only for American publishers, but for the English as well. It is reported that in the 1840s at least forty to fifty percent of all books published in America were English productions. Although the movement toward establishing American branches of British publishing firms began before the Civil War, the real expansion began afterwards, when Macmillan, Oxford University Press, Frederick Warne, and John Lane established branches in New York City. For Kate Greenaway the United States became an even better client than England.

It may seem surprising that the popularity of Greenaway, Crane, and Caldecott did not stimulate the immediate issue of comparable American picture books. On the contrary, these pretty English books tended to *discourage* indigenous efforts. The state of printing technology was abysmal—even the Englishman W. J. Linton's attempts to rescue American engraving from an appalling fate at the end of the 1860s did not have lasting success—the publications for children produced in America were homely by comparison to their English counterparts. The lack of copyright protection gave American publishers a free hand at the wealth of illustrated books from abroad at no greater cost than the cutting of new blocks. Why bother to rival the English books, therefore, when they were so accessible, so inexpensive, and so obviously superior? After all, whatever was imported to the United States was always better anyway!

To be fair, this exchange was not entirely one-sided. There *were* some American children's books that enjoyed favor in nineteenth-century England as well. The conservative Samuel Griswold Goodrich, known as Peter Parley, was read and widely imitated in England during the first half of the nineteenth century, and he was succeeded by other favorites, including *Uncle Tom's Cabin* (1852) by Harriet Beecher Stowe, *Uncle Remus* (1881) by Joel Chandler Harris, *A Wonder-Book* (1852) and *Tanglewood Tales* (1853) by Nathaniel Hawthorne, *Huckleberry Finn* (1884) and *Tom Sawyer* (1876) by Mark Twain, and *Little Women* (1868) by Louisa May Alcott. Meanwhile, the American magazine for children, *St. Nicholas*, edited by Mary Mapes Dodge (author of *Hans Brinker and the Silver Skates*), enjoyed a considerable English readership from 1873 to nearly the end of the century.

What the Americans were sadly lacking was not good writing but good pictures. While Crane and Evans were working together on their toy books, American styles of illustration continued to be based on the rigid requirements of black-and-white reproduction in popular magazines, and the results were stilted and derivative. After the Civil War a number of competent illustrators working in black and white did emerge, most notably Thomas Nast, Felix Darley, A.B. Frost, E.W. Kemble, Edwin Abbey, as well as Howard Pyle, of course, but there was still little evidence of good work in color. It was not until the very end of the century that the Americans showed any signs of establish-

ing their own tradition of artistic books in color. W.W. Denslow, beloved of children but condemned by librarians who felt his work was "of the comic poster order," and therefore "should be banished from the sight of impressionable children," incorporated Walter Crane's ideas into his own work to create the fully-designed picture book. With Pyle's diligent teaching of illustration, moreover, an American tradition soon evolved that was continued by N.C. Wyeth and his colleagues, representing the entry of the United States into its own expression of picture-making.

By the end of World War One, America had assumed a position of leadership in publishing books for the nursery, and national pride had replaced the anglophilia of earlier years. Yet the eminence of the English tradition remained fixed forever in the American concept of the fine children's book. In 1922 an annual award was established to honor the best American children's book of the year. It was named the Newbery Medal, after the Englishman John Newbery who published the first children's book in the eighteenth century. And in 1936 an award was established to honor the best illustration for a children's book. It was named the Caldecott Award.

The Illustrators

To classify every artist in this volume as an illustrator of children's books may be misleading. In fact, not all illustrators were exclusively engaged in books, any more than all book illustrators confined their activities solely to children's literature. The specialized field referred to as children's illustration is a modern-day classification which has little application here.

"Robin Hood and his Companions Lend Aid from Ambush,"
original oil painting for *Robin Hood*, by N.C. Wyeth.

he Great Red Fox goes
to call on neighbour Cock at his
house because he will crow in the
morn.

From *The Wonder Clock* (1888) by Howard Pyle.

These illustrators did, of course, share some common traits worth noting. First, they illustrated stories, which means they were necessarily sensitive to the written word. Just how they chose to illustrate the text is another matter entirely. N.C. Wyeth preferred to illustrate the scene as it was described in words, a literal visualization of the text repeated in pictures. Arthur Rackham preferred to illustrate the indescribable, to use the text merely as a hint at pictures that were meant to exist independently of the words. Randolph Caldecott chose to weave his pictures in and out of the words, filling in what the words omitted, interpreting the words where suitable, playing a carefully orchestrated duet with the pictures and text. For Walter Crane and W.W. Denslow, the words themselves were part of the total picture, exquisitely designed letterforms integrated within the format of the unit of a decorated book. But words they were, and in making pictures for stories or verses, all illustrators were distinctly apart from the studio artist whose picture is stimulated by a single idea rather than a written narrative.

Secondly, the illustrators were preparing their pictures for the printed page, not for exhibition in gallery halls. A concern for better reproduction required their knowledge of printing technology, and the degree to which they took the time to bother with the process frequently determined the final results. Walter Crane, for example, was apprenticed to W.J. Linton, one of the finest engravers of his day, for three years in order to learn how to render designs on the wood block. On the other hand, John Tenniel generally took little interest in the procedure, relying heavily on his engravers to interpret his drawing for him, until he worked

closely with the Brothers Dalziel in preparing *Alice's Adventures in Wonderland*. This involvement with the printing process may explain why much of Tenniel's work reproduced in *Punch* is so uneven in comparison to the consistently fine results of his *Alice* illustrations. Even when photo-reproduction replaced the engraver, distancing the artist from the process, attention to technical matters was still mandatory. Arthur Rackham and Edmund Dulac heightened their palette considerably in preparation for the deadening consequences of the color reproduction process employed at the time. And Rackham's exhortations to the printer, marked in large letters on the color proofs sent to him for approval, suggest that the results rarely met the artist's standards of perfection.

Beyond these two ingredients—an appreciation of words and a concern with printing procedures—there is little else these illustrators share in common. What drew them to be illustrators in the first place, for example? For Crane, illustration was a craft, a laudable profession endorsed by his father who was a portrait painter. Kate Greenaway's father was also "in the trade," an engraver who encouraged his daughter to pursue a training in art. Beatrix Potter's bourgeois Victorian parents, on the other hand, regarded *any* trade—especially for a *woman*—with contempt, and it was only a frustration intensely seeking outlet that drove Potter to the easel and to her writing. For a long time, Caldecott and Rackham were obliged to study art merely as a sideline to their employment as office workers, and they joined the ranks of illustration only after years of studying evenings and holidays.

If a career in illustration developed out of different patterns, a penchant specifically for children's

Ernest H. Shepard.

Kay Nielsen.

books derived from equally divergent intentions. Surely, a love of children does not seem to be the governing principle. There is no indication that the childless Dulac, Tenniel, Nielsen, or Greenaway particularly sought out the company of children. On the other hand, the work of Edward Lear and Beatrix Potter—who also happened to be childless—was inspired by joyful contact with specific children. What seems more significant here was not whether they had children of their own, nor even whether they had *contact* with children, but rather that they seemed to take pleasure in remembering the child within. After all, they had all been children themselves. "I write to please myself," Beatrix Potter admitted, echoing a sentiment frequently expressed by all illustrators.

Writing anything at all was also a matter of individual choice. Although Greenaway occasionally made pictures for books written by others, she preferred to create her own simple verses for illustration. The independent Beatrix Potter would *only* illustrate her own text, working "to order" being altogether unthinkable. Edward Lear's superb writing frequently overshadowed his drawing, countless other illustrators making new pictures for the words Lear wrote over a century ago. Howard Pyle adapted folk tales and legends, but with his own text. By contrast, Crane and Caldecott were perfectly content to illustrate old nursery rhymes just as they found them; Dulac, Rackham, and Nielsen favored the classic fairy tales, while Tenniel, Shepard, Wyeth, and Denslow illustrated many books written by contemporary writers.

How large a portion of the illustrator's career was occupied in producing pictures for children varied with each. Few illustrators made pictures

"I have had such a terrible dream," she declared,
"... a pretty bird swooped down, snatched it from my hands
and flew away with it," from "Rosanie or The Inconstant Prince"
in *In Powder and Crinoline* by Kay Nielsen.

From *Winnie-the-Pooh*, illustrated by E.H. Shepard.

exclusively for children throughout their professional lives, not that the work done for children differed much from that offered to adults. For Tenniel and Shepard, illustrating children's books was simply an extension of their central activity as illustrators for *Punch*, although Tenniel abandoned any connection with *Alice* immediately after completing the two books, while Shepard continued to create the characters from *Winnie-the-Pooh* for many years until he died in his nineties. Like Shepard, Arthur Rackham continued to make pictures for children's stories until he was too frail to work any longer at all. But several illustrators were preoccu-

pied with other matters entirely. Walter Crane's children's illustrations, for example, were largely an expression of his fascination with design in general, fostering also his mission as an educator. But he became far too involved in the Arts and Crafts movement to confine himself exclusively to the domain of the nursery, or even to the illustrated book, extending his talents to the design of wallpapers, fabrics, tapestries, ceramics, plasterwork, mosaics, and stained glass. Beatrix Potter wrote about twenty books for children over a period of only thirteen years, but abandoned the practice totally in her late forties when she married.

Designing sets and costumes for the theater attracted Dulac, Nielsen, and Denslow. For N.C. Wyeth, who spent most of his life making dramatic pictures of epic tales, illustration itself was an unworthy profession, and he longed to give it up entirely in order to paint tranquil interpretations of the countryside surrounding him. Even Wyeth's teacher, Howard Pyle—who was a serious professional all his life—decided to leave illustration in order to take up the challenge of mural decoration.

Pyle's restlessness, his eagerness to find new avenues of expression, was a necessary means of fighting off boredom. For the satanic force that threatens every artist is repetition, a threat only heightened by success. Public acclaim is fickle, and its whims are governed by an appallingly conserva-tive appetite. Once an illustrator has become beloved by his public, invention is discouraged. In the 1920s, Rackham was urged to return to his familiar linear style after experimenting with a softer watercolor technique in *Irish Fairy Tales* and *The Tempest*. Edmund Dulac encountered the same resistance when he altered his approach in *The Bells*. If the artists in this volume have endured the test of time, therefore, it is precisely because they wrestled with the devil of repetition every time they lifted the brush. They may have illustrated to please the children, it's true, but above all they had to please themselves first. "So when we have put forth our best efforts," Arthur Rackham said modestly, "let us quietly retire to our workshop again and try to do better next time."

From *Winnie-the-Pooh*, illustrated
by E.H. Shepard.

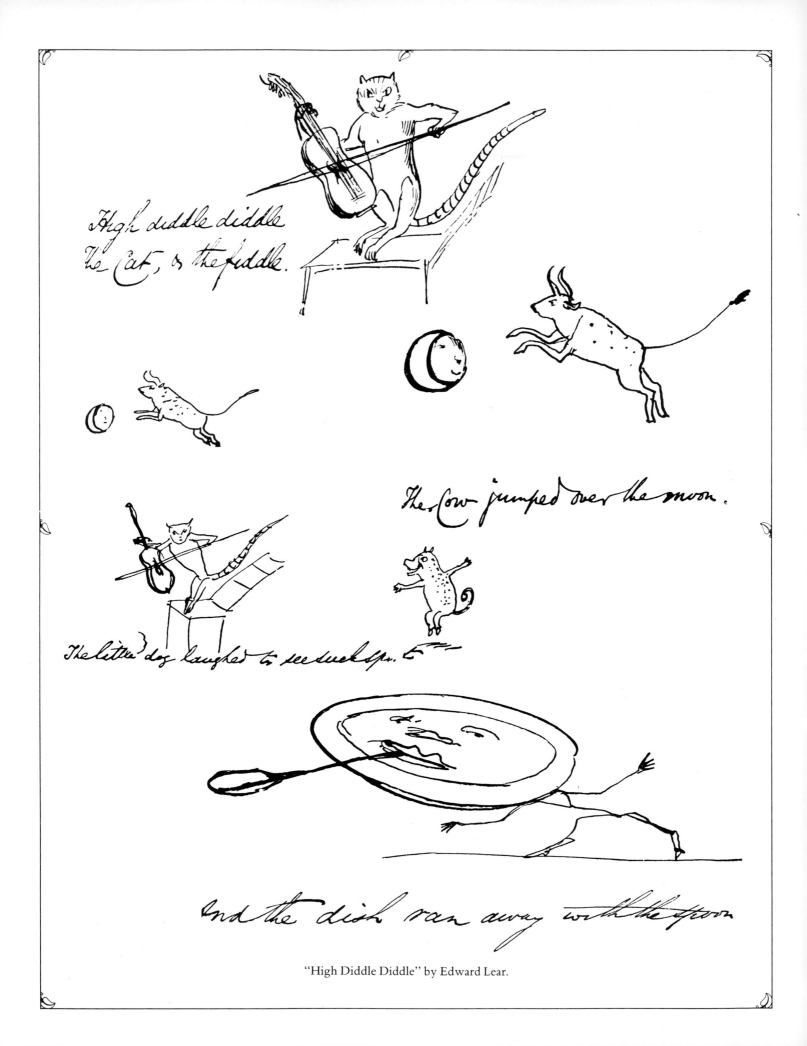

High diddle diddle
The Cat, & the fiddle.

The Cow jumped over the moon.

The little dog laughed to see such sp.

And the dish ran away with the spoon

"High Diddle Diddle" by Edward Lear.

Edward Lear

"The Owl and the Pussycat," from *Nonsense Songs,
Stories, Botany and Alphabets* (1871).

THE MOST LASTING IMAGES created for children's
books are those that amplify the words—pictures
that enhance the story with greater meaning. Together words and pictures combine to form a
magical union linked forever in the mind of the
child. Although the images may seem perfectly
entwined with the prose, the artist who interprets
the words with such visual eloquence is seldom the
one who writes the story itself. In fact, many of
the greatest illustrators may have had extraordinary visual imaginations, but little talent for assembling words. In this respect, Edward Lear was a
notable exception. He also possessed a remarkable
gift for poetry, and for generations his writing
has continued to inspire other artists to create
new images for his ever-popular verses.

Like Beatrix Potter, who created *Peter Rabbit*
fifty years later for the children of her former

governess, Edward Lear created poems and pictures simply to entertain boys and girls, with no
thought of publication. He was the "Adopty
Duncle" of countless children, although he never
had any of his own. During joyful moments, he
created delightful verses and drawings, finding
here a welcome release from the melancholy that
afflicted him through the years. Late in life, Beatrix
Potter was lucky enough to marry, fulfilling her
deepest yearnings, and she ultimately abandoned
her writing and illustration altogether, no longer
seeming to require a creative outlet for her frustrations. Lear never managed to find such peace,
leaving one to ponder the extent to which the
imagination may actually be fired by unhappiness.
Surely, Lear's empathy for children derived in part
from his inability to overcome the sadness of his
youth, and if he understood children it may have

been because he never felt he left his own childhood very far behind.

Lear liked to say that he could remember "every particle" of his life from a very early age. Born in 1812—the same year as Charles Dickens and Robert Browning—Lear remembered being wrapped in a blanket and taken to the window to see the celebrations of the Waterloo Victory when he was three years old. He was the twentieth child born in the family; many of his siblings had died as babies, and twelve survived. His father was a successful stockbroker and the large Lear family lived comfortably in a prosperous London suburb. This came to an end in 1816 when his father went bankrupt as a result of some unfortunate financial investments.

Although he eventually managed to get himself out of debt some months later, the family never returned to the state of affluence they had enjoyed earlier, and Edward's mother felt unable to cope with the burdens of caring for so many children. She entrusted her four-year-old son Edward to her eldest daughter, Ann. Twenty-two years his senior, Ann Lear never married and cared for her brother with unfailing devotion for the rest of her life. Meanwhile, it appears that Edward's mother had nothing more to do with the upbringing of her son, and he only rarely saw his father, even though they all lived in the same house.

These depressing upheavals were intensified because of the boy's ill health. Edward's eyesight

Edward Lear self-portraits.

was poor, he suffered from chronic asthma and bronchitis and, most upsetting of all, experienced almost daily attacks of epilepsy (which he called "the Demon" in his diaries). If the crosses he marked in his journals are an accurate account of the frequency of these seizures, he seems to have endured up to eighteen a month, generally in early morning and in late evening, throughout his entire life. Because he refers to "the Demon" quite frequently in his private journals and never in his letters, there is good reason to believe that the nature of his illness remained secret from all but his immediate family. Sensing when a seizure was coming on, he had sufficient warning to withdraw into a private room, so that he could spare himself the embarrassment of any witnesses. He followed a careful diet and a program of regular exercise in the expectation that a diligent regimen would diminish the intensity and frequency of his seizures. Superstitions surrounding epilepsy were prevalent during the Victorian era, and it is not surprising that Lear would choose to conceal his affliction. But the cost of his secrecy was high, forcing him into isolation and depriving him of the kind of intimacy he so deeply craved. "I suppose the ever-presence of the Demon since I was seven years old, would have prevented happiness under any sort of circumstances," he wrote in his journal. "It is a most merciful blessing that I have kept up as I have and have not gone utterly to the bad mad sad."

In fact, the emotional strain on the boy plunged him into frequent bouts of depression and irritability which he called "the Morbids." He was a lonely child, overprotected by his elder sister, unwanted by his mother, and frequently ill. To ward off "the Morbids" he developed his own resources for distraction. In one room of the house his father had a collection of original paintings that fascinated him, and Ann taught him to paint flowers, butterflies, and birds. By reading aloud to him, Ann shared her love of literature and history, and he discovered the modern poets, particularly Byron, as well as natural history and classical mythology.

Throughout his adolescence, Edward went frequently to stay in Sussex with his married sister Sarah. During what appear to be the happiest periods of his youth he developed an affection for the comforting English countryside. Here he also discovered his talent for making people laugh and referred to himself as a lovable oddity, "three parts crazy—and wholly affectionate." Not far from his sister lived the Earl of Egremont, a wealthy patron of the arts whose private collection of English landscape paintings was among the best in the country. Overwhelmed by the paintings of J.M.W. Turner he beheld at Egremont's home, and later by the Turners in the collection of Walter Ramsden Fawkes, Lear was determined to become an artist also.

Having inherited a small annual income from her grandmother, Ann was able to provide some support for her brother while he set out to earn a living as an artist. He was not yet sixteen when they rented modest rooms in London, ready to launch his career. While he looked for work he began to do "uncommon queer shop-sketches—selling them for prices varying from ninepence to four shillings; colouring prints, screens, fans; awhile making morbid disease drawings for hospitals and certain doctors of physic."

Lear was aware, of course, that there were a number of opportunities at the time for artists who rendered birds and animals, subjects he had so diligently practiced under his sister's tutelage. Lavishly illustrated books on birds and animals had become fashionable. For several years, naturalists had been classifying the exotic specimens brought to England from throughout the British empire, work that had stimulated the study of local species as well. John James Audubon began his research on the birds of North America in 1820, and in England Prideaux Selby and Sir William Jardine were preparing a major series of books, *Illustrations of British Ornithology*. The first volume of this lavish set appeared in 1825, and future volumes were underway when Lear was hired as an assistant by Selby.

Lear's apprenticeship with Selby gave him the skills and confidence to undertake a book of his own, for which he confined himself to the study of parrots. His project was ambitious. Lear was given permission to work from life in the newly formed Zoological Gardens in London, where he made drawings that established the details of each bird. Back in his studio, he transferred these details in reverse onto a lithographic plate. (Lear preferred lithography to the more common method of reproduction, wood engraving, because lithography permitted him to make his *own* drawings on a plate rather than rely upon the efforts of a professional wood engraver who might have been less meticulous in execution than the artist.) Lear then brought the finished plates to the printer. After the run was complete, Lear hired an assistant to color the prints by hand. Called *Illustrations of the Family Psittacidae or Parrots*, the book was originally planned to be

published for 175 subscribers in fourteen folios, a remarkable feat for an eighteen-year-old boy. In 1830 the first two were ready and by the end of 1831 he had finished twelve, but he found the effort too costly and time-consuming to complete the remaining two. Nevertheless, the series had served its purpose: the lithographs were very well received, securing his reputation as a capable zoological draftsman, and he seemed to have found work that suited him.

As it happened, Lord Stanley, heir to the twelfth Earl of Derby, had been looking for an artist to help in his plans to publish an illustrated book on his rare collection of birds and animals at Knowsley Hall, near Liverpool. Impressed by Lear's sensitive and accurate parrot lithographs, Lord Stanley in-

The Rural Runcible Raven,
who wore a White Wig and flew away
with the Carpet Broom.
From *An Alphabet.*

vited the young artist to come and live at Knowsley and to make drawings of the private collection there. Lear jumped at the offer to work at one of the most famous menageries in Europe, an ambitious project that occupied the artist for much of the subsequent five years.

Lear's time at Knowsley represented the major turning point in his personal and professional life. At twenty, when he first arrived at the estate, he was a tall, ungainly young man with little self-esteem. Only the year before, alongside a self-portrait drawing made in a letter to a friend, he described himself this way: " . . . this is amazingly like; add only—that both my knees are fractured

The Good-natured Grey Gull,
who carried the Old Owl, and his Crimson Carpet-bag,
across the river, because he could not swim.
From *An Alphabet.*

from being run over which has made them peculiarly crooked—that my neck is singularly long—and a most elephantine nose—and a disposition to tumble here and there—owing to being half blind and you may well imagine my *tout ensemble.*" Although his penchant for self-mockery persisted through the years, at Knowsley Lear found compensations for his shortcomings. He discovered how much he enjoyed children, a pleasure that would nourish him wherever he traveled, and he learned to feel at home with nobility of the highest order, from which group he found lifelong patrons and intimate friendships that sustained him.

Lord Stanley's father, the twelfth Earl of Derby, was an elderly, warm-hearted man who always enjoyed the company of family and friends. The Earl's children, grandchildren, and great-grand-children would arrive at the estate for extended visits, and at any one time between forty and one hundred guests might be seated at the dinner table.

Permanent residents of the household included a retinue of nurses and governesses who supervised the children, and the nursery became a happy refuge to which Lear paid daily visits. To the delight of these children, Lear drew odd-looking birds and animals (caricatures of the beasts he was drawing each day at the menagerie) and people with funny noses (like his own), adding nonsense rhymes to go with the drawings.

Early in his stay at Knowsley, Lear was treated as a member of the staff and took his meals down-stairs with the servants. Before long, Lord Derby noticed that the children were dashing from the

The Queer Querulous Quail,
who smoked a Pipe of Tobacco on the top of
a Tin Tea-kettle.
From *An Alphabet.*

dinner table as soon as it was permissible, down to the stewards' room where the young artist would greet them with his rhymes and drawings. Discovering this, the Earl promptly invited Lear to join the rest of the family for dinner upstairs, and thereafter Lear was treated as a guest in the noble-man's home. Lear felt at ease with these patricians, whom he called the "swells," and his jocular and open manner immediately won him many friends. He complained that the intensely social atmo-sphere at Knowsley could be oppressive at times (Lear liked to say that he enjoyed company, not

There was an old person of Skye,
Who waltz'd with a Bluebottle fly:
They buzz'd a sweet tune,
To the light of the moon,
And entranced all the people of Skye.

From *One Hundred Nonsense Pictures and Rhymes*.

society), and he wrote to a friend, "the uniform apathetic tone assumed by lofty society irks me *dreadfully*. Nothing I long for half so much as to giggle heartily and to hop on one leg down the great gallery—but I dare not." Lear never lost this sense of the absurd.

Hearing of Lear's talent for entertaining children, one of the guests at Knowsley presented the artist with a copy of *Anecdotes and Adventures of Fifteen Gentlemen*. Published in 1822, the book contained amusing illustrations to a text, consisting of verses cast in a form that has come to be called the limerick, although no one knows exactly why. The limerick is a humorous verse, in which two rhyming three-beat lines are followed by two rhyming two-beat lines, and concluded by a fifth line that rhymes with the first two. Lear found this "a form of verse lending itself to limitless variety for rhymes and pictures," and immediately began to create limericks for children at Knowsley. (Lear, to

There was a Young Lady whose bonnet
Came untied when the birds sate upon it;
But she said, "I don't care!
All the birds in the air
Are welcome to sit on my bonnet!"

From *The Book of Nonsense* (1861).

There was a Young Lady whose nose,
Was so long that it reached to her toes;
*   So she hired an Old Lady,*
*   Whose conduct was steady,*
To carry that wonderful nose.

From *The Book of Nonsense* (1861).

be sure, did not *invent* the limerick, as is commonly believed. The popularity of his limericks in later years brought the form to wide public attention and for this reason it has come to be associated with his name.)

In these limericks, Lear would write about an "Old Man" or "Old Person" and sometimes about a "Young Lady" or "Young Person." He poked fun at what he felt were silly people, particularly bores and stuffed shirts, and busybodies. Some of the characters may be greedy, some vain, some self-righteous, but they were designed to make children laugh, not tremble: Lear's gentleness is evident everywhere. In these verses, Lear joyfully tinkered with the English language, shaping words and spellings with irreverence—the more familiar the word, the more likely to be turned on its head. Punning, which was already a favorite English pastime, was elevated into a real art form with Lear's handling. He loved to create odd spellings

There was an old man of Dumbree,
Who taught little owls to drink tea;
*   For he said, "To eat mice,*
*   Is not proper or nice,"*
That amiable man of Dumbree.

From *One Hundred Nonsense Pictures and Rhymes.*

and to invent words for children, descriptive words that needed no definition: "runcible," "flumpy," "gromphibberous," "scroobius," "pomskizillious," "ombliferous," to name only a few.

No less witty than the words, Lear's pen drawings embellished each limerick. Here he invented a form never before attempted and virtually impossible to imitate. Like children, Lear's drawings are in perpetual motion. The whimsical figures leaping across the pages were the antithesis of his meticulously rendered zoological drawings, yet his training as a naturalist certainly gave him the ability to express himself freely in the simplest terms. No wonder that birds and animals appear in so many of the limericks. In fact, Lear could not resist the temptation to transform even the humans into birds, and the birds into humans, obviously amusing himself while he entertained his audience. (It was like Lear to caricature himself as an owl, for example, beaked and bespectacled, never missing

The aged & obese Landscape=
=painter will rejoice to come
to H. Excellency tomorrow. —
he hopes EB ΛAADC will go
to Athens next Monday weak

an opportunity to ridicule his own appearance.) These elegantly designed, lyrical drawings—deceptively naïve—are as contemporary in feeling today as they were more than one hundred years ago.

The limericks and drawings made at Knowsley were created just for fun, and Lear had no plans to publish them at the time. It was not until twelve years later, in 1846, long after he had left Knowsley, that Lear published the *Book of Nonsense*.

In the first edition, there is no mention of Lear's name, the author credited simply as "Derry down Derry," taken from the limerick by that name reproduced on the frontis of the book. Just why Edward Lear preferred to keep his identity secret is unclear. Perhaps he feared that the nonsense verses and drawings would interfere with his career as a serious artist. There is no question that he was proud of these light drawings, however, and he did eventually claim authorship in the 1861 edition of the book. The immediate popularity of the *Book of Nonsense* naturally prompted his readers to speculate about the identity of the author. There was a widespread theory that Lord Derby himself wrote the verses. To Lear's irritation, this rumor persisted even after the author had revealed his identity. On his travels one day Lear encountered a gentleman and two ladies and discovered the reasoning behind this theory. By coincidence, the strangers sharing Lear's train compartment happened to be reading a copy of the *Book of Nonsense*, laughing in delight at the verses and pictures.

"How grateful," said the old gentleman to the two ladies, "all children and parents too ought to be to the statesman who has given his time to composing that charming book!"

With his hat, handkerchief, and stick, Edward Lear manages to prove his identity.

(The ladies looked puzzled, as indeed was I, the author.)

"Do you not know who is the writer of it?" asked the gentleman.

"The name is Edward Lear," said one of the ladies.

"Ah!" said the first speaker; "so it is printed, but that is only a whim of the real author, the Earl of Derby. 'Edward' is his Christian name, and, as you may see, LEAR is only EARL transposed."

"But," said the lady doubtingly, "here is a dedication to the great-grandchildren, grand-nephews, and grand-nieces of Edward, thirteenth Earl of Derby, by the author, Edward Lear."

"That," replied the other, "is simply a piece of mystification; I am in a position to know that the whole book was composed and illustrated by Lord Derby himself. In fact, there is no such person at all as Edward Lear."

"Yet," said the other lady, "some friends of mine tell me they know Mr. Lear."

"Quite a mistake! Completely a mistake!" said the old gentleman, becoming rather angry at the contradiction. "I am well aware of what I am saying. I can inform you, no such person as 'Edward Lear' exists!"

Hitherto I had kept silence, but as my hat was, as well as my handkerchief and stick, largely marked inside with my name, and as I happened to have in my pocket several letters addressed to me, the temptation was too great to resist, so, flashing all these articles at once on my would-be extinguisher's attention, I speedily reduced him to silence.

The *Book of Nonsense* was a revolutionary development in children's literature. Until Lear, books for children were stilted and sentimental, saturated with moral undertones. Lear's sole intention was to amuse children, not to make them good. Nearly twenty years after the publication of the first *Book of Nonsense*, Lewis Carroll's *Alice in Wonderland* joined Lear's volume in creating a body of nonsense and wit for children, but until Lear children's literature seemed bereft of any fun. The impact of Lear's contribution did not go unappreciated. The

Manypeeplia Upsidownia

Tureenia Ladlecum

Tigerlillia Terribilis
From *Nonsense Botany*.

Book of Nonsense was reprinted many times during Lear's own lifetime, and the course of children's literature changed forever. Even John Ruskin, the most famous critic in England, acknowledged the significance of Lear's book: "Surely the most beneficent and innocent of all books yet produced is the *Book of Nonsense*, with its corollary carols—inimitable and refreshing, and perfect in rhythm. I don't know of any author to whom I am half so grateful for my idle self as Edward Lear. I shall put him first of my hundred authors."

Edward Lear seemed to be on the threshold of success. He had a gift for making and retaining loyal friends, he had a promising career, and inexhaustible energy. Yet his potential was never realized. Ill health, unrequited love, and misdirected talents prevented him from achieving fulfillment. For a man who could so easily make people laugh, it is ironic that Edward Lear seemed always destined for a life of sadness and solitude.

A career as a zoological draftsman was out of the question. Lear's poor eyesight could not withstand the strain of the exacting work required for accurate rendering. While he was still at Knowsley he knew he couldn't continue doing this work much longer. "My eyes are so sadly worse," he wrote, "that no bird under an ostrich shall I soon be able to do." If his eyesight represented a physical hardship, his respiratory condition was even more worrisome. Suffering from chronic asthma and bronchitis, Lear found it increasingly difficult to tolerate the cold, damp winters in England. With the financial assistance of his friends at Knowsley, Lear departed for Rome in 1837 to recover his health and to begin a new career as a landscape painter. Thus began a lifetime of exile, partly as a result of physical necessity, partly self-willed. From the time he was twenty-five, until old age, Lear never settled long in any one place. Over the years, an insatiable quest for new travel experiences took him to Calabria, Sicily, Kingdom of Naples, Greece, Albania, Corfu, Egypt, Palestine, Corsica, even India. He returned to England for periods of time, but his longest stay was for four and a half years, much too long for his restless temperament and frail health. Lear had become a wanderer, at home wherever he traveled, but lost and lonely wherever he remained.

Lear and his famous cat Foss in San Remo.

Although he lived well into his seventies, Lear regarded himself as an invalid all of his life. Although he traveled far and wide, worked long and intense hours each day, Lear's fear of illness plagued him continually. Although he was never destitute (and actually managed to set aside a fair amount of money for retirement), financial problems were a constant irritant. Although he yearned for intimacy, he retreated from every real opportunity to achieve a fulfilling relationship. In fact, Lear seemed to have a knack for depriving himself of what he most craved, and for craving what was unobtainable.

Lear was a caged animal, hopelessly seeking

release, yet capable only of pacing off the limits of the barriers surrounding him. Like his drawings, he was in perpetual motion, fearing that idleness might expose him to boredom and loneliness. Was it epilepsy that induced him to exercise so diligently —walking fifteen to twenty miles a day, perhaps—or was it a need for distraction? "After all, one isn't a potato," he would say. It is no surprise that what he most disliked about painting was its sedentary nature: "No life is more *shocking* to me than sitting motionless like a petrified gorilla as to my body and limbs hour after hour—my hand meanwhile, peck peck pecking at billions of little dots and lines, while my mind is fretting and fuming through every moment of the weary day's work."

Considering his restlessness, it seems remarkable that Lear was capable of sustaining such profound friendships through the years. Distance did not prevent him from remaining a loyal friend to those he left behind in England, and his correspondence (much of which has since been published) represented a kind of lifeline to the intimacy he lacked in his immediate surroundings. He liked to complain about the number of people who wrote to him, but it was evident that he also depended on them. "Every human capable of writing ever since the invention of letters must have written to me," he grumbled, "with a few exceptions perhaps, such as the prophet Ezekiel, Mary Queen of Scots, and the Venerable Bede." It is no wonder that his correspondence was so extensive, however. After all, he devoted several hours each day to writing letters, generally in early morning before breakfast, completing as many as thirty-five in a day! This correspondence reveals the qualities that made him endearing. His humor, boundless curiosity, thoughtfulness, and vulnerability emerge in the letters he wrote to his dear and distant friends. The letters reveal his shortcomings as well, particularly his irascible nature. He was eccentric in his likes and dislikes—having a special aversion to noises, crowds, bores, large dogs, clerics, and Germans—and he could be self-indulgent and excessive, particularly with a bottle of Marsala. But he was a loveable grump, and his friends adored him.

While he was fortunate in having so many good friends, he seemed unable to secure what he most wanted: a permanent and mutually rewarding relationship with one individual. Twice he entertained the thought of marriage, but his journals reveal that he was unable to summon the courage to propose. Both women married other men, altogether unaware, no doubt, of Lear's anguish. And so his loneliness continued. "The 'marriage phantasy,'" he wrote in his diary, "will not let me be. —Yet seems an intangible myth. To think of it no more, is to resolve on all the rest of life being passed thus—alone—and year by year getting more weary—to encourage it, is to pursue a thread leading to doubt and perhaps to more positive misery. . . ." Perhaps his mother's rejection prevented him from ever trusting another woman. Perhaps the secrecy surrounding his epilepsy discouraged him from revealing what seemed most shameful. Perhaps a bout with syphilis early in adulthood scared him off from future physical relations, although he seems to have been totally cured of the disease. Perhaps if his friends Franklin Lushington or Hubert Congreve had returned the ardor he had felt for them, he might have settled into a homosexual liaison that would have satisfied his longings. Whatever the circumstances, it seems apparent that Lear was never to enjoy the comfort of a loving relationship. Only his servant, Giorgio Cocali, remained at his side for twenty-seven years of service and was eventually buried alongside Lear's own gravesite in San Remo, Italy.

With the years, "the Morbids" plagued Lear even more intensely. At times his despair seemed insufferable. Nearing a mental breakdown in 1877, he wrote in his diary:

Tears, idle tears—always. In vain I resolve and re-resolve: —gloom contracts and convulses me. But I am gradually getting to see that the past must be past, and buried: —yet I can by no means think of anything to put forward as the future. Meanwhile the present is a fearful blank—cutting of heart strings the only serious order of the day. . . . In vain I work for an hour—tears blind me. In vain I play on the Piano,—I get convulsed: in vain I pace the large room—or try to sleep.

Nor did Lear derive much satisfaction from his accomplishments as a painter. His decision at twenty-three to become a landscape artist was based on practical necessity—his ill health and the need to earn an income—as well as his love for travel. But he did not take pleasure in painting. "Yes," he wrote to a friend, "I certainly *do* hate the act of painting, and although I go steadily on, it is like grinding my nose off." To achieve recognition as a serious painter he felt it necessary to create large canvases in oil, landscapes that would be exhibited at the Royal Academy and sold at high prices. Following the advice of a good friend, Holman Hunt (one of the most distinguished of the Pre-Raphaelite painters), he made every effort to study nature closely and to paint precisely what he saw before him. In spite of Lear's hard work, and two years of arduous study at the Royal Academy Schools, he was unable to develop his oil painting beyond the most pedestrian level.

If Lear had not applied so much pressure on himself to produce major canvases in oil, he might have taken greater pride in his watercolors, which were far superior. There were also opportunities here for an artist of Lear's talent and zest for travel. Illustrated travel books were quite fashionable in England, and Lear's particular eye for the un-spoiled landscape and for classical antiquities was appealing to English taste. He showed promise when, in 1841, he published *Views in Rome and Its Environs*, which consisted of lithographs taken from his drawings. And his second book, *Illustrated Excursions in Italy*, impressed Queen Victoria so greatly that she invited Lear to give her a course of twelve drawing lessons in 1846.

In spite of this fine beginning, Lear seemed unable to make much of a success of his career. Dismissing his watercolor drawings as mere "topo-graphical landscapes," he charged so little for them that they did not inspire the confidence of collectors. Only by selling a large volume was he able to stay afloat financially, and he might turn out anywhere from 60 to 250 at one time! These "Tyrants," as Lear called them, were produced so rapidly that he released many that would have been better destroyed. Yet it would be unfair to discredit the watercolors simply because Lear had such a low opinion of them. His importance as a painter was overlooked until the end of the 1920s, when the sale of several thousand watercolors from the estates of his friends Lushington and Lord Northbrook aroused new critical appraisal,

Lear's cat Foss.

and his reputation has increased ever since.

During his lifetime, Lear's fame—and a portion of his income—derived not from his paintings, but from his books of nonsense. Even here, his business judgment could betray him. Having published the first *Book of Nonsense* himself, he decided to take the revised edition to a publisher in 1860. When both Smith & Elder and Routledge & Warne turned it down, Lear produced it with his own funds, this time using wood engraving produced by the Brothers Dalziel, which was less expensive than the earlier lithographic edition. Routledge took 1000 copies for distribution, of which 500 sold within a few days. Their success with the book prompted them to offer £100 for the copyright. Lear settled only on £125. It was a bad deal for Lear: in his own lifetime the book went into nineteen editions, for which he received no further income.

To his first *Book of Nonsense*, consisting primarily of happy and light-hearted limericks written for the children at Knowsley, he added *Nonsense Songs, Stories, Botany, and Alphabets* in 1871, includ-ing stories about travel and wandering, such as "The Owl and the Pussy Cat," "The Duck and the Kangaroo," and "The History of the Seven Families of the Lake Pipple-Popple." In later years he wrote more serious verse—"The Dong with the Luminous Nose" and "The Pelican Chorus"—in which he looked back on a happiness gone forever. In the end, Lear made no distinction between what was written for himself and what was meant for children. They were one and the same. To children he gave what he most longed for in his own life: laughter and love. In sharing with them what was most tender in him, he gave children the greatest gift he had to offer.

In 1871, Lear decided finally to settle in San Remo, Italy, where he built a home called Villa Emily (after his dear friend Emily Tennyson, the wife of the poet). When a hotel was built on the adjoining property, blocking his light and view to the Mediterranean, he built another home, called Villa Tennyson, where he lived until his death in 1888. He died, as he had lived, beloved by friends and children, but alone to the end.

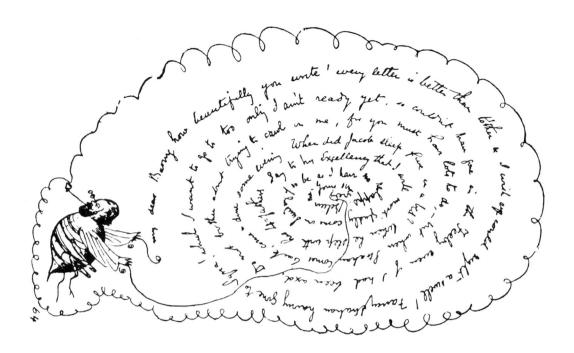

"How pleasant to know Mr. Lear!"
    Who has written such volumes of stuff!
Some think him ill-tempered and queer,
    But a few think him pleasant enough.

His mind is concrete and fastidious,
    His nose is remarkably big;
His visage is more or less hideous,
    His beard it resembles a wig.

He has ears, and two eyes, and ten fingers,
    Leastways if you reckon two thumbs;
Long ago he was one of the singers,
    But now he is one of the dumbs.

He sits in a beautiful parlour,
    With hundreds of books on the wall
He drinks a great deal of Marsala,
    But never gets tipsy at all.

He has many friends, laymen and clerical,
    Old Foss is the name of his cat;
His body is perfectly spherical,
    He weareth a runcible hat.

When he walks in a waterproof white,
    The children run after him so!
Calling out, "He's come out in his night-
    gown, that crazy old Englishman, oh!"

He weeps by the side of the ocean,
    He weeps on the top of the hill;
He purchases pancakes and lotion,
    And chocolate shrimps from the mill.

He reads but he cannot speak Spanish,
    He cannot abide ginger-beer:
Ere the days of his pilgrimage vanish,
    How pleasant to know Mr. Lear!

Edward Lear

"'Begin at the beginning,' the King said very gravely, 'and go on till you
come to the end: then stop.'" From *Alice in Wonderland*.

John Tenniel

From *Alice's Adventures in Wonderland*.

"And what is the use of a book without pictures or conversations?" wondered Alice as she looked at the volume her sister was reading. Since 1865, when Alice uttered these thoughts in the very first paragraph of *Alice's Adventures in Wonderland*, well over one hundred artists have taken up Alice's challenge to illustrate her fantastic story. Yet none has supplanted the original version illustrated by John Tenniel whose pictures appear in simple harmony with the prose, as if words and images were created by one hand to form the perfect union. So perfect, in fact, is this union that it is tempting to assume author and illustrator must also have been in perfect harmony. Nothing could be farther from the truth. Like Tweedledum and Tweedledee, Lewis Carroll and John Tenniel are linked forever in the public's mind. But, like Tweedledum and Tweedledee, Lewis Carroll and John Tenniel also "Agreed to have a battle." For *Alice's Adventures in Wonderland* and *Through the*

Looking Glass, John Tenniel produced a total of ninety-two drawings, of which Carroll liked only one—Humpty Dumpty. Perhaps this was more praise than the author would have bestowed on any other illustrator, but it was not an auspicious evaluation.

To be fair, Lewis Carroll's grievances against his illustrator were only human. After all, Carroll (or Charles Dodgson, which was his real name) was already a man of enormous accomplishment by the time he was thirty. An ordained deacon, he lectured on mathematics at Christ Church, Oxford, and was a serious writer on mathematics and logic well before he began to write children's stories. Infatuated with an eleven-year-old girl named Alice Liddell, Carroll created *Alice's Adventures Under Ground* to entertain the child in 1863. The first draft of 18,000 words was handwritten and garnished with thirty-seven illustrations by the author, loving testimony of his feelings for her. Persuaded

"She was now rather more than nine feet high,"
from *Alice's Adventures in Wonderland*.

by his friends to publish the manuscript, Carroll enlarged the draft to 35,000 words and committed the time and funds to printing the book, supervising every aspect of the illustration, production, and publication. By nature an exacting and methodical man—if not downright prim—the author was particularly fretful over the publication of the book because of his special feelings for Alice Liddell.

It must have been a difficult decision for Carroll to follow the advice of his friends not to use his own illustrations for the Alice book. He took pride in his artistic efforts, although he knew he was a more accomplished photographer than draftsman, and so he agreed to compromise by preparing his own illustrations for the shorter manuscript as a private gift for Alice Liddell.

Alice was already partially in galleys when John Tenniel was introduced to Lewis Carroll in 1864. For nearly fifteen years Tenniel had been one of the chief contributors to *Punch* and it was Tom Taylor, an editor at the publication, who introduced the writer to the illustrator. Carroll had admired Tenniel's rendition of *Aesop's Fables* and thought him suitable for the beasts in the Alice book. Although Tenniel was extremely busy with his work for *Punch*, he was attracted to the notion of illustrating *Alice* because it gave him the opportunity to create more animal drawings, a subject that had fascinated him since he was inspired years before by the work of the French illustrator J.J. Grandville.

After reading the manuscript, Tenniel agreed to do forty-two illustrations, for which Carroll insisted on giving detailed instructions concerning the subject, size, and position on the page. The wood engravings would be prepared by the Brothers Dalziel and printed at Oxford by Clarendon Press, all at Carroll's personal expense. Originally planned for Christmas publication, they both soon agreed the date was unrealistic and prepared instead for release in 1865.

From the outset there were difficulties.

Harry Furniss, who also encountered problems with Lewis Carroll years later when he illustrated Carroll's *Sylvie and Bruno*, described the author as "a wit, a gentleman, a bore and an egoist," qualities Tenniel no doubt faced as soon as he began to illustrate *Alice*. Rankled that he was unable to execute his own illustrations, Carroll demanded the artist execute his vision precisely. He was adamant that the artist not introduce any alien elements into the story; there was only one truthful portrayal possible. "Don't give Alice so much crinoline," he cautioned Tenniel. "The White Knight must not have whiskers; he must not be made to

"Her eyes immediately met those of a caterpillar,"
from *Alice's Adventures in Wonderland.*

look old," he insisted. In evaluating the artist's work, Carroll's orientation as a mathematician was likely to intrude. Harry Furniss reported that when Carroll would receive one of the drawings for *Sylvie and Bruno*, the author—using a magnifying glass, if necessary—would count the number of lines to the square inch and compare this figure with the number of lines to the square inch of a Tenniel before making an assessment of the drawing.

Carroll surely met his match with John Tenniel. The illustrator could be every bit as disagreeable as the author. The two were alike in many ways, in fact. Were it not for their differences over a project they both took so seriously, it is possible they might have actually admired each other. Both men were truly products of the Victorian age. Both were insular, even provincial; Carroll's territory confined to Oxford, Tenniel's to London. (Tenniel spent his youth in Kensington and lived there until his death.) Both were conservative. Carroll was opposed to any kind of reform—although he was on friendly terms with modern poets, painters, and actors—and Tenniel remained conservative all his life.

Their taste in art was similar as well. Tenniel shared Carroll's drive for perfection, and his appreciation for exquisite line and modeling. Tenniel even followed closely a few of Carroll's Alice drawings, such as the pool of tears, long-necked Alice, and Father William. Where they differed, however, was in regard to the Pre-Raphaelites. These radical friends of Lewis Carroll were convinced that only the close study of nature would produce truthful art. Too much the product of academic training, John Tenniel preferred to rely

"You are old, father William," from
Alice's Adventures in Wonderland.

on visual memory. Carroll pleaded with Tenniel to draw animals from life, but Tenniel adamantly refused, insisting that the animals in *Alice* must be fanciful creations from the imagination, not shapeless renditions of nature. Carroll finally surrendered, but with great reluctance. "Mr. Tenniel is the only artist who has drawn for me," he wrote, "who resolutely refused to use a model and declared he no more needed one than I should need a multiplication table to work a mathematical problem." The argument was too logical for Carroll to refute.

If Carroll took an unreasonable approach to pictorial content, Tenniel could be equally tyrannical about literary content. "A *wasp* in a *wig*," he wrote to Carroll when he read this passage in the galleys of *Through the Looking Glass*, "is altogether beyond the appliances of art.... Don't think me brutal, but I am bound to say that the 'wasp' chapter doesn't interest me in the least, and I can't see my way to a picture. If you want to shorten the book, I can't help thinking—with all submission—that *there* is your opportunity." And so the wasp chapter was removed. Carroll felt that he was also generous when Tenniel objected to the walrus and the carpenter. The author recollected this incident when Harry Furniss questioned a word choice in *Sylvie and Bruno*: "... I made the very same offer to Mr. Tenniel when he remonstrated against the walrus and the carpenter as a hopeless combination and begged to have the carpenter abolished—I remember offering 'baronet' and 'butterfly' (which, by the way, might suit *you*), but he finally chose 'Carpenter.'"

In spite of their disputes over pictures and text, the book was moving along without delay. It was necessary to select a suitable title. *Alice's Adventures*

"The Duchess was sitting on a three-legged stool," from *Alice's Adventures in Wonderland*.

Under Ground was eliminated because it was "too like a lesson book about mines." Carroll wavered over *Alice's Golden Hour*, then dismissed it because there was already a published book entitled *Lillian's Golden Hours*. Then he considered various Elf-land alternatives—*Alice Among the Elves, Alice's Hour in Elf-Land, Alice's Doings in Elf-Land*—before he finally settled on *Alice's Adventures in Wonderland*. To Carroll's good fortune, Macmillan, a large publishing firm that would ensure the finest distribution for the book, agreed to handle it on a commission basis.

With everything now in place, all that remained was the production.

"There never was an author more elaborately careful than Lewis Carroll for the details of production," wrote Charles Morgan in his history of the Macmillan Publishing Company, "or one that can have more sorely tried the patience of his publisher." Carroll's obsession for perfection extended into every aspect of the production process,

from the selection of the binding (he preferred *bright red*) to the packing of the books (a diagram showing how the parcels should be wrapped and tied was sent to the Macmillan mailroom). But the area of greatest concern was the quality of the printing. And in this domain John Tenniel was the tyrant.

Tenniel was accustomed to working with wood engravers, having prepared his drawings for the foremost engravers in London, the Brothers Dalziel and Joseph Swain. Each week, under great pressure, he made a new drawing to be reproduced in *Punch*. In an interview with M.H. Spielmann, the author of *History of Punch*, published in 1895, Tenniel described his method of preparing his drawings for reproduction in *Punch*:

I get my subject on Wednesday night; I think it out carefully on Thursday, and make my rough sketch. On Friday morning I begin and I stick to it all day, with my nose well down on the block. By means of tracing

"She was a little startled by
seeing the Cheshire Cat sitting on a bough of
a tree a few yards off," from *Alice's
Adventures in Wonderland.*

*paper—on which I make such alterations of composition
and action I may consider necessary—I transfer my
design to the wood and draw on that. The first sketch I
may, and often do, complete later on as a commission . . .
well, the block being finished, it is handed over to
Swain's boy at about 6:30 to 7 o'clock, who has been
waiting for it for an hour or so, and at 7:30 it is put in
hand for engraving. That is completed on the following
night, and on Monday night I receive by post the copy of
next Wednesday's paper.*

Tenniel was fortunate in being able to depend
upon engravers as expert as Joseph Swain and the
Brothers Dalziel, because the artist was not particularly concerned with the technique of drawing on
wood, nor was he skillful in this respect. In fact, it
appears that he had little, if any, training in drawing at all! After he made the drawing on paper
with pencil, he would transfer it to the wood
simply by using tracing paper and a hard pencil.
Spielmann noted that Tenniel's drawing on the
block was so faint that "it looked as if you could
blow it off the wood." The artist refused to take

responsibility for the quality of the reproduction—he complained constantly that Swain's engravings distorted the original—because he had little understanding or interest in the technical process. According to Spielmann, "Swain always *interpreted* John Tenniel's work, not simply facsimile'd his exquisite grey drawings. So Swain would thicken his lines . . . and otherwise bring the resources of the engraver's art to bear upon the work of the master in pencil."

Tenniel must have taken greater pains in preparing his illustrations for *Alice*, sparing the Brothers Dalziel some of the hardships imposed on Swain. Using tracing paper as a guide, Tenniel first placed only the heavy outlines of the drawing on the block, and then completed the finer details directly on the block itself, working closely with the engravers in the process. The precision and delicacy of Tenniel's drawing represented a challenge for the Dalziels and they worked with great care in meeting the exacting demands of author and illustrator. Tenniel marked the proofs with pencilled comments, occasionally in red, and corrections with Chinese white. (Corrections on the block could be made by cutting out the portion of the block and inserting a plug to re-cut.) The approved blocks were then signed with Tenniel's monogram and with Dalziel's name.

Although proofs were pulled from the wood blocks, these originals were not used for printing *Alice's Adventures in Wonderland*. Instead electrotypes were made for printing: a wax mold was first made of each block and on the surface of the mold a thin shell of copper was deposited by electrolysis. Reinforced and mounted, the electrotypes could provide an exact and durable substitute for the original wood block, ideal for large editions.

While the plates may have been prepared properly, the printing was another matter. Clarendon Press had little experience with such a complex printing assignment, but Lewis Carroll didn't seem to notice. When they presented him with a sample copy in May 1865, he said he liked "the look of it exceedingly" and approved the publication of 2,000

"The March Hare and the Hatter were
having tea: a Dormouse was sitting between them,"
from *Alice's Adventures in Wonderland*.

"'Who is this?' the Queen said to the Knave of Hearts,"
from *Alice's Adventures in Wonderland*.

copies, urging the printer to proceed quickly for his young friends who "are all grown out of childhood so alarmingly fast." The edition was printed, but the sample sent to Tenniel was altogether unacceptable, and he urged Carroll to reject the printing. He wrote a stern letter which Carroll showed to Macmillan, groaning, "He is entirely dissatisfied with the printing of the pictures, and I suppose we will have to do it all again." Although Carroll feared considerable financial loss, he did agree to suppress the edition, and turned over the printing to Richard Clay, a London firm better equipped to do the job. (The 1,952 copies printed by Clarendon lay as unbound sheets until Carroll sold them—with Tenniel's consent—to

Appleton in New York in 1866, evidence of the low opinion they held of American cultural standards.) With the type completely re-set, *Alice's Adventures in Wonderland* was reprinted and finally issued in November 1865. Tenniel had won his case and boasted about his triumph in a letter to the Dalziels: "I protested so strongly against the disgraceful printing . . . [Carroll] *cancelled the edition*."

Lewis Carroll had taken a fair financial risk with *Alice's Adventures in Wonderland*, but the risk paid off. The reviews were pleasant enough—not overwhelming—but the refreshing little book, delightfully free of moral overtones, appealed to the public immediately and its fame quickly spread by word of mouth. From 1865 to 1868 a new edition appeared every year and in two years Carroll had made a profit of £250 on his initial investment of £350 (which included Tenniel's fee). During Carroll's lifetime 159,000 copies of *Alice's Adventures in Wonderland* were printed in Great Britain alone, and many other editions appeared on the Continent and in America as well.

The success of the first *Alice* naturally prompted a demand for a sequel, and Lewis Carroll was forced to admit that no one was better qualified for the job than Tenniel. Tenniel refused, however, claiming he was occupied with other work. In despair Carroll approached three other artists— Richard Doyle, J. Noel Paton, and W.S. Gilbert— but all politely turned him down and Carroll returned to Tenniel, pleading that he take the assignment. Reluctantly, Tenniel agreed to do the pictures "at such time as he can find." After innumerable delays, *Through the Looking Glass* finally appeared six years later.

"And certainly the glass was beginning to melt away, just like a bright silvery mist," from *Through the Looking Glass*.

Tenniel's abrasive relationship with Carroll persisted through the second volume as it had through the first, and Tenniel was not likely to undertake a similar assignment again. "It is a curious fact," he wrote to Lewis Carroll some years later, "that with *Through the Looking Glass* the faculty of making drawings for book illustrations departed for me. . . . I have done nothing in that direction since." This disdain for book illustration probably had more to do with his contempt for Lewis Carroll. When he heard that Harry Furniss was about to illustrate *Sylvie and Bruno*, Tenniel dashed off a letter to his colleague, warning him, "Lewis Carroll is impossible. . . . I'll give you a week, old chap; *you* will never put up with that fellow a day longer."

For all the fame they brought John Tenniel, which *was* flattering, the two *Alice* books represented a disruption in the artist's quiet life. In every respect, Tenniel was a man of moderation, the more reason he was so unnerved by that peevish

"'Let's pretend there's a way of getting through into the glass, somehow.'" from *Through the Looking Glass*.

"And still the Queen kept crying, 'Faster! Faster!'"
from *Through the Looking Glass.*

Lewis Carroll, "that conceited old Don." Tenniel's life had been a paradigm of Victorian restraint. Happily married to Julia Giani, he was bereft when she died suddenly in 1856, only two years after their wedding. He did not re-marry. For twenty-three years Tenniel's mother-in-law cared for his home. After she died, his sister stepped in to care for him. Throughout his life he followed a modest routine, enjoyed riding, hunting, rowing, and performing now and then in amateur theatrical productions. In his professional life he was also steadfast. Tenniel spent fifty years on the staff of *Punch*, for more than half that time its principal cartoonist. During this long career, his illustrations appeared in more than thirty books and he produced some 2,000 cartoons. The general public remembers Tenniel for his two *Alice* books, while his illustrations for *Punch* were also a great inspiration to future illustrators, including Ernest Shepard, who eventually sat in his place at the *Punch* table, and Arthur Rackham, who eventually illustrated his own version of *Alice's Adventures in Wonderland.*

It was from his father, John Tenniel, Sr.—the fencing master of the Angelo School—that the artist must have inherited the ingredients required for success: discipline, hard work, and a quick mind. If he didn't happen to apply these qualities to athletics, as his father would have liked, he did adopt all the features of a model Victorian gentleman —manliness, honor, dignity, and good humor, tempered by extreme self-control. "Few men have been so reserved," noted a *Punch* colleague. "Even his most intimate friends knew nothing of him in the intimate sense." The extent to which he controlled his emotions was demonstrated during a fencing bout with his father when he was twenty years old. When the button from his father's foil accidentally dropped to the ground, the blade swept across John Tenniel's eye. Seeing no unusual emotional response, the elder Tenniel never suspected that his son had been blinded in the right eye by this unfortunate stroke of the foil. Tenniel only made light of his injury. Years later, he quipped, "It's a curious thing, is it not, that two of the principal men on *Punch*, du Maurier and I, have only two eyes between them?'' (George du Maurier, the famous black-and-white artist, had lost the sight of his left eye, probably the result of a detached retina.)

The blind eye never deterred Tenniel from continuing his career as an artist, his ambition since boyhood. Except for a few lessons at the Royal Academy Schools, Tenniel was essentially self-taught. He joined the Clipstone Street Art Society, where he drew from life and attended anatomy lectures, and he studied the drawings and prints at the British Museum. His skills in academic painting earned him a commission in 1846 to paint one of the frescoes—Dryden's St. Celia—in the Houses of Parliament. The government's commission took him to Munich where he studied fresco techniques, one of only two trips abroad Tenniel ever made.

" 'I'll see you safe to the end of the wood,' said the White Knight,''
from *Through the Looking Glass*.

"Humpty Dumpty leant forwards and offered Alice his hand," from *Through the Looking Glass.*

"Tweedledum and Tweedledee agreed to have a battle," from *Through the Looking Glass.*

Tenniel's early start in painting proved not to be the direction he would eventually take in his career. From the early 1840s he earned additional income by working in black and white, contributing illustrations to books, and in 1848 he illustrated a book of his own, *Aesop's Fables*, containing the delicate drawings of animals that ultimately led to his introduction to *Punch*, and attracted the eye of Lewis Carroll.

When Tenniel first came to *Punch*, in 1850, the paper was in its most radical days, still under the leadership of Douglas Jerrold. At the time John Leech was the principal cartoonist and soon Tenniel's old friend Charles Keene would join as well. Tenniel replaced the cartoonist Richard (Dicky) Doyle, a Catholic who had resigned from *Punch* in protest to the paper's anti-papist policies. During his long tenure at the paper, Tenniel saw the publication drift away from the ideals of the founders, becoming a more conservative publication that upheld Victorian virtues of rank and wealth. For his part, Tenniel professed no political ideology, "At least, if I have my own little politics, I keep them to myself, and profess only those of my paper." In the early days of the publication, the artists had something to say about the subjects they would draw for the next issue, decisions that were made in the weekly meetings held at the *Punch* "table." Tenniel did not participate in these decisions, although he attended the meetings, preferring instead to accept whatever assignments were given him every Wednesday evening.

When Leech died in 1864, Tenniel became the principal cartoonist, a position he held until his retirement in 1901. During this long tenure, Tenniel's cartoons appeared each week, consistently humorous and generally in very good taste. He was at his best when he created his humorous animal drawings; his figures were less effective. Apart from the time at Clipstone Street, he never drew from life, working from other pictures or photographs if he needed reference. This practice enabled him to render imaginative animals from his extraordinary visual memory, but meant that he was less successful with human anatomy. (In the *Alice* volumes, for example, the anthropomorphized beasts are more convincing than Alice herself, whose head is slightly too large for the delicate body below.)

Tenniel's *Punch* cartoons and *Alice* books earned him a popularity seldom accorded an illustrator in England. Yet fame never altered the steady beat of his routine. Tenniel was probably the only one who was surprised, therefore, when the Gladstone government announced in 1893 that they had conferred John Tenniel's knighthood. Thereafter he would be known as Sir John Tenniel.

Tenniel was eighty when he retired from *Punch*. Although the eyesight in his left eye was failing from overwork, he continued to paint occasionally in watercolors for amusement until he became totally blind. Except for colleagues from *Punch* who came to visit now and then, his only diversion was the quiet sound of the housekeeper's voice as she read aloud to him. Lewis Carroll had long since died and no further disruptions of any sort were anticipated. It was nearly a half-century since the publication of *Alice's Adventures in Wonderland* when Sir John Tenniel passed away quietly on February 25, 1914. He died in his Kensington home just three days before his ninety-fourth birthday.

"Queen Alice," from *Through the Looking Glass*.

From *The Frog Prince* (1874). For Walter Crane, book
illustration represented the ideal collaboration of artist and craftsman and a means of expressing his own ideas about
design and education.

Walter Crane

From *Flora's Feast* (1892)

NOTHING IRRITATED WALTER CRANE more than hearing reviewers describe him as the "Academician of the Nursery." For one, his designs for children represented only a part of his total output as an artist and designer. For another, he felt he had dedicated his entire career to innovation and experimentation, achievements that represented to him the very antithesis of the term, academician.

Walter Crane was a rather shy, slender man whose personal life seemed to be a chapter from one of his nursery books. For many years he lived in Kensington with his wife and two children (Beatrice and Lionel, for whom Crane created several charming unpublished picture books), and a menagerie that contained at one time or another a jerboa, golden pheasant, alligator, marmoset, owl, rabbits, guinea pigs, mongoose, and sundry cats and dogs. While he worked, a squirrel would sit perched on his shoulder.

Although his colorful and delightful books have entertained children for over 100 years, his achievements are more remarkable than these little books might suggest. In only ten years—between 1865 and 1875—Crane transformed the children's book as it was known until then by applying his considerable design skills to a more advanced method of production, raising the quality of inexpensive picture books as no one before him had done. While he was, it is true, a charming illustrator, he also represented a new breed of designer whose work and ideas influenced many generations of artists that followed him.

Born on August 15, 1845, the son of a locally respected portrait painter, Walter Crane was encouraged to paint and draw from the very outset. In the studio, the boy sketched the hands and faces of the subjects of his father's portrait commissions, and pored over the journals and papers displaying the work of contemporary illustrators and fine artists. At thirteen he decorated books for amusement, creating delicate watercolors surrounded by borders of flowers and embellished with decorated initials. His father, sensing a potential career for his son, presented young Walter's efforts to William James Linton, whose printing and engraving company was among the best in England. (Linton's firm prepared the engravings for such prominent artists as John Tenniel, J.E. Millais, and George du Maurier.) Guiding his son to Linton was wise: as England was entering a decade of extraordinary growth in publishing, wood engraving was assuming an artistic importance of its own, and Walter Crane's talents could be put to good use. Linton was so impressed by the lad's designs that he agreed to take him on as an apprentice without charging the usual premium.

In his *Reminiscences*, Crane described the atelier:

It was a typical wood-engraver's office of that time, a row of engravers at work at a fixed bench covered with green baize running the whole length of the room under the windows with eyeglass stands and rows of gravers. And for night-work, a round table with a gaslamp in the centre, surrounded with a circle of large clear glass globes filled with water to magnify the light and concentrate it on the blocks upon which the engravers (or "peckers" or "wood-peckers," as they were commonly called) worked, resting them upon small circular leather bags or cushions filled with sand, upon which they could easily be held and turned about by the left hand while being worked upon with the tool in the right.

Linton first employed about six engravers and an equal number of apprentices who studied from three to six years to master the craft. This was the period required to develop skills that demanded speed, efficiency, and high standards. Two levels

of engravers were employed to create an ordinary print: a "tint" or "facsimile" person to do the easier, mechanical work (such as shadow areas), and a master engraver to work on the more difficult passages, such as faces. Crane, as it turned out, was essentially apprenticed to make drawings on wood for others to engrave. Here he began to study under Linton's partner Orrin Smith. "He set me at his table," wrote Crane of his first day,

to draw one of my own pen-and-ink sketches on a small block of boxwood, showing me the way to prepare it with a little zinc-white powder (oxide of bismuth was generally used) mixed with water and rubbed backwards and forwards on the smooth surface of the boxwood until dry. On this the design was traced in outline, and then drawn with a hard pencil to get the lines as clear and sharp as possible for the engravers. . . . My chief work was to make little drawings, on fragments of boxwood, for the apprentices to practise upon. The outside edges of the boxwood, after the square block had been sawn out of a cross section of the tree, were used up in this way.

Because Linton had perceived Crane's talent for drawing and for inventive design, he gave the lad work to develop this talent—assignments at the zoological gardens for practice in drawing animals, and assignments to improve the faulty animal drawings of others drawn on the block, and even an occasional assignment as a press artist.

When Crane's apprenticeship ended in 1862, Linton provided him with introductions to potential clients, which landed him some respectable commissions. The following year, one of these clients introduced Crane to the man who would be responsible for establishing Crane's reputation as a children's book illustrator: Edmund Evans.

But he had brought with him
a green Christmas-tree,
And sprigs of crisp holly,
And all that was jolly
In puddings and presents, as
there you may see.

Now, if this party is such as
may please one,
We hope you'll receive them,
For here we must leave them,
Wishing you all the good things
of the season

From *King Luckie Boy's Party* (1871). Like the Japanese artists whose work he admired, Crane adopted a rebus for his signature, a symbol of a crane.

With an eye for talent and an instinct for business, Edmund Evans was the proprietor of the finest color printing firm of his day. By the 1860s, color printing with wood blocks represented one of the most exciting aspects of the growing book market, and Evans was a master at producing attractive productions with economy. For nearly ten years he had been printing so-called "yellow backs" (also called "mustard plaisters")—inexpensive railway novels put out by many publishers to meet the growing demands of an expanding literate class. Perhaps the earliest equivalents of mass paperbacks for adult readers, these books were bound between inexpensive boards and clad in a glossy yellow paper with a picture printed on the front. The name, "yellow backs," derived from Evans' introduction of a yellow enamelled paper after he had received complaints from the trade about how easily the paler paper covers were spoiled. Although Evans also printed more expensive publications, the yellow-back productions were largely responsible for his firm's prosperity.

Evans employed several artists to create designs for these yellow backs, and first hired the eighteen-year-old Walter Crane to provide cover illustrations for this purpose. Until this time, Crane had little experience with color work, but he soon adapted. On his part, Evans immediately took note of Crane's talents, with a single qualification: "The only subjects I found he could not draw," Evans wrote, "were figure subjects of everyday life." Since so many of the yellow backs portrayed just these everyday life scenes, Evans decided that the illustrator's gift for imaginative subjects would be better applied to children's books. As it turned out, Evans had already considered extending his own color printing activities to include inexpensive children's books, and so he embarked on a program of printing a new line of books, using new methods of production.

He devised a means of creating an eight-page form designed from cover to cover, and printed in color throughout, so economically planned that these slim, large-format volumes could sell for sixpence. For a toy book—as these sixpenny editions were called—the front cover was pictorial and the last page carried advertisements.

The toy-book idea was not new. Designed simply to entertain, these slender, inexpensive picture books appeared soon after the accession of Queen Victoria in 1837 and were devoured by the Victorian middle-class readers almost immediately. Dean and Son claimed to have published over 200 titles by 1858 and Routledge had already issued thirty-six toy books by the time Crane and Evans undertook their own. Crane, however, did not find these early picture books terribly commendable; "They were not very inspiring. These were generally careless and unimaginative woodcuts, very casually coloured by hand, dabs of pink and emerald green being laid across faces and frocks with a somewhat reckless aim."

Working under Evans' technical direction, Crane was able to produce sixpenny toy books that were attractive and imaginative, and he created an average of three a year. His training with Linton had prepared him for these experiments, as Crane himself observed: "I consider it was an advantage to me thus to have been assisted with a definite handicraft, as well as an art like wood engraving, instead of going through the usual academic or art course." His efforts surely paid off: during the ten years he worked in tandem with Evans he became the most famous children's book illustrator of his day. Although Crane's achievements after that period extended into many other areas of design, these books he created with Evans clearly identified him as the "father of the illustrated children's book."

They made a good team. For each book, Evans handed Crane a precise layout of the entire volume, and the illustrator made his drawings following the pattern set forth in this dummy. After Evans transferred the drawing to the block, he pulled a proof and gave it to Crane for coloring. Then Evans mixed the colors with the same powdered pigment the artist had used on the colored proof. To keep down the printing costs, Evans used just three colors at first—not ten to twenty as many of the other printers did—although he increased this number with later publications. As Crane became more adept at designing with color, his books revealed greater imagination and fluency in their execution. Because the paper lacked opacity, each sheet was printed on one side only, the reverse left blank. A heavier sheet of paper was employed for the cover, pasted on both sides, and stitched through the center of the book in a single gathering. To receive any profit at all from these carefully produced picture books (and it was a small profit at

Ali Baba's son, who one day invited him to his father's house. On hearing that the new guest would eat no salt with his meat, Morgiana's suspicions were aroused, and she recognised him as the captain of the robbers. After dinner she undertook to perform a dance before the company, and at the end of it pointed a dagger at the captain, and then plunged it into his heart. Ali Baba was very much shocked, until Morgiana explained the reasons for her conduct; he then gave her to his son in marriage, and they lived in great prosperity and happiness ever after.

From *The Arabian Nights* (1873).

"No, Master," said Puss, "give me boots to my feet—
A pair of top-boots—and please leave me alive,
And you shall just see how we'll flourish and thrive."

From *Puss in Boots* (1874). The correct integration of picture and text was vital to Crane's plan, with each page in turn subordinate to the design of the book as a whole.

that) a minimum edition of 10,000 had to be printed.

Evans contributed more than technical assistance to Crane: he acted as Crane's artistic and business adviser as well. Evans advised Crane about subject matter, about layouts and design, and he managed the business transactions with the publishers. At the outset, both Crane and Evans worked for Frederick G. Warne and for Ward Lock Publishers, but soon Routledge took over the publication of all Crane's children's books. In addition to the Sixpenny Toy Series created for Routledge, Crane also produced a Shilling Series of picture books. By 1875, Crane had created twenty-nine sixpennies for Routledge and eight shilling books, and their sales were so good that the publisher issued composite volumes of several toy books.

The variations in subject were vast: he illustrated several alphabet books and other primers and illustrated stories written by himself and in collaboration with his sister, Lucy. He illustrated the Charles Perrault stories, which were among the stories first collected in France during the seventeenth century: *Cinderella, Little Red Riding Hood, Blue Beard, Puss in Boots, Sleeping Beauty*. He illustrated traditional English tales, such as *The House That Jack Built, Cock Robin, Story of Jenny Wren*; and traditional English rhymes, such as *One, Two, Buckle My Shoe, The Fairy Ship*, and *The Three Little Pigs*. He illustrated a compendium of eastern stories called, *The Arabian Nights*, introducing Ali Baba and Aladdin. And he illustrated contemporary nursery stories, such as *Goody Two Shoes* and *My Mother*.

In 1876, Crane's contract with Routledge expired and when the publishers refused to renegotiate a contract that would give Crane royalties—instead of the flat fees they had paid previously—Crane

From *Goody Two Shoes* (1874).

From *Beauty and the Beast* (1874). In the elaborate
interior settings of his illustrations, Crane expressed his ideas
about good design.

From *The Princess of Belle Etoile* (1875).
Crane shared with the Pre-Raphaelites an affection
for medieval design and subject matter.

went on to illustrate different kinds of children's books, working independently with Evans, including *Baby's Opera, The Baby's Bouquet,* and *The Baby's Own Aesop.* From 1875 to 1889, Crane also illustrated many books in black and white by Mrs. Molesworth, a popular Victorian writer for children. Although there are some fine examples in this series, the work is uneven, leaving Crane's toy books as the most enduring contributions.

Crane devoted a great deal of thought to the kind of designs that would appeal to children, and his particular style is consistent with these theories:

Children, like the ancient Egyptians, appear to see most things in profile, and like definite statements in design. They prefer well-defined forms and bright, frank colour. They don't want to bother about three dimensions. They can accept symbolic representations. They themselves employ drawing . . . as a kind of picture-writing, and eagerly follow a pictured story. When they can count, they can check your quantities, so that the artist must be careful to deliver, in dealing with, for instance, "The Song of Sixpence," his tale of twenty-four blackbirds.

Crane was seriously concerned with the power of the picture to educate and to inform, and he felt the illustrator had an important responsibility in shaping the child's intelligence. Long before children can read or write, children can learn "definite ideas from good pictures." Over the years, Crane created three primers, in addition to his alphabet books, which were used specifically for instruction. In 1884, for example, he collaborated with the educator J.M.D. Meiklejohn to create *The Golden Primer,* with text and illustrations designed to teach children words through their association with pictures. On the endpapers, the reader is advised:

"Teach only words, teach them as wholes: never mention the names of a letter unless the child demands it."

During the first years of life, the child's imagination must be continually fresh and stimulated with bright color, sensitive line, and symbolic imagery. (In later years, Crane would be distressed by some of Arthur Rackham's illustrations of ghouls and monsters because he suspected they disturbed the child's development.) "The best of designing for children," he wrote, "is that the imagination and fancy may be let loose and roam freely, and there is always room for humour and even pathos, sure of being followed by that ever-living sense of wonder and romance in the child heart—a heart which in some cases, happily, never grows up or grows old."

Not only the content, but the very way in which the books were presented—from cover to cover—was a matter of consequence. Nothing was left to accident. Crane regarded each volume as a designed work, in which every element—text, ornaments, and pictures—was a detail that was subordinate to the whole concept. The entire volume represented a unified design, including the covers and endpapers as well. Regarding any one of these elements as simple decoration—rather than part of an organic whole—was tantamount to erecting a shanty in the woods. He, on the other hand, preferred to surround his home with a garden, leading to a porch, then to a welcome hallway, and from there taking his reader on a pleasant journey from room to room and "weaving dreams in the changing lights and shadows to forget life's rough way and the tempestuous world outside."

If Crane felt the elements within each book were subordinate to the total design concept, he also felt that book design itself was subordinate to aesthetic theories that applied to *all* aspects of design. In addition to his work as a fine artist, Crane also turned his attention to branches of the decorative arts other than books, directing his skills to the design of textiles, ceramics, embroidery, tapestries, stained glass, mosaic and gesso reliefs, wallpapers, and interiors. In each, he emphasized the importance of sound craftsmanship and a respect for the specific materials. Even his book illustrations provided a means for him to exercise his concepts in the decorative arts. ("I was in the habit of putting in all sorts of subsidiary detail that interested me, and often made them the vehicle for my ideas in furniture and decoration.") Indeed, these books were read not only by children, but by artists and architects who followed the latest modes of the reform aesthetics and who presented them to clients for decorating ideas.

At the foundation of Crane's work lay a powerful conviction that the designer's purpose ran deeper than mere decoration, that the designer's function was to rescue Victorian society from the "heavy and vulgar taste borrowed from the French empire which had for twenty years or more dominated Victorian taste in English house decoration and furniture." In elevating taste, the designer assumed a role of moral significance. According to Crane, the artist must be a reformer.

Crane joined with the charismatic William Morris in leading the Arts and Crafts Movement to re-establish the importance of the craftsman in society. Crane became the first president of the Art Workers Guild in 1884 and the president of the Arts and Crafts Exhibition Society in 1888, and

From *The Yellow Dwarf* (1874). "Children," maintained
Walter Crane, "prefer well-defined forms and bright, frank colour.
They don't want to bother about three dimensions."

remained in this position until 1912 (except for the years 1893–1896, when Morris held the office). In the catalog for the first exhibition of the Arts and Crafts Society, Crane wrote:

Of late years . . . a kind of revival has been going on, as a protest against the conviction that, with all our modern mechanical achievements, comforts and luxuries, life is growing "uglier every day" as Mr. Morris puts it. Even our painters are driven to rely rather on the accidental beauty which, like a struggling ray through a London fog, sometimes illumes and transfigures the sordid commonplace of everyday life★ . . . The true root and basis of all Art lies in the handicrafts. . . . If there is no room or chance or recognition for really artistic power and feeling in design and craftsmanship—if Art is not recognized in the humblest object and material and felt to be as valuable in its own way as the more highly rewarded pictorial skill—the arts cannot be in sound condition; and if artists cease to be found among the crafts there is great danger that they will vanish from the arts also, and become manufacturers and salesmen instead.

From his days as an apprentice, Crane had witnessed the virtues resulting from the collaboration between artist and craftsman, and he was eager to see all handicraftsmen, designers, architects, and artists unified toward a new era of shared interest and cooperation. "We must turn our artists into craftsmen and our craftsmen into artists," he urged. Like his colleagues—John Ruskin, Edward Burne-Jones, and William Morris—Crane reached to the earlier traditions of English Gothic for inspiration, feeling that here lay the honest and sincere efforts of the craftsman. Gothic gables,

★The reference here, of course, is to the paintings of James McNeill Whistler.

finials, and painted decoration worked their way into Crane's imagery. This appreciation of the Medieval craft was consistent with Crane's preference for engraving, a technique that favored a style using strong black lines. He disliked Caldecott's sketchy line illustrations, preferring instead a completely outlined contour drawing, framed with figures and placed within a fully designed setting, a style commonly seen in the work of Albrecht Dürer. (For his part, Randolph Caldecott was critical of Crane's style also. "He is a clever man," Caldecott wrote to a friend, "but he does not enough follow his natural bent. He is in the thrall of the influence of the early and most intellectual Italian painters and draughtsmen.")

It is true that Crane tended to be eclectic in his taste, borrowing from many historical sources. He studied the line work on classic Greek pottery and the flat decorative work of the Japanese. He studied the decoration of the Renaissance and was consistently inspired by the Pre-Raphaelites. His design vocabulary, therefore, derived from other artists and other designs, rather than from direct observation of nature. (In this respect, of course, he was in direct opposition to the Pre-Raphaelites who felt a close study of nature was the key to truthful rendition.) "I feel convinced that in all designs of a decorative character, an artist works most freely and best without any direct reference to nature," Crane maintained.

Crane's training as an engraver introduced him to the plight of the laborer who, if not phased out altogether by technology, was at least the victim of the division of labor that pervaded all factory systems. His mentor, W.J. Linton, had been a socialist and had inspired Crane by his ideas. Not surprisingly, Crane became a socialist, William Morris being primarily responsible for this conversion. "I imagine," said Crane, "that as people can be roughly divided into Socialists and Individualists, so they can be sub-divided into conscious Socialists and unconscious Socialists. I believe I really belonged to the latter class long before I knew I belonged to the former." Crane joined Morris' Socialist League shortly after its establishment in 1885 and in the same year became a member of the Fabian Society. Although Morris continued to be a far more familiar personality to the working man, Crane became the movement's most active artist. For the rest of his life, he frequently placed his versatile talents at the service of the socialist cause.

Crane's design achievements and leadership in the Arts and Crafts and socialist movements, as well as his extensive teaching and writing, propelled him into the status of international celebrity. His signature—a rebus incorporating a crane —became a familiar trademark throughout the Western world, and his work was sought from every sector. (Lewis Carroll was one of many to offer Crane a commission. In 1878, unable to work any longer with John Tenniel, Carroll approached Crane to illustrate his *Sylvie and Bruno*. Although Carroll did not entirely admire Crane's "rather sick wood cut sort of line," the author wrote Crane a very persuasive letter in which he espoused his own theories of design to the master. Carroll failed in his efforts to engage Crane's service. Besides being fully occupied with other work, Crane thought Carroll "a most peculiar person."

Harry Furniss eventually illustrated the book.)

Walter Crane had an exceptionally strong following in America, and in 1891 he accepted an invitation to the New World to accompany a traveling exhibition of his work. Expressing his socialist sentiments at a speech in Chicago aroused the contempt of many conservatives, and Crane was surprised "in what I had supposed was a free country" to find that he was banned from several clubs and cancelled out of several public engagements. In spite of this unfortunate occurrence, it was generally agreed that his exhibition and presence gave impetus to the revival of handicrafts at a time when American designers were prepared to take advantage of his example. On his journey to Boston, Chicago, St. Louis, Philadelphia, New York, Los Angeles, and San Francisco, Crane met many of his distinguished American colleagues, including Howard Pyle, whose *Otto of the Silver Hand* the English illustrator had particularly admired.

By the time of Crane's death in 1915, his work and ideas had been felt in France, Italy, Holland, Belgium, Germany, Scandinavia, and Hungary. Determined to lead his flock out of the darkness into a new era, this reformer promoted English theory and design to a wide audience, inspiring new generations of artists and designers. Yet his most ardent followers were oblivious to his polemics. Innocently turning the pages of his slender picture books, children throughout the world would remember Walter Crane not for his theories, but for his simple gift of joy, for giving them these cherished moments in an imaginary universe where reason has no place.

From *The House That Jack Built* (1878). This book was Caldecott's
first commission for Edmund Evans' Picture Book Series.

Randolph Caldecott

From *The House That Jack Built* (1878).

On the surface, Walter Crane and Randolph Caldecott had much in common. They were born within months of each other, came from Old Chester families, and eventually settled in the Kensington section of London. Each became renowned largely as a result of working with Edmund Evans. In fact, for many years—until Caldecott died—the two artists were very good friends. Yet here their similarity ends.

The son of an artist, Crane was from the outset a member of the English art community and his public leadership in that community was a natural outcome of his heritage. By contrast, Caldecott's modest family background might have discouraged a lesser man from becoming an artist at all. Crane was an activist, a reformer, whose ideas were widely published; Caldecott remained a private and retiring individual, even after becoming famous, and his ideas were expressed in writing

only in his personal correspondence. Their differences were especially apparent in their work: Caldecott's drawing is sketchy and spontaneous; Crane's is decorative, stylized, frequently mannered. Crane spurned nature as a source of inspiration and looked instead toward the art of ancient Greece, medieval England, the Italian Renaissance, Japan, and the Pre-Raphaelites for his ideas, while Caldecott found in eighteenth- and nineteenth-century England all he needed for subject and style. Crane was a decorator; Caldecott was an illustrator.

If Caldecott agreed with Crane that English culture had been corrupted by the vulgarity of Victorian taste, there is no such evidence. Rather, Caldecott's art suggests that he held great affection for his environment and drew the scenes and simple events he had observed around him every day of his life. The sketches he made when he was a small boy may well have gone unnoticed by his parents, but his work—even at that time—expresses the joy of someone feeling very much at home in his surroundings.

The city of Chester in Cheshire, where Randolph Caldecott was born on March 22, 1846, was enveloped by a gentle, English countryside. The Caldecott family lived near the center of town in quarters above the shop where John Caldecott conducted his business as a tailor and hatter. When he was not attending school, young Randolph was seen whittling wood, modeling in clay, or sketching the figures and landscapes around him. Seeing little future in this pursuit, his parents sent their fifteen-year-old son off to begin work as a bank clerk in the nearby town of Whitchurch. Randolph seems to have performed acceptably during the five years he spent at the Whitchurch and Ellesmere Bank, and he restricted his drawing to a spare-time activity, amusing his colleagues with his humorous caricatures. Living in a hamlet located two miles from the bank, the young man walked through the countryside each day, as he went to and from the office. He regularly made the rounds to the country squires and farmers with whom the bank conducted its trading. He made friends easily, attended fairs, went hunting and fishing, became a competent horseman, and joined the hunt and steeplechase. The country scenes and his sportive activities recorded in the sketches made during these daily routines and hours of relaxation would be used for material years later when he reconstructed them for his illustrations.

It was not until he was twenty-one, when he left Whitchurch to take a position at the head office of the Manchester and Salford Bank, that Randolph Caldecott encountered anything that resembled an artistic community. In Manchester he finally met others who appreciated his abilities and encouraged him to develop his talents further by studying evenings at the Manchester School of Art. After successfully placing some drawings in a humorous weekly called *Will o' the Wisp*, Caldecott began to see an opportunity for a career as an illustrator.

Caldecott was introduced to a Manchester artist living in London—Thomas Armstrong—who showed the young man's portfolio to the editor of *London Society*, Henry Blackburn. Blackburn bought a sufficient number of Caldecott drawings for publication to encourage the young artist to leave his life as a "quill driver" and make his way to London as a professional illustrator. Within two years, Caldecott became established in his profession, taking on every assignment that came his way.

Throughout his life, Caldecott waged a constant battle with ill health—the result of a childhood bout with rheumatic fever. Blackburn—a distinguished author, critic, lecturer, and editor—turned out to be a good friend as well as a major client. He directed Caldecott away from the rigors of a life exclusively as a press artist, suggesting instead assignments that would enable him to travel to benign climates where he would avoid the cold and damp English winters. The two traveled together, collaborating on a series of articles that took them to the Harz Mountains, to Vienna, and to Brittany.

It was during these first two years in London that Caldecott's sprightly drawings caught the attention of a prominent wood engraver named James Cooper. Cooper approached the young artist with a challenging assignment: to illustrate extracts from Washington Irving's *Sketchbook*, the

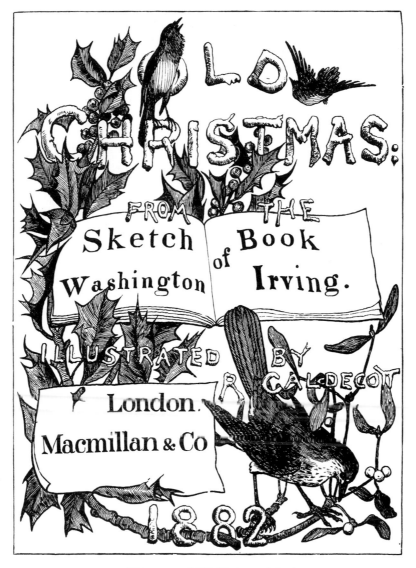

Title page of *Old Christmas* (1875).

first volume of which was called *Old Christmas*. For the book, nearly 120 drawings depicting scenes from a period of seventy years earlier were needed, a demanding assignment that occupied Caldecott for most of 1874 and required nearly a year for Cooper to complete the engravings. Macmillan agreed to publish *Old Christmas*, and Caldecott's reputation as a book illustrator was launched, other book assignments following immediately.

When Walter Crane's contract with Routledge had expired, it was evident that Edmund Evans would need to find illustrators to continue the series of inexpensive children's books that had been so lucrative to his business for the past ten years. With his talent for detecting promise, Evans was attracted to Randolph Caldecott's illustrations in *Old Christmas*, although the artist had never done children's books and these spontaneous little sketches bore no resemblance whatsoever to the decorative work of Walter Crane that had been so popular. (Evans described Caldecott's drawings as "slight illustrations . . . little more than outlines . . .

Cow

Lightning sketches for *The House That Jack Built*, published posthumously with the widow's consent in 1899. Creating a guide for his book illustrations, Caldecott entered lightning sketches into a blank dummy. In order to retain the spontaneity of these lively sketches, they were included in the picture books, a balance to his more formal full-page finished color illustrations.

racy and spontaneous.'') The engraver called on Caldecott's London studio, and proposed a collaboration, a meeting which Evans recalled years later in his memoirs:

He liked the idea of doing them as I proposed, and fell in with me very pleasantly, but he would not agree to doing them for any fixed sum: feeling sure of his own powers in doing them, he wished to share in the speculation —said he would make the drawings—if they sold and paid, he would be paid, but was content to bear the loss if they did not sell, and not be paid.

For the toy books, now selling for one shilling, Evans devised an innovative layout that would present an appealing publication for the price: nine pictures in color and a minimum of twenty line drawings printed on the text pages. Heavier paper would make it possible to print on both sides of the sheet, eliminating blank pages. They discussed a procedure for executing these prints:

I agreed to run all the risk of engraving the key blocks which he drew on wood: after he had coloured a proof I would furnish him, on drawing paper, I would engrave the blocks to be printed in as few colours as necessary. This was settled, the key block in dark brown, then a flesh tint for the faces, hands, and wherever it would bring the other colours as nearly as possible to his painted copy, a red, a blue, a yellow and a grey.

By the time he met Evans, Caldecott's only experience with color had been his work on two pages of illustrations for the *Graphic* Christmas issue two years previously. This did not discourage him from venturing immediately into an ambitious pair of books with Evans: *The House that Jack Built* and *The Diverting History of John Gilpin.*

From *The House That Jack Built* (1878). Like the English
artist Thomas Rowlandson, whose work he admired, Caldecott
was particularly fond of scenes from humble eighteenth-century country life.

Thirty thousand copies of each were released in time for Christmas 1878.

Caldecott discovered a procedure that worked extremely well for his toy books. First he made up a blank book in the correct size, with the precise number of pages. On each page he made "lightning sketches" to indicate the picture and its placement with text, which he followed carefully as he made the final drawings for Evans. He never labored over his drawing. If it wasn't right, he threw it away (or gave it away to a friend), moving onto a

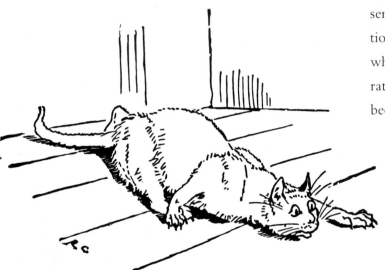

Both from *The House That Jack Built* (1878).

new sketch immediately. For drawing he preferred using brown ink, though he complained to Kate Greenaway that his favorite ink was not ideal for colored work because it was not waterproof and therefore could not withstand the applications of watercolor placed over the lines. This required his conversion to brown india ink which, he reported, would "stand any number of deep assaults."

For a color illustration, Caldecott handed over his final sketch to Evans, who in turn transferred it to the wood block, perhaps by hand, more likely photographically. The block was engraved, a proof pulled, and the image colored by Caldecott. Simulating the effect of Caldecott's delicate watercolors, Evans engraved six colors in a variety of techniques designed to re-create the subtle colors and textures of the originals. Their success was immediate. Within seven months of publication, Routledge sold 60,000 copies of *The House that Jack Built* and *John Gilpin*.

Caldecott's years at the bank gave him a fair sense of financial matters. He discussed the question of remuneration with his friend Walter Crane, who advised him to take a royalty wherever possible, rather than a flat payment as the older artist had been compelled to accept in previous years. It had

become more common practice for an artist to receive a royalty, though the percentage was low. ("I get a small royalty," Caldecott wrote to a friend, "—a small, small royalty.") In his first

From *The Diverting History of John Gilpin* (1878).
Caldecott adopted subtle pastel shades in his color work, preferring a brown outline to the black used by his colleagues Kate Greenaway and Walter Crane.

From *The Diverting History of John Gilpin* (1878). Unlike Walter
Crane—whose work was inspired primarily by classical European and Oriental
traditions—Caldecott drew his inspiration from his own experience in
the English countryside and from his English predecessors: William Hogarth,
Thomas Rowlandson, George Cruikshank, and John Leech.

From *Sing a Song for Sixpence* (1880). Caldecott's
penchant for personal interpretations of familiar stories is revealed in his shifting the title of this old rhyme from
"Sing a Song *of* Sixpence" to "Sing a Song *for* Sixpence."

publications he received three farthings for each copy sold, which amounted to 6¼ percent of the shilling list price. Because of the success of *The House that Jack Built* and *John Gilpin*, he managed to earn £375 within the first year, but it always irked him that the creator's revenue was disproportionate to the profits earned by the publisher, and he persisted in his efforts to improve that ratio. In 1881, his royalty was raised somewhat, and two years later again raised to 12½ percent of the sale price. His income grew steadily each year.

From 1878 to 1885 Evans and Caldecott worked together on the toy books, publishing a pair of titles each year until a total of sixteen small books had been issued. (The books were also issued in volumes combining four titles in each.) During this eight-year collaboration, Caldecott created his most memorable work, including *Hey Diddle Diddle*, *The Frog Would A-Wooing Go*, and *Sing a Song for Sixpence*. Where Walter Crane had initiated the concept of the decorated children's book—a unified design from cover to cover—Caldecott created a new kind of picture book for children. A single story stimulated many associations, ideas which Caldecott set down on the page as they came to him. He enlarged the story by interpreting the words with his pictures. The illustrations fill in what the words leave out, and the words fill in what the pictures leave out—both closely interwoven, each enhanced by the other.

The rhythm of picture to text was carefully planned by Caldecott, as his lightning sketches for *The House that Jack Built* so marvelously demonstrate. A few lines of verse are embraced by a series of pictures that leap from one page to the next, as if the words are a musical refrain propelling the pictures to dance. The movement from page to page is animated, unrestricted by heavy borders or decorations, spontaneous and unexpected. While these little sketches may be unassuming, they are never naïve. Only a supremely sophisticated artist is capable of executing convincing drawings with such economy. "The art of leaving out is a science," Caldecott wrote. "The fewer the lines, the less error committed." It was not modesty, for example, but an appreciation for the delicacy of his drawings that influenced his decision about omitting his signature from much of his work. "I would rather leave out my initials than to have them interfere with the drawings—and I often do—and in these slight drawings every little tells." Caldecott's work has all the charm of the nursery rhymes he pictures and all of the elegance of modern-day illustrations.

Caldecott's talents attracted more offers than he could handle. He became a frequent contributor of humorous sketches to *Punch*, the *Graphic*, and other periodicals, and provided illustrations for popular Victorian writers such as Mrs. Juliana Horatia Ewing and Mrs. Frederick Locker. Even his original drawings were sought out by collectors. (One of those to collect Caldecott originals was Rupert Potter, father of Beatrix. The thirty or so drawings he managed to acquire made it possible for his daughter to study these first-hand. Two Caldecott drawings from *Sing a Song for Sixpence* are still on view at Hill Top, Beatrix Potter's home.)

Caldecott met his success with modesty, and only his health prevented him from producing even more work than the substantial amount he managed to execute. According to Walter Crane, Caldecott "never looked strong, and his quiet

From *Hey Diddle Diddle* (1882). Caldecott's rendition of this familiar old nursery rhyme established a tradition that others followed for generations.

From *The Frog Would A-Wooing Go* (1883). Beatrix Potter was a great admirer of Caldecott. Among Caldecott's work that her father purchased were two small pen-and-ink sketches from this book.

From *Ride a Cock Horse* (1884). Here again, Caldecott altered the
traditional meaning of the old English rhyme. Until then, "riding a cock horse"
signified straddling a toy or an adult's knee.

manner, low voice, and gentle but serious and
earnest way of speaking did not suggest the extraordinary vivacity and humour of his drawings."
Caldecott's health could not keep pace with the
demands of his popularity and he frequently suffered from overwork. To adopt a slower pace, the
illustrator bought a home in Kent in 1879 and it
was here that he met and married a local resident,
Marian Brand. They returned to London in 1882—
living near Walter Crane in Kensington—and passed
each winter in the milder climates of Italy or the
south of France. In view of Caldecott's frail health,
it seems surprising that he decided to make a

sketching trip to America in the late autumn of
1885. The cross-Atlantic voyage proved exhausting,
leaving him in a weakened state by the time the
ship pulled into the New York harbor. With the
goal of spending the cold winter months in Florida,
the Caldecotts traveled from New York to Philadelphia, to Washington and Charleston, arriving in
Florida in mid-December. By then, Caldecott was
too ill to regain his strength, and he died in St.
Augustine on February 13, 1886. He was thirty-
nine years old.

In the fourteen years Caldecott spent as an
illustrator, he managed to leave a legacy of outstand-

ing achievements. When, in 1936, the directors of the American Librarians Association decided to inaugurate an annual award to an illustrator of children's books, they agreed to call it the Caldecott Medal after the great illustrator. Here was recognition that Randolph Caldecott had been an inspiration to the generations of artists who followed him. Yet he would have been embarrassed by this accolade. Caldecott was as unpretentious as his drawings. He was thoroughly English, drawing upon the English country and outdoor life, satirizing everyday events with a humor altogether free of contempt. His tenderness for his subjects continues to transmit a warmth that all children find irresistible. The joy in his work was genuine, after all. In having the good fortune to make a living from doing what he most loved, Randolph Caldecott was a lucky man. And he knew it.

From *The House That Jack Built* (1878)

"Where waters gushed and fruit trees grew, and flowers put forth a fairer hue," original watercolor illustration for *The Pied Piper of Hamelin* (1887) by Robert Browning. John Ruskin was critical of this scene: "I am more disappointed in the 'Paradise' than I expected to be—a *real* view of Hampstead ponds in spring would have been more celestial to me than this customary flat of yours with the trees stuck into it at regular distances."

Kate Greenaway

"A Child's Prayer," original watercolor
illustration for *A Day in a Child's Life* (1881).

AMONG THE NINETEENTH-CENTURY illustrators of children's books none is more familiar than Kate Greenaway. Her images of idyllic pastoral scenes—in which boys and girls frolic and romp—are untouched by time. They appeal as much to the twentieth-century eye as they did to the Victorian readers of the 1870s, as charming to the English sensibilities as to the French, American, German, Belgian, or Dutch. The bucolic world presented by Kate Greenaway is infinite, remote from the distressing upheavals of a rapidly industrializing society or by the ravages of war. Their apparent innocence may be misleading, however; while these serene pictures bear no resemblance to contemporary life, they are more complex than they appear. And so was their creator.

In fact, these charming children dancing in the countryside seem strangely dispirited, almost melancholy. Like china dolls, they are always well-behaved, smile only occasionally, and never laugh or cry. Their dreamy figures seem disembodied in time and space, moving through a world populated primarily by little girls, a place where few ever grow old. Even the vaguely eighteenth-century costumes, dainty and picturesque as they may be, seem other-worldly, detached from period or place.

Through the imagination, the artist reshapes something seen or felt, creating a world that is an echo—no matter how distant—of something real. The children in Kate Greenaway's world have been transformed from fragments of childhood memories: her doll collection, the fabrics and bonnets she fondled in her mother's millinery shop, and her summer visits to a rural village some 130 miles from London. Her gardens, so pretty in her delicate watercolors, were originally inspired by the backyard of her childhood home, a small patch of ground where a few neglected flowers survived among the weeds. With her imagination, Kate

Greenaway idealized her immediate environment, but also expressed a sadness and solitude that remained with her throughout her life.

From the publication of her first children's book in 1879, Kate Greenaway became the rage. Throughout Europe and America her books were widely published; her pictures were reproduced on handkerchiefs, plates, vases, and caskets; her costumes

From *Under the Window* (1879).

became the fashion; imitators surfaced everywhere. In spite of this celebrated status, Greenaway despised publicity, insisting on absolute privacy. To the overtures of a prospective biographer she responded, "You must wait till I am dead; till then I wish to live my life privately—like an English gentlewoman." What *was* known about Miss Greenaway did not seem so fascinating anyway. A spinster living with her parents and unmarried brother, a dowdy woman seldom seen in society, indicated that her life was uneventful. If it had not been for the vast amount of personal correspondence she wrote and the letters she saved, one would safely assume the years had passed with

little emotional upheaval. Even after her death, her privacy was respected by her friends who wrote a biography without revealing any information the illustrator would have preferred to keep secret. Only in recent years—in a compelling biography of Kate Greenaway by Rodney Engen—have the contents of those letters been made public. What emerges is the picture of a complex woman whose deepest longings were left unsatisfied.

Born in 1846, less than a week before Randolph Caldecott and only a few months after Walter Crane, Kate Greenaway was very different in temperament from either of her rivals. "I was never told I was tiresome when I was young, but I was constantly told I was *odd*," she said. It is not surprising that she displayed unusual traits in her youth, because her youth was so unusual. As her father struggled to keep his wood-engraving firm in business, the financial pressures were great. The family moved several times. When Kate was five or six she was sent to live with relatives in the country, a little village called Rolleston, and in London she knew a half-dozen different homes before they finally settled when her mother opened a millinery shop and left the eldest daughter, Lizzie, with the task of watching the other children in the family.

Kate seems to have inherited her mother's resourcefulness, finding in each of these relocations some detail that would later appear in her illustrations. Left to cultivate her own fantasies, Kate explored her surroundings and allowed herself to daydream. She was devoted to her dolls—whose names included Gaurca, Prince Albert, and Queen Victoria, among others—and dressed them in scraps from her mother's store. She loved to pore through her father's engravings and the picture books and periodicals that found their way into the busy household. In later years Greenaway recalled the rewards she received from her imaginary life:

I had such a very happy time when I was a child, and curiously, was so very much happier than my brother and sister, with exactly the same surroundings. I suppose my imaginary life made me one long continuous joy —filled everything with a strange wonder and beauty. Living in that childish wonder is a most beautiful feeling—I can so well remember it. There was always something more—behind and beyond everything—to me, the golden spectacles were very very big.

If her imaginary life sustained her, it also distanced her from her surroundings, a fact that had both favorable and unfavorable results. She tended to be excessively shy and awkward, given to great swings of emotional extremes. ("Joy surfeited turns to sorrow," she once said.) She found school intolerable, being too sensitive to withstand the strain of the lessons, and was overcome with unexplained illnesses each time she was taken to a new instructor. When she was eleven, she succeeded in persuading her mother to send her to evening classes at the Finsbury School of Art nearby, and her sincere applications in this classroom were sufficient evidence of her serious intent that she was permitted to attend Finsbury as a full-time student for six more years. After completing the course, she continued on for an additional six years of study at the National Art Training School in South Kensington, simultaneously attending life classes at Heatherley's School of Art and Slade School of Art in the evenings. She was dedicated and industrious, receiving several awards for

her ornamental design work. Like her parents, she was determined in her career and pressed ahead, despite disappointments, already making the rounds to sell her illustrations while still an art student.

At the time she was ready to leave her formal art training, the greeting card industry had taken hold in England. The first Christmas card was issued the year of Greenaway's birth, 1846, but until the 1870s design work was created primarily by journeymen artists. With improved production techniques, greeting cards became extremely fashionable and illustrators of the highest repute were commissioned to design cards.

Among the most established firms in this field was Marcus Ward, a Belfast-based company with a London office. The artistic director of the firm was Thomas Crane, Walter's brother, and some prominent artists were already being engaged to create greeting cards for them, including Walter Crane himself. Ward was interested enough in Greenaway's work to assign her the design of a Valentine's card, which—to everyone's astonishment—sold 25,000 copies within the first weeks of its issue. For six years, Greenaway continued to design Valentine's, birthday, and Christmas cards for Ward—her earliest cards being floral decorations, then pictures of fairies and children. Most of these designs were anonymous, the initials K.G. inserted only occasionally.

Greenaway's most successful cards depicted children dressed in historical costumes placed against plain backgrounds. Here she began to devise the costumes that became so familiar in her children's books, interpretations of the old-fashioned clothing she had observed at Rolleston, where the local citizens wore costumes that had long since disappeared from the more sophisticated English communities. Partly from memory, but primarily from invention, she created the ribbons and ruffles, bonnets, jackets, prim aprons, buttoned breeches, high-waisted dresses, sashes, and muffs that became the vogue only a few years later.

Marcus Ward took a strong hand in her artistic development, destroying whatever work he felt inadequate. She accepted his opinions unhesitatingly, but she continued to write poems even after Ward had declared her verses were "rubbish and without any poetic feeling." Although she looked to Ward for support and direction, it was also typical of her independent nature that she ultimately severed her relations with him when he refused to return her original drawings after they were reproduced.

By the time she was thirty-three years old, Kate Greenaway was fairly prosperous, but still unrecognized. She had illustrated books written by others and she had published any number of greeting cards, always subjected to the business terms dictated to her. Determined to alter this direction in her career, she brought her verses and pictures to Edmund Evans. Evans had known her father since he was fourteen, and he had seen Greenaway's earlier work, so he was warmly receptive to her visit. "About 1877–78 K.G. [as she was called by her friends] came to see us," wrote Evans, "bringing a collection of about 50 drawings she had made, with quaint verses written to them. I was fascinated with the originality of the drawings and the ideas of the verse, so I at once purchased them and determined to reproduce them in a little volume. The title *Under the Window* was selected afterwards from one of the first lines." Evans offered to buy the drawings outright and to give her one-third of

the publishing profits, to which she agreed.

Evans presented the verses and drawings to Routledge and the publisher agreed to take on the book, but not until the following year, after the verses were looked over by the poet Frederick Locker, author of *London Lyrics.* According to Evans' report, "Locker was very much taken with the drawings and the verses, and showed them to Mrs. Locker with quite a gusto; he asked me many questions about her, and was evidently interested in what I told him of her. I do not think he did anything to improve the verses, nor did K.G. herself."

Evans was admiring of the meticulous care Greenaway had taken with the costumes in her drawings. "Miss Greenaway had made costumes to put on her models before drawing them; she was expert with the needle and did this often when she wanted something quaint to paint her pictures." In fact, Evans' enthusiasm for the project emboldened him to take considerable financial risk in the production of *Under the Window.* He used several color blocks—red, flesh tint, blue, and yellow—to reproduce the quality of the original watercolors, the cost of which was sufficiently high to drive the price of the book up to six shillings. Against the advice of Routledge, Evans decided to publish 20,000 copies of the book, a daring decision that paid off immediately. "We soon found that we had not printed nearly enough to supply the first demand; I know booksellers sold copies at a premium, getting ten shillings for each of them: it was, of course, long out of print, for I could not print fast enough to keep up the sale." For the second edition, 70,000 copies were printed, which, with the German and French editions, brought the

POLLY's, Peg's, and Poppety's
    Mamma was kind and good ;
She gave them each, one happy day,
    A little scarf and hood.

A bonnet for each girl she bought,
    To shield them from the sun ;
They wore them in the snow and rain,
    And thought it mighty fun.

But sometimes there were naughty boys,
    Who called to them at play,
And made this rude remark—" My eye !
    Three Grannies out to-day ! "

From *Under the Window* (1879). For all their playfulness and
charm, Greenaway's girls are actually melancholy, dispirited, and strangely
detached from period or place.

Randolph Caldecott and Kate Greenaway were guests of a friend in a country house in 1868 when Caldecott made this quick sketch and remarked, "I have lost *all* powers working in my own style, everything comes out Kate Greenaways."

total sales up to 100,000 copies within Greenaway's lifetime.

With *Under the Window* Kate Greenaway's reputation was established, and a mutual agreement between Evans and Greenaway resulted in the publication of several children's books and almanacs for the ensuing decade. Greenaway improved the financial arrangement in the partnership, receiving £5 for the use of each drawing and increasing her share of the profits to half.

Catapulted into fame, Greenaway was joined in celebration with Walter Crane and Randolph Caldecott, artists naturally linked because of their association with Edmund Evans, although all three were not comrades. According to Caldecott, he and Greenaway had met at the home of Evans prior to the publication of *Under the Window.* "Many charming drawings," he wrote, "—coloured —did I see on Sunday of children and child-life done on paper by Kate Greenaway, in whose company I passed the weekend at Witley, near Godalming." Reputed to be a handsome bachelor

with a roving eye, Caldecott's observations about her may have suggested she was impervious to his charm. "We were staying in the same house, I mean. She had not a sunny smile; but the book which will contain the drawings—added to bits by herself—ought to be a success." Until Caldecott's death the two illustrators remained friendly, offering each other professional advice about models and technique, although Caldecott did express concern about how her success had hurt the sales of his books, forcing him to sacrifice "some of the necessary luxuries of life."

Walter Crane was less generous toward Greenaway, finding her harmless drawings and verse frivolous and without instructional merit. "May I confess that (for me, at least) I think she overdid the big bonnet rather, and at one time her little people were almost lost in their clothes." He was outraged when Routledge announced *Under the Window* as a companion volume to his own *Baby's Opera,* and demanded the advertising be dropped. Actually, Crane met Greenaway only on one occa-

SCHOOL is over,
　　Oh, what fun!
Lessons finished,
　　Play begun.
Who'll run fastest,
　　You or I?
Who'll laugh loudest?
　　Let us try.

K.G.

From *Under the Window* (1879). Immediately after the publication of this, her first book
made in collaboration with Edmund Evans, Greenaway's reputation was secured.

Original watercolor illustration for *Under the Window* (1879). Ruskin adored Greenaway's "girlies" and she presented him with countless drawings of these subjects to charm him.

sion, reporting, "My impressions of Kate Greenaway were of a very quiet and unobtrusive personality, probably observant, self-contained, reserved, with a certain shrewdness."

Crane did not exaggerate when he said, "The grace and charm of her children and young girls were quickly recognized and . . . captivated the public in a remarkable way." Just as the young girls seized the affection of the public, so did their creator. Almost overnight, the name Kate Greenaway became synonymous with style. She was invited to tea at Buckingham Palace, was wined and dined at the most fashionable soirées, escorted by the elegant Frederick Locker. She was introduced to the most eminent literary and artistic figures of her day, including Robert Browning and Alfred Lord Tennyson. Throughout Europe she became the vogue as well. "It has occurred to me that you are about the only English artist who has ever been the fashion in France," observed Frederick Locker. The Germans claimed she was actually from Düsseldorf, and gossip had it that she was secretly married to Randolph Caldecott.

It may have seemed odd, perhaps, that the illustrator of these sweet children in quaint costumes was so absent of style herself, causing a friend to observe, "Her delicate taste in dressing her subjects failed to give any suggestion, or she did not know how or did not take the trouble to make the best of herself." Unlike her little girls, Kate Greenaway was dowdy and plain, and consistently timid in the presence of strangers. On the other hand, she had much in common with her creations, for like them she was obedient and compliant. Her resolute—often obstinate—character was in contrast to her submissiveness, particularly when it came to her relations with the men in her life, a pattern that began with her father.

There had always been a deep bond between John Greenaway and Kate and the choice of her profession was clearly inspired by her father's own passion for his work as an engraver. Frequently obliged to work around the clock in order to meet the deadlines for timely publication, he and Kate would savor the early hours of the morning together as they shared a breakfast before his departure at dawn. He admired her strong will and determination and was even amused by her eruptive temperament, calling her "Knocker" to describe how her face resembled the door knocker when she cried. John Greenaway introduced her to clients, advised her on her work, helped her with her faulty perspective drawings, and remained throughout her life a guiding force. If the little girls in Greenaway's illustrations are convincing, it may be the result of her own unwillingness to leave her childhood far behind. She "lives with her girlhood as with a little sister," wrote John Ruskin. She herself admitted, "I hated to be grownup and cried when I had my first long dress."

As she grew up, this childishness transformed into an extreme dependence on the leadership— even tyranny, at times—imposed by the men around her. Her submission to the proprietary Marcus Ward resembled the relations she later developed with others—her engraver Edmund Evans, her colleague H. Stacy Marks, her friend Frederick Locker and, most notably, her lover-in-writing, John Ruskin. From them she craved criticism and support, always plagued by the feelings that her work was inadequate. There seemed to be little cause for her fears. No illustrator of her time was

From *Kate Greenaway's Birthday Book* (1880).

so adored by her public. Superlative reviews in England, Europe, and America described her as "a genius," compared her to the greatest artists of the century, and predicted that her work had all the makings of a classic. Nevertheless, she was convinced her illustrations were inferior to those of her colleagues Crane and Caldecott. "I wish I had such a mind," she wrote of Randolph Caldecott, continuing, "I'm feeling very low about my own powers just now, for I have been looking at the originals for the new Crane book. Some of them are literally dreams of beauty."

To H. Stacy Marks—a distinguished greeting card designer, illustrator, and Royal Academician—she turned for criticism of her work. And she got it. "I am not going to be 'severe,'" he wrote, "but I *must* ask you not to repeat those funny little black shadows under the feet of your figures—looking in some places like spurs, in others like tadpoles, in others like short stilts."

Frederick Locker, who became a diverting companion and adviser, corrected her verse, and commented on her pictures: "Do you think the Bride sitting under the tree is so feeble that she could not stand up?" or "Are the young ladies' arms like cloth sausages?" or "You must make your faces look happy." But he also advised her not to take criticism too harshly: "You must be influenced by what the critics say up to a certain point—but not beyond." To Locker Greenaway turned for advice in business and in this department he was firm, insisting, "You are to be treated on as handsome terms as those two gentlemen [Crane and Caldecott]." Greenaway was torn between the pressures exerted by Evans to create more work and by Locker's persistent urging "to do moderate work." Locker, whose affections for Greenaway may have transcended those of pure friendship, was in rivalry with still another dominant male in Greenaway's life: John Ruskin.

The history of Greenaway's intense relationship with John Ruskin has all the ingredients of Victorian romance: suppressed desires, rapture suffused with frustration and melancholia, cruelty and tenderness, unfulfilled passions expressed in a tempestuous poetic discourse that spanned a period of nearly twenty years.

The famous art critic—by then nearly sixty, and already the victim of mental instability—had a well-known obsession for young girls. When he first laid eyes on the delightful creatures in Greenaway's pictures he was still mourning the loss of his beloved Rose La Touche, a young woman with whom he'd been enamored since she was nine years old. On Rose's seventeenth birthday (when he was thirty-nine), he had proposed to her, reluctantly agreeing to wait a few years for the marriage to take place. The wedding never occurred: Rose La Touche discovered the nature of his first marriage to Effie Gray (who later became Mrs. John Millais), a marriage that had been annulled two decades earlier because he had failed to consummate it. In horror, Rose broke off the engagement and retreated into religious devotions, suffering from frequent bouts of madness until her death in 1875. Ruskin's devotion to Rose became an obsession after her death, and he surrounded himself with prepubescent girls to evoke her presence. While his interests may appear prurient to the contemporary observer, in fact his desires were—in a typically Victorian manner—only uttered, never performed. No doubt he became entranced with Kate Greenaway's suggestive drawings when he saw *Under the Window* because the images must have aroused his longings for his "pet" Rose.

H. Stacy Marks, always happy to promote Greenaway's work among his influential artistic and literary friends, urged Ruskin to express his admiration for *Under the Window* directly to the author. Ruskin's first letter, written just a few months after the 1879 publication of the book, set the stage for what would develop into a feverish correspondence:

My Dear Miss Greenaway—I lay awake half (no, a quarter) of last night thinking of the hundred things I want to say to you—and never shall get said!—and I'm giddy and wary—and now can't say even half or a quarter of one out of the hundred. They're about you—and your gifts—and your graces—and your fancies—and your—yes—perhaps one or two little tiny faults. . . .

Thus ensued an active exchange in which he

Original watercolor illustration of "P Peeped in It," from *A Apple Pie Alphabet* (1886). It has been suggested that the Apple Pie so eagerly coveted by these children was actually meant to represent John Ruskin who was pursued by so many ladies for a share of his affection.

assumed full authority for correcting her "little tiny faults." If Marks had been gentle in drawing her attention to the shadows painted under the feet by calling them "spurs," "tadpoles," or "short stilts," Ruskin was more brutal: her feet were like "mussel-shells," "paddles," "flappers," "real deformities." Her shoes were like "butter boats," her legs "lumpy at the shin and shaky at the knees." Although her strength lay in imaginary conceptions, Ruskin pressed for greater realism. At school she had never excelled at meticulous draftsmanship and she'd grown careless with details, leaving out essentials and concealing form with drapery. Ruskin commanded, "You must cure yourself of thinking so much of hair and hats and parasols—and attend *first* (for some time to come) to toes-fingers-and-wrists." At another time he scolded her, "You must give up drawing round hats. It's the hats that save you from having to do backgrounds." He urged her to paint from nature, and gave her exercises to perform, demanding she paint rocks and landscapes to sharpen her skills. "What you ABSOLUTELY need," he wrote, "is a quantity of practice from things as they *are*—and hitherto you have ABSOLUTELY refused even to draw any of them so." (One wonders, of course, if it was only for educational purposes that he urged her to disrobe the little figures in order to draw the full form beneath the costumes!)

The fact that it was two years before Ruskin and Greenaway actually met already hinted that their involvement was more chimerical than actual. While Ruskin may have been hopelessly infatuated with her "girlies," as he called them, he found little in the plain—even frumpy—spinster Greenaway to charm him except for her talents.

Nevertheless, their stormy postal exchange continued for nine years—interrupted by his increasingly frequent bouts of madness—and persisted on Greenaway's part for the remaining nine years of his life, during which time Ruskin's mental state rendered him incapable of writing letters in return. She saved every letter and telegraph that he wrote, some 500. To Ruskin she probably wrote twice that number, although he managed to save only one of her letters until he created a Greenaway drawer in 1887, into which he placed all her letters, some unopened.

With the years, Kate Greenaway grew increasingly dependent on Ruskin, and he grew inordinately punishing, a result of his deteriorating mental condition as much as his distaste for her needful entreaties. For her part, she adored him. "Words cannot say the sort of man he is," she wrote to a friend, "perfect—simply."

The neurotic pattern of their communication repeated itself over and over during the course of nine years. In response to his silence, she would give way to tantrums, provoking him with her need for reassurance. Impatient with her pleading, he would admonish her: "I wish you liked my books and wanted more of them and not so much of me." She would then quell his anger by plying him with more drawings of his cherished girlies, gifts which inevitably sent him into rapture: "I could contentedly and proudly keep you drawing nice girls in blue sashes with soft eyes and blissful lips, to the end of—my poor bit of life." Begging for forgiveness, he would retreat into self-pity, writing, "I never mean to be cross, but am—so also I'm sorry when you waste your precious hours in trifling with me." Then he would resume

THE CATS HAVE COME TO TEA.

From *Marigold Garden* (1886). As evidence of her international fame, more
copies of this book were shipped initially to America than reserved for English sales.

Original watercolor illustration of April for the 1887 *Almanack*. This delicate watercolor is reproduced more than twice actual size, demonstrating Greenaway's painstaking efforts at technical control.

the flirtation, beg her to visit him, sign his letters with kisses, and lament, "How I wish I *could* write you a real love-letter! and to think of all the foolish girls everywhere that get them, (—not from me, I mean, but in general—) and poor Kate Greenaway —not one—only lectures and teasers and dreadful silences!" He relished her attention until it became tiresome, then he would reject her entreaties and the pattern would repeat. He was often cruel, particularly when he was about to slip into another bout of depression. He cancelled her visits with excuses made last minute, he teased her by comparing her unfavorably to other females in his life, and once he informed her that he had decided to burn her letters, some even unopened, "for fear of their lying about."

While he was demanding her total submission, he was also her most vocal champion, extolling her work to the public. In his lectures at Oxford he ranked her among the old masters and most important contemporary artists. Although he admitted that he felt her design "has been restricted by being too ornamental...contracted into any corner of a Christmas card, or stretched like an elastic band around the edges of an almanac," he declared that her value was inestimable: "In her drawings you have the radiance and innocence of reinstated infant divinity showered again among the flowers of English meadows."

Their tempestuous correspondence must have been a relief from the monotony of her routine. When she was not filling a commission or writing her verse, she was painting for Ruskin's own approval. Her income had increased substantially through the years, but so had the financial strain. She moved her family—parents and brother—into a large home in Hampstead, a move, incidentally, that irritated Ruskin: "I am against the house in Hampstead and quite resolved that you *shan't* live in London." Financial pressures drove her to work even harder and her brother described what appears to be a rather dreary routine:

Of my sister at work, we saw very little. She very wisely made it a fixed rule that, during working hours, no one should come into the studio save on matters of urgency. Her great working time was the morning, so she was always an early riser and finished breakfast by

"And out of the houses rats came tumbling," original watercolor illustration for *The Pied Piper of Hamelin* (1887) by Robert Browning. Illustrated with an eye
toward pleasing her beloved John Ruskin, this demonstrates Greenaway's
acquiescence to the principles set forth by the overbearing critic. She worked in an
uncharacteristic Pre-Raphaelite style, creating thirty-five watercolors with
a palette of rust, ochre, and olive tones rather than with her usual pastels. Although he
deplored the Paradise scene, Ruskin praised her efforts elsewhere in the
book, stating "It is all as good and nice as it can be, and you really have got through
your rats with credit—and the Piper is sublime—and the children lovely."

Original watercolor of two girls
in a garden, one on a swing.

eight o'clock. Her most important work was done between then and luncheon time (1 o'clock). Practically
she never went out in the morning. After luncheon she
usually worked for an hour or two, unless she was going
out anywhere for the afternoon; and then went for a
walk on the Heath, and came back to tea. The evenings
up to eight o'clock, when she had a meal that was a sort of
compromise between dinner and supper, were spent in
letter-writing, making dresses for models, occasionally
working out schemes and rough sketches for projected
books and such-like things; but all finished work was
done in the morning or afternoon. In the summer, too, a
good deal of this time was spent in the garden seeing to
her flowers. After supper she generally lay on a sofa and
read until she went to bed at about 10 o'clock.

She could not stand late hours and seldom went out in
the evening. For the same reason she very seldom dined
out. Tea-time was always her time for going out to see
friends, or for them to see her.

To meet her financial obligations, she wrote and
illustrated books at a rapid rate and continued to
illustrate books written by others. Her books
included *The Birthday Book*, *A Day in a Child's Life*,
Mother Goose, *The Language of Flowers*, *Marigold
Garden*, *A Apple Pie*, as well as *The Queen of Pirate
Isle* by Bret Harte, *The Pied Piper of Hamlin* by Robert
Browning, and *Little Ann* by Jane and Ann Taylor,
to name only a few. In addition, she created a new
almanac for Routledge each year until 1897.

By the mid-1880s she had become disgusted by
the array of imitators who copied her books,
draining her of enthusiasm for illustrating. Her
work became a financial necessity to her, purely a
commercial venture, and the results of her efforts
were frequently uneven. The death of Randolph
Caldecott came as a shock. "It looks quite horrid
to see the black-bordered card with his books in
the shop windows—it feels horrid to want to sell

his books somehow, just yet. I'm very sorry." By 1886 her fame was diminishing in England, although it continued to flourish in America, and by 1889 she was unable to get any illustration work at all, turning instead to gallery painting.

Nine years of exchanging letters with Ruskin came to an end as he fell into a final depression. She continued to write to him almost every day—jotting down her thoughts as they came to her, a piece of paper always placed by her side, which she would mail off to him as soon as the paper was filled. But she had finally come to accept his silence as a sign of illness rather than rejection. She was bereft. "I often wonder at the way I do miss *him*," she wrote to a friend. "It is such an unutterable loss as if the best of everything has gone and nothing so nice or so happy or so interesting again. You would think in all this time I should have got used to it—used to doing without him—but I have not one bit."

She entered the most dismal period of her life when her father died in 1890, and her mother not long after. Beset by financial worries and bitterness, she continued to paint and write verse, but in despair.

Deserted, cast away, my work all done,
Who was a star that shone a little while,
but fallen and all its brightness gone—
A victim of this world's brief fickle smile.
Poor fool and vain, grieve not for what is lost,
Nor rend thy heart by counting up the cost.

By the time Ruskin died—early in 1900—Greenaway was already ill herself. She died the following year, cremated according to her wishes, her ashes scattered in the family plot next to her beloved parents. She died, as she lived, in solitude.

A lonely soul, I am ever alone.
If love ever comes it is quickly gone—
Nothing abides and nothing stays.
I think I have found it, but only to know
How very soon it is all to go.
The sunshine is followed by falling snow.

From *Marigold Garden*.

"The mice stitching buttonholes," original watercolor illustration for *The Tailor of Gloucester* (1903). Potter demonstrated her gifts as scientist and story-teller, combining naturalism with imagination to express real animals free of distortion or sentimentality.

Beatrix Potter

"The Tailor Mouse," original watercolor illustration
for *The Tailor of Gloucester* (1903).

ALTHOUGH SHE WAS BORN a full generation after Kate Greenaway, Beatrix Potter was every bit as much a daughter of the Victorian era as her predecessor. Like Greenaway, Beatrix Potter was introspective, her inner life nourished by her solitary creations. Each of them accomplished an independence of spirit through her writing and art, liberated from her oppressive Victorian milieu by exercising her rich imagination. Potter was more fortunate than Greenaway, however: ultimately she realized in her personal life a fulfillment that altogether supplanted the need for any private expressions of spiritual freedom. The pleasure she had derived through her imagination for fifty years was replaced by the pleasure she received from adopting a way of life that satisfied all her earlier intellectual and emotional longings.

Beatrix Potter was born in 1866, the second generation following an enterprising group of individuals that made its fortunes in the Lanca-shire textile industry. Typical offspring of the industrial age, her parents adopted the stodgy piety of the bourgeoisie without having inherited any of the fiery spirit that had characterized their entrepreneurial forebears. Although Beatrix's father, Rupert, had taken the trouble to qualify as a barrister, he never bothered to practice law, choosing instead to live in fashionable retirement. He belonged to a number of London clubs, where he socialized with respectable members of the establishment, and he passed through life essentially as a dilettante—an amateur photographer, fisherman, and an occasional artist.

During the summer the Potters left their London home in Bolton Gardens ("my unloved birthplace"), moving with the servants to furnished houses in Scotland or in the Lake District of northern England. For Beatrix these summer months were a relief from the winter monotony of spending so many hours alone, or with nursemaids, or obediently greeting her mother's friends in the parlor. In London there were no neighborhood children to play with; her brother Bertram, born when Beatrix was five, was her only constant companion until he was old enough to be sent off to boarding school. Her own schoolroom was confined to the nursery where she worked alone with a governess, a course of education she did not find unfavorable in retrospect. "Thank goodness, my education was neglected," she wrote many years later. "I was never sent to school . . . the reason I am glad I did not go to school—it would have rubbed off some of the originality (if I had not died of shyness or been killed with over pressure). I fancy I could have been taught anything if I had been caught young; but it was in the days when parents kept governesses, and only boys went to school in most families."

These solitary hours were consumed by three interests: her writing, her art, and a study of the flora and fauna surrounding her. When she was thirteen years old she began to make almost daily entries into a journal, a ritual that continued until she was almost thirty years old. Although it has since been published, the journal was intended for her eyes only, and to protect her privacy she invented her own secret code for recording each entry. Apparently the journal was unknown to everyone, including her immediate family, lying undiscovered in a drawer until 1952 when a cousin who had inherited her house happened to come across a bewildering package in the attic that contained "a most extraordinary collection of papers . . . a large bundle of loose sheets and exercise books written in cipher-writing which we can make nothing of . . . ." The job of decoding this

200,000-word journal was taken up by Leslie Lindner—a devoted collector of Potter's work— but six years passed before he was able to break the code. Every attempt—even assisted by a professional code-breaker—proved unsuccessful, until a single sentence containing a date gave Lindner the clue that enabled him to unlock the entire code. Six more years were required to decipher the minute handwriting that filled so many pages.

The pains taken to keep these notes private may suggest that the journals revealed some surprising details of Beatrix Potter's life, but such was not the case: the pages were filled with matter-of-fact reports, impersonal details, and records. (Occasionally there is an entry that reveals Potter's sharp perceptions and directness. For example, her humorous description of John Ruskin, whom she observed at a Royal Academy exhibition, provides an amusing contrast to the way he was perceived by the adoring women in his circle. She described him as "one of the most ridiculous figures I have ever seen. A very old hat, much necktie and aged coat buttoned up on his neck, humpbacked, not particularly clean looking. He had on high boots, and one of his trousers was tucked up on the top of one. He became aware of this half way round the room, and stood on one leg to put it right, but in so doing hitched up the other trouser worse than the first one had been.") With the exception of these occasional sparks of humor and pertinent insights, Potter's writing in her journal seemed to contain little of the poetic quality that characterized the books written later. Even she was mystified by these journals when she looked them over in later years, declaring "When I was young, I always had the itch to write, without having any material to write about . . . . I used to write long-winded descriptions, hymns (!), and records of conversations in a kind of cipher-shorthand which I am now unable to read even with a magnifying glass."

For a child inclined to pass the hours in solitude, the journal served its purpose, and painting and drawing provided another engrossing activity. What started as a casual pastime when she was nine years old developed into a compelling occupation. "It is all the same," she wrote, "drawing, painting, modelling, the irresistible desire to copy any beautiful object which strikes the eye. Why cannot one be content to look at it? I cannot rest, I must draw, however poor the result." As an amateur artist himself, her father was amused by Beatrix's artistic curiosity. Occasionally he might take her to the museum or to an exhibition at the Royal Academy, or to the studio of his good friend, John Millais. The distinguished painter praised Beatrix for her gift of "observation," a compliment she valued greatly because she had taken such pains to record visual fact. (This was, perhaps, her only connection to the Pre-Raphaelites whose work she had studied closely. "When I was young it was still permissible to admire the Pre-Raphaelites; their somewhat niggling but absolutely genuine admiration for copying natural details did certainly influence me," she reported.)

Eclectic in his tastes, Rupert Potter had admired the work of Randolph Caldecott and collected many of the illustrator's original drawings and watercolors, which Beatrix happily studied first hand. "I did try to copy Caldecott," she confessed, "but I agree I did not achieve much resemblance." In fact, she valued these originals so highly that she retained many of them throughout her life, and at

"You may go into the fields or down the lane, but don't go into Mr. McGregor's garden," original watercolor illustration for *Peter Rabbit* (1901). Although she observed animal life with the objective eye of a scientist, Potter also formed strong emotional attachments to her many pets. Peter Rabbit and Benjamin Bunny were special favorites: "It is this naturalness . . . that I find so delightful in Mr. Benjamin Bunny, though I frankly admit his vulgarity. At one moment amiably sentimental to the verge of silliness, at the next, the upsetting of a tea-cup . . . will convert him into a demon, throwing himself on his back, scratching and sputtering."

"First he ate some lettuces," original
watercolor illustration for *Peter Rabbit* (1901). Confined to the
respectable yet solitary life of an unmarried daughter,
Potter plunged her creative energies into
her journals and nature studies, sharing these
private talents in her letters to children. The small
books she eventually published resembled these
letters, printed in the scale she assumed
children preferred.

least two are still in her now-historic home, Hill
Top, located in Sawrey, England. Caldecott's illustrations, she was convinced, towered over those of
his contemporaries; and she claimed "the greatest
admiration for his work—a jealous appreciation;
for I think that others, whose names are commonly bracketed with his, are not on the same
plane at all as artist-illustrators. For instance Kate
Greenaway's pictures are very charming, but compared with Caldecott she could not draw."

Beatrix Potter had no shortage of material to
inspire her writing and painting. She was fascinated by a number of subjects, including history,
literature, geology, botany, and zoology. Sharing
her intense love of nature, brother Bertram joined
in undertaking a serious investigation of wildlife.
In their rooms, at any one moment, the governess
might stumble across spiders or beetles, toadstools,
caterpillars, minnows, frogs, birds, hedgehogs,
snakes—dead or alive, intact or dismembered.
Brother and sister skinned the dead specimens,
examined what they could under the microscope,
boiled what was beyond skinning in order to
obtain the bones. Then they painted and drew
every morsel, every follicle and fin, every eyeball
and toenail. In one summer house they came
across an old printing press and they made wood
engravings of their victims which they then
printed. Beatrix also photographed rocks, flowers,
and animals with her father's old camera, filing
away the prints for future reference.

Beatrix's appetite for detailed information about
her specimens was insatiable. For about six years—
while Bertram was off at school—she made an
intensive study of fungi, creating over 250 paintings of her samples. She entertained the notion of

creating a book out of these paintings and research, an idea she soon dismissed because she predicted the book would be dull to anyone but her. She did manage to prepare a paper bearing the formidable title, "On the Germination of the Spores of Agaricina Agaricineae," which was read at a meeting of the Linnaean Society of London in 1897, but was received with skepticism by the conservative members because she had dared to advance too many of her own theories.

While the animals in Beatrix Potter's home were objects of study, they were also pets, and her attachments to them were no less emotional because of her clinical interest in them. As specimens they were examined for their generic patterns of behavior; as pets they possessed unique personality characteristics that charmed her. While she recorded the hibernation process of her pet hedgehog with meticulous attention to detail, for example, she also observed how the animal (whom she called "Mrs. Tiggy Winkle") seemed to enjoy traveling by train in a basket. While she observed that the breathing system of newts was markedly different from that of toads or frogs, she also mourned the passing of her pet rabbit who was "an affectionate companion and a quiet friend."

Her love for these pets was shared by her brother and they each prepared strange luggage for transporting their favorite animals to and from the ritual holidays. One winter Bertram took his pet jay to Oxford "crammed into a little box, kicking and swearing. Momma expressed her uncharitable hope that we might have seen the last of it." At another time, Bertram left behind "the responsibility of a precious bat." The pet snails—Lord and Lady Salisbury, Mr. and Mrs. Camfield, Mars and Venus

—occupied quarters near the pet frog Punch, the tortoise, and the weasel. She adored her Mrs. Mouse who was "in many respects the sweetest little animal I ever knew," but her favorites were the two Belgian rabbits named Benjamin Bunny ("Bounce") and Peter, "creatures of warm volatile temperament, but shallow and absurdly transparent."

As Beatrix entered her twenties, these animals represented a welcome source of amusement in an otherwise solemn household. During the months her brother was off at school, Beatrix lived a solitary existence under the watchful eye of her dour parents, and continued to flee from the relentless monotony of her daily routine by writing in her journal and painting. "I can't settle down to anything but my painting," she lamented. "I lose patience with everything else." She was frequently depressed, falling into what she called "odious fits of low spirits," and restlessly searched for a way to direct her private interests toward something meaningful. Setting aside her work on fungi, resigned to the fact that her scientific investigations would be of little interest to anyone except herself or her brother, she would amuse herself by scribbling casual sketches on scraps of paper, adding verses to little fantasy watercolors, experimenting with designs for greeting cards. She was attracted to Edward Lear's *Owl and the Pussy Cat* and illustrated the verses, creating a small booklet that was never published. She also did some illustrations of Alice from Lewis Carroll's text, intrigued by the creatures that lay behind the looking glass. She sold an occasional drawing, and even managed to find a publisher for six of her Christmas card designs in 1890, but failed to sustain interest in

Eastwood Dunkeld
Sep 4th 93

My dear Noel,

I don't know what to write to you, so I shall tell you a story about four little rabbits

whose names were —

Flopsy, Mopsy Cottontail

and Peter

They lived with their mother in a sand bank, under the root of a big fir tree.

'Now my dears', said old Mrs Bunny 'you may go into the field or down the lane, but don't go into Mr McGregor's garden.'

Flopsy, Mopsy & Cottontail, who were good little rabbits went down the lane to gather black berries. but Peter, who was very naughty

creating any others, finding the work hackneyed and sentimental. Instead she began to write picture-letters to the children of friends, an activity undertaken for diversion which magically presented a commercial challenge she pursued in later years.

Beatrix Potter began writing these illustrated letters to children when she was twenty-six years old, favoring in particular the children of a former governess, Miss Annie Carter, who had served in the Potter household many years before. Beatrix had always been fond of the governess and they maintained their friendship after Miss Carter became Mrs. Moore and produced a sizable family of eight children. To "the little Moores" Beatrix wrote imaginative letters, illustrated by charming drawings of her pets. In 1893, the eldest Moore child, Noël, was confined in bed for several months with a childhood ailment. To amuse the five-year-old, Beatrix wrote him a picture-letter featuring rabbits as the central characters. "My dear Noël," it began, "I don't know what to write you, so I shall tell you the story about four little rabbits, whose names were Flopsy, Mopsy, Cottontail and Peter. . . ."

It was not until seven years later that the thought of publishing these letters occurred to Beatrix Potter. When she wrote to Noël—who was by then twelve years old—she had only a faint hope that the letter might have survived, and was amazed to learn that he had actually saved his letter, just as his brothers and sisters had kept so many of theirs, tied in a ribbon and safely stored away. Using the letter as a basis, Potter copied the drawings almost exactly, added a few others, and lengthened the story slightly. Entitling it *The Tale of Peter Rabbit*, she submitted manuscript and drawings to Frederick

Warne & Co., soon receiving a courteous, but firm rejection. She offered the book to five other publishers with the same result. Undaunted, Potter decided to have the book privately printed at her own expense, an edition of 250 copies, which she would sell at a modest price to "obliging aunts." She planned the book according to what she felt best suited the young child reader: a small format, with only one or two sentences accompanying a new picture on each page. The book was printed in black and white, with only the frontis in color, recreating the same features that made her picture-letters so appealing to her young readers. The plan seemed to work. Ready in December 1901, the book was already sold out by February, so she had another 200 printed to satisfy the demand.

Meanwhile, because they had sent such a courteous reply to her initial submission of *Peter Rabbit*, Potter decided to send off a fresh copy of her little book to Warne, secretly hoping they might reconsider the book for publication, which is precisely what did happen. Warne would be happy to publish the book, they wrote, if she would agree to provide colored drawings instead of black and white, adding, "of course we cannot tell whether the book is likely to run to a second edition or not." Thus followed a happy exchange of arrangements, in which the drawings were discussed, as well as royalties, copyright, and printing. The year 1901—Beatrix Potter was already thirty-five—was the beginning of a new life. For the first time, some joy had entered the Potter household and her activities began to assume a purpose, presenting challenges she'd never imagined possible. Even before *Peter Rabbit* was completed, Potter eagerly began sketches for a new book, *The Tailor of Glouces-*

In a letter addressed to a seven-year-old boy, Noël Moore, Potter started her story of Peter Rabbit, having no thought of publication at the time.

"Lady Mouse in Mop Cap," original
watercolor illustration for *The Tailor of Gloucester* (1903).

ter, based on a story she had heard while visiting her cousin several years before. She chose not to submit the second book to Warne, suspecting it was too soon after the first (or fearing that they might not approve it). Instead she had a full-color edition of 500 printed at her expense. Writing to Warne she said, "I will send you the little mouse book as soon as it is printed. Except the children's rough copy I have not showed it to anyone, as I was rather afraid people might laugh at the words." Remaining her own favorite among all her books, *The Tailor of Gloucester* was published by Warne two years later, when it had become apparent that Beatrix Potter was a success.

Excited by the creative opportunities that now lay open to her, Beatrix Potter resumed her careful study of Caldecott's work, writing Warne, "We go to the Lakes for three months tomorrow. I will try to bring one of the frames of Caldecott's to Bedford Street in the autumn; I have been looking at them a great deal. They seem to have been drawn with brown ink and a very fine pen—I wonder if it's the habit of Evans' line blocks to come out thicker? . . . It may sound odd to talk about mine and Caldecott's at the same time, but I think I could at least try to do better than *Peter Rabbit*, and if you did not care to risk another book, I could pay for it. I have sometimes thought of trying some of the other nursery rhymes about animals, which he did not do. . . ."

The energy and enthusiasm she had once confined to the private entries in her journal and to her solitary scientific investigations were now directed to the creation of these little books for children.

"The Mice hear Simpkin outside," original
watercolor illustration for *The Tailor of Gloucester* (1903).

With each new book she developed, the ideas were shared with her editor Norman Warne, the youngest member of the Warne family to join the publishing firm. In detail, Beatrix Potter presented her concepts, and he tactfully offered advice. His sound, critical judgment encouraged her to develop confidence in her strongest capabilities, gradually giving her the courage to leave behind her reliance on nursery rhymes, riddles, and Randolph Caldecott. With Warne's guidance she completed, from 1903 to 1905, *The Tale of Squirrel Nutkin, The Tale of Benjamin Bunny, The Tale of Two Bad Mice,* and *The Tale of Mrs. Tiggy Winkle.* It seems remarkable that she could be so productive, considering the number of interruptions during the year as she accompanied her parents on trips back and forth to the Lake country during the summer and Easter and on

numerous seaside excursions made during the year, but these books were a joy, and they ended too soon. "I do so hate finishing books," she wrote to Warne, "I would like to go on with them for years."

Beatrix Potter and Norman Warne were temperamentally suited to each other. Both approaching forty, their friendship was supportive and comfortable. Several times Potter visited the Warne house in London, where Norman Warne lived with his sister and mother, and where the two older brothers and their families often came as well—a household full of interest, laughter, and children, so different from the solemn atmosphere in her own home. One would assume that Norman Warne's proposal of marriage to Beatrix Potter in June of 1905—and her acceptance—would come as a welcome relief to her parents who might have abandoned any hope of their daughter's betrothal. On the contrary, the Potters flatly opposed the union, appalled by the thought that Beatrix could wed a mere "tradesman." Defying her parents' wishes for the first time in her life, Beatrix pronounced herself engaged, declaring, "Publishing books is as clean a trade as spinning cotton."

As fate would have it, this period of independence was brief. Stricken suddenly with acute leukemia, Norman Warne died at the end of August, just three months after Potter had declared the engagement.

Beatrix Potter was not likely to forfeit the independence she had begun to earn. With the money she had acquired from a little legacy left to her by an aunt, and with her own accumulated earnings, she invested in a small farm called Hill Top, located in the Lake District. She had decided to buy the farm before Norman Warne died, but the purchase took on even greater meaning after his death. She did not intend to make Hill Top her permanent home, since it would be out of the question for an unwed daughter to leave her family for a farm as her brother had done. Nevertheless, having her own property, in a section of the country she adored, was sufficiently symbolic of her breaking away. "My brother and I were born in London . . . but our descent, our interest and our joy were in the north country." For her Hill Top represented freedom.

"She found some tiny canisters upon the dresser,"
original watercolor illustration for *Two Bad Mice* (1904).

"Mrs. Tiggy-Winkle with an Iron in her Hand,"
original watercolor illustration for *Mrs. Tiggy-Winkle* (1905).

Grief-stricken over the loss of Norman Warne, Potter buried herself in her work, completing *The Pie and the Patty-Pan*, a book begun with Norman earlier that year. The new farm provided solace during the melancholy months following the summer of 1905. She prepared to make alterations in the structure to provide a wing for the tenant farmer's quarters, reserving the farmhouse for herself. She continued to live with her parents, as was expected, but she slipped away to Hill Top at every acceptable opportunity.

By 1905 Beatrix Potter was indeed a success. The sales from her first two books continued to be brisk and the animal characters from these titles had already become heroes in the nursery. Stuffed Peter Rabbits appeared in store windows; and Nutkin squirrels were in the toyshops. *Peter Rabbit* was being translated into several languages, now dubbed *Il Coniglio Pierino, Pieter Langoor,* or *Petro Cuniculo* by children throughout Europe. (The piracy of her books in America was a matter of some concern. "The difficulties about 'copyrighting' an English book in America," she wrote, "are now so very great that we are obliged to engrave and print *in* America all copies intended for American use.") *Benjamin Bunny* and *The Two Bad Mice* were as successful in sales as their predecessors, and *Mrs. Tiggy Winkle* sold 30,000 copies within the first few weeks of publication.

Beatrix Potter took pride in this success ("It is pleasant to feel I could earn my own living"), and understood that the popularity of the books rested largely on the authenticity of her subjects. The specific knowledge she had of the animals enabled her to translate their appearance and behavior into convincing portrayals, free of distortion or sentimentality. Her devotion to real life in the real world was conveyed through these altogether believable animals, as real as Hunca Munca, her pet mouse, or Peter, her pet rabbit. The clothing they wear is only a superficial disguise of the real animal. "I can't invent. I can only copy," she reported, referring to her painstaking efforts to achieve fidelity. And she felt this was the only true course, disparaging those who did otherwise. "Kenneth Grahame ought to have been an artist," she said about the author of *Wind in the Willows*, "at least all writers for children ought to have sufficient recognition of what things look like —did he not describe 'Toad' as combing his *hair*? A mistake to fly in the face of nature—a frog may wear galoshes, but I don't hold with toads having beards or wigs."

Just as the animals populating the pages of her books were actually the pets in her home, so, too, do the settings describe what she actually observed in her own surroundings. With her father's old camera she photographed the landscapes in the north country, bringing them back to London for reference. The books consistently express her affection for the countryside and for farm life, and a trip through the house at Hill Top (now open to the public) will reveal how many of the interiors in her books were actually based on her own home—the

"The chimney stack stood up above the roof like a little stone tower," original watercolor illustration for *The Roly-Poly Pudding* (1908). As she spent more time in her beloved country home, Hill Top, Potter's books became larger and fuller. The domestic countryside became a more dominant feature of her illustrations.

kitchen, the staircase, the fireplace. And the Constable-like watercolor landscapes and farm-yard scenes are those seen from the back of the very same house.

Her writing, too, was concrete, meant for a specific child. "It is much more satisfactory to address a real child," she maintained. "I often think that was the secret of *Peter Rabbit*, it was written to a child—not made to order." Knowing the reader, she was able to relate believable incidents, never straying too far from what was familiar. She took great care to place precisely the correct phras-ing with the precise pictures, selecting words that were appropriate, if not always predictable. (The word "soporific" in *The Flopsy Bunnies* created quite a stir with her publishers, but she refused to make a substitute, convinced it was the perfect choice.) The writing served a visual purpose as well, and she might delete or add a word to improve the appearance of the page. Above all, she wrote, as she always had, for the sheer pleasure of writing. "I think I write carefully because I enjoy my writing and enjoy taking pains over it. I have always disliked writing to order; I write to please myself. My usual way of writing is to scribble, and cut out, and write it again and again. The shorter and plainer the better. And I read the Bible (un-revised version and Old Testament) if I feel my style wants chastening."

Norman Warne's death may have come as a blow to Potter, but she did not falter. He had given her the confidence to continue creating her unusual books for children and one followed the other in rapid succession. In eight years she produced thir-teen books considered her best work: *The Pie and the Patty Pan*, *Jeremy Fisher*, *Tom Kitten*, *Jemima*

"But the sales were enormous," from *Ginger & Pickles* (1909). After Potter's move to Sawrey, barnyard animals populated her stories, reflecting her love for the farm life surrounding her.

Puddle-Duck, The Roly-Poly Pudding, The Flopsy Bunnies, Ginger and Pickles, Mrs. Tittlemouse, Timmy Tiptoes, Mr. Tod, Pigling Bland, A Fierce Bad Rabbit, and *Miss Moppet.* Many of these describe Hill Top Farm and the town of Sawrey where the farm is located. Her connection to this town became more and more deeply felt with the years and whenever she could manage it, she would flee to Hill Top, gradually loosening the ties with her parents.

In 1909 she bought another property in Sawrey, called Castle Cottage, a small farm adjoining Hill Top. The office transferring the property for Miss Potter was W. Heelis and Sons, and Mr. William Heelis was the partner who handled the arrangements. A native of the region, he was very helpful in advising Potter on details about Castle Cottage. Over the next four years a friendship developed between them, a pleasant rapport based on their mutual affection for the area, and they exchanged letters during the cold winter months while she remained in London. When he proposed marriage, she accepted, a move that inevitably provoked the predictable response from her parents: the man was not worthy of her class. The fact that her brother arrived in London at the same time to declare that for several years he had been secretly married in Scotland to a wine merchant's daughter did not help her cause. But Beatrix Potter was now forty-seven years old, and determined to live as she pleased. Finally, her parents weakened and withdrew their objections. Beatrix Potter was married in autumn of 1913.

With the exception of a half dozen books patched together from previously prepared fragments, Beatrix Potter never wrote another book. There was no need. "The earlier books were written in

picture-letters of scribbled pen-and-ink for real children; but I confess that afterwards I painted most of the little pictures mainly to please myself. The more spontaneous the pleasures, the more happy the result. I cannot work to order: and when I had nothing more to say I had the sense to stop."

Beatrix Potter's books, created over a period of only thirteen years, offered her a gateway to freedom. Their function ceased after her marriage as she enjoyed the most fulfilling period of her life. Spurning her celebrated maiden name, she lived in Castle Cottage simply and happily as Mrs. William Heelis for thirty years, applying herself to the farm with the same willful energy she had given to her books. ("I seldom sit down except to meals," she reported.) Having abandoned her former life forever, Mrs. Heelis refused any visitors from outside, except for an occasional American who might have taken the trouble to travel to the Lake District to find her. (She always preferred her American admirers to the English, feeling they "understood and liked an aspect of my writings which is not appreciated by the British shopkeeper.")

Toward her final years in Sawrey, Potter was determined to see that her beloved countryside would remain preserved as she remembered it. With this intention, she purchased large parcels of land for donation to the National Trust or arranged for their purchase by the government. In her will she bequeathed 4,000 acres of Lake District property —including Hill Top itself—to the National Trust, preventing forever the land from being desecrated by development. What she was unwilling to share in her lifetime, she made available to the public after her death. Slipped in with her papers or attached to backs of pictures on her walls, she left behind notes for future students of her work.

Until an attack of bronchitis ended her life in 1943, she would spend hours alone sorting through the papers in the library of her cherished Hill Top, which she had kept intact all these years, though she did not live there. The housekeeper observed Mrs. William Heelis as she came into the empty house: "She liked to come and go unnoticed, and to be left quite alone with her memories of the past; and I would never come into that part of the house when Mrs. Heelis was there, although on cold dark, winter afternoons I often wished I could bring in cups of hot tea or cocoa to warm her." Left undisturbed, Beatrix Potter Heelis was preparing a legacy that would remain with us forever.

"She rather fancied a tree-stump amongst some tall fox-gloves," original watercolor illustration for *Jemima Puddle Duck* (1908). After marrying, Potter was no longer compelled to write and paint. "I am *very* happy," she wrote, "and in every way satisfied with Willie [her husband]. It is best now not to look back."

"And in a moment I heard Winnie-the-Pooh—*bump,
bump, bump*—going up the stairs behind him," from *Winnie-the-
Pooh* (1926). Regarded as the last of the great English
"black and white artists," Ernest Shepard eventually yielded to
popular demand for colored renditions of the favorite characters for the world of Christopher Robin.

Ernest H. Shepard

From *Now we are Six* (1927).

"ERNEST SHEPARD was a professional," his colleagues agreed. Drawing from the time he could first hold a pencil nearly to the day he died at ninety-six, Shepard's output of illustrations was constant and consistent. Although he suffered the untimely loss of four close family members—his mother, brother, wife, and son—Shepard's work continued uninterrupted, perhaps even *accelerated* by his sorrow, a steady pulse beat of drawing, drawing, drawing. Over the years he illustrated nearly 100 books and was a regular contributor to *Punch* and other periodicals, but he is still celebrated primarily for his little black-and-white drawings that appeared in four slender volumes about Christopher Robin and Winnie-the-Pooh. Shepard himself was rather surprised by the overwhelming popularity of these books, a reaction that was typical of the illustrator's modesty in these matters. When, during his own lifetime, he witnessed the sale of a single Pooh drawing escalate from only a few pounds to £1700, he simply donated the remaining 300 drawings in his collection to the Victoria and Albert Museum so that they might remain together. Shepard was, by nature, a moderate man, and his success never blinded him to what he knew to be his most enduring reward: a job well done. Ernest Shepard was, indeed, a professional, first and foremost.

"Father had quite decided that I should be an artist when I grew up," Ernest Shepard wrote in his autobiography, *Drawn from Memory*, "though I considered an artist's life to be a dull one and looked for something more adventuresome." When he was seven years old, he found his adventures in the form of a wooden horse named Septimus who was perched on top of three wheels. Introduced within the first pages of this charming autobiographical sketch, Septimus represented the union of Ernest Shepard's real and imaginary life, not a wooden toy at all, but a magnificent steed capable of transporting his master from one heroic episode to the next. Septimus remained Ernest's proud possession until he was obliged to abandon the horse when his mother died three years later.

Shepard's accounts of his early life suggest that this was a happy, stimulating, and active period. Ernest's father, Henry Shepard, was an architect who had come from a highly respected family, one of four sons and seven daughters. Henry and his brothers continued the Shepard name, but their sisters never married, which meant that Ernest

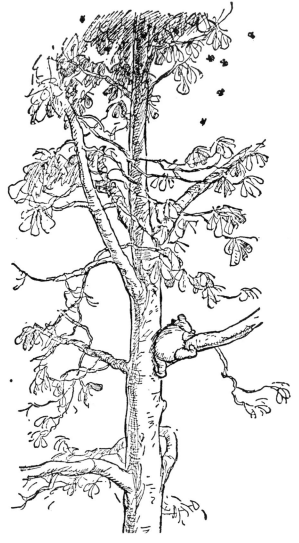

"Isn't it funny
How a bear likes honey?"
from *Winnie-the-Pooh* (1926).

was surrounded by doting maiden aunts. Ernest's mother, Jessie, was the daughter of a distinguished watercolorist, William Lee, and was friendly with many artists and actresses, especially the painter Frank Dicksee and the actress Ellen Terry. Henry and Jessie had three children, the youngest of whom—born in 1879—was Ernest. The happy period of Ernest's childhood came to a close in his tenth year when Jessie Shepard died and the three children were sent to live in the home of four spinster aunts. "It was years before the cloud seemed to lift and the natural buoyancy and happiness of youth revived itself in me," Shepard wrote.

In spite of financial hardship, Henry Shepard managed to raise the necessary funds to purchase a home in Hammersmith where the three children could come to live with him. While their sister Ethel studied the piano, Ernest and his brother Cyril attended St. Paul's, a fortunate choice made possible because their favorite uncle Willie was a master at the school and was able to arrange for their admission and reduced tuition.

Recognizing Ernest's talent for drawing, St. Paul's seized the opportunity to groom him for the prestigious prizes and scholarships he might win, and he was placed immediately in the Special Drawing Classes for this purpose. "What pleased me most," Shepard recalled, "was the encouragement I was given to put my own visual thoughts on paper. I drew every sort of subject with a preference for battle scenes, and I usually produced one or two by way of homework." Shepard's training at St. Paul's, coupled with less satisfying classes on Saturdays at Heatherley's, paid off: he won a scholarship to the Royal Academy Schools and went on to win the distinguished Landseer

" 'Oh, help,' said Pooh;
as he dropped ten feet,"
from *Winnie-the-Pooh* (1926).

he delighted his friends with his performances in amateur theatrical productions. The wanton life of an art student was temporary, and he knew it, but he enjoyed the experience while it lasted. "We all thought we were going to be oil painters," he recalled, "but we all had to give it up to start earning a living."

In fact, earning a living became Shepard's most important goal, the very thing he needed to give him license to propose marriage to the woman he loved, Florence Chaplin. A talented art student, three years older than himself, she agreed to marry as soon as they had accumulated sufficient funds. Happily, that time came sooner than expected. She received payment for a mural commission at the same time one of his paintings was accepted to the Royal Academy exhibition of 1904 and sold for £100. Feeling sufficiently prosperous, they made plans for marriage, despite the admonitions of Shepard's conservative Uncle Willie, who felt they were acting recklessly.

Although one of his paintings had been accepted for exhibition at the Royal Academy the very year he had completed his art studies, and another accepted at the Paris Salon the same year, Shepard never painted again for the public. "Well, I'm no good, you see," he said in an interview many years later, "that's the thing. I know that I can't handle the medium as I should. I'm perfectly sure I couldn't have competed as an oil painter." It was not that Shepard was timid, mind you. He was doggedly persistent with *Punch*, pestering them with two or three ideas a week until he finally succeeded in placing two drawings in 1907, and even after this triumph, the publication accepted only one in ten ideas he submitted. No, Shepard

Scholarship and a British Institutions Prize for his accomplishments in painting and drawing.

The scholarships were not sufficient to keep Ernest financially comfortable, but poverty was the state common to all art students in those days. The conviviality of friendship more than compensated for any financial worries that may have beset them. Shepard recalled with good humor his first steak in the Chelsea studio he shared with a friend. The meat was so tough he had to hammer it out with a t-square until it was the size of a small blanket, which then had to be folded several times to fit into the frying pan. During those days, Shepard's irrepressibly high spirits earned him the nickname "Giddy-Kipper," current slang for indulging in carefree behavior, and the shortened version "Kipper" or "Kip," stuck with him the remainder of his life. The nickname was well deserved: Shepard was mischievous, fond of practical jokes, and was not sensitive about rejection. Being an illustrator was what he had set out to do for a living, and what he was determined to do for the rest of his life.

The Shepards rented a home in Shamley Green, Surrey, and the two of them worked, drew, painted, and raised two children—Graham, born 1907, and Mary, born 1909. Until 1914, Shepard worked continuously, illustrating numerous books that included *Tom Brown's Schooldays* by Thomas Hughes, *David Copperfield* by Charles Dickens, *Henry Esmond* by W.M. Thackeray, *Aesop's Fables*, and *Smouldering Fires* by Evelyn Everett-Green. Then the War came.

Shepard was determined to apply for a commission in the Royal Artillery, in spite of his meager qualifications for the military ("I couldn't ride; I couldn't shoot; I was bad at maths; I didn't even know how or when to salute," he reported). He admitted that he had always been fascinated with guns and soldiering, and the cause was important, so he lost no time in signing up. Joining the 105 Siege Battery, he had to learn fast. Over the next four years he would see combat at the Somme, Arras, the Third Battle of Ypres, and in Italy. By the end of his service, he had been awarded a Military Cross and retired with the rank of Major.

It was typical of Shepard that throughout the time he served in the military, he continued to send in his humorous drawings to *Punch* on a regular basis, and he quietly drew and painted the countryside around him in his leisure hours, giving little evidence of the dangers he had experienced or the casualties he witnessed. In his autobiography, Shepard refers only briefly to a single sad episode in France when a battalion of Welsh Fusiliers passed him. They were singing a hymn: "I was standing by the roadside, close to what had been Fricourt, when they passed. I was grateful for their song. It seemed as if the men were singing a requiem. For that day I had found my dear brother's grave in Mansell Copse. The spot was marked by simple wooden crosses bearing the names of the Fallen roughly printed on them. It was, and is still, the resting place of over two hundred men of the Devons who fell that Sunday morning in July 1916." (Twenty-seven years later he would lose another beloved relation: his son Graham was killed in action during World War Two.)

Not long after returning home, Ernest Shepard received the greatest thrill of all: *Punch* invited him to join the "table," a regular staff position in which he would meet each week with twelve or fourteen members of the staff to decide the two political cartoons for the coming issue. For Shepard this appointment would mean a regular income; it also represented a great honor: he would sit at the same table where Sir John Tenniel had once been seated, where his wife's grandfather, Ebeneezer Landells, had once presided. "I nearly fell off my perch when I got the letter," Shepard recalled when he received the invitation to the *Punch* table. "Being accepted by the Academy the year I left school, that was a great thing of course. That first picture we got married on, oh, that was wonderful. But being accepted by *Punch*, being taken on the table, that was a permanent, lifetime job."

At the weekly dinners (which soon became weekly luncheons instead), it was customary for the proprietor to sit at one end of the table, and the editor (then Owen Seaman) at the other. Shepard sat alongside E.V. Lucas, a distinguished figure in the world of *belles lettres* who was chairman of the publishing company Methuen. Lucas was a friend and colleague of A. A. Milne, a prominent playwright, poet, and essayist, and a former assistant editor at *Punch*. In 1923 Lucas received an unusual submission from Milne: a book of child's verses called *When We Were Very Young*. Milne had started to compose light verse about his three-year-old son as a diversion during a rainy summer holiday in Wales, returning from the holiday with a sense of guilt because he had written for fun when he should have been applying himself to a book that would make some money for the family. Nevertheless, Milne was proud of his compositions and defended them years later when he felt they had been misunderstood by the critics. "*When We Were Very Young* is not the work of a poet being playful, nor a lover of children expressing his love, nor of a prose-writer knocking together a few jingles for the little ones. It is the work of a light-verse writer taking his job seriously even though he is taking it to the nursery. It seems that the nursery, more than any other room in the house, likes to be approached seriously."

After receiving Milne's manuscript at Methuen, E. V. Lucas happened to mention the poetry to Owen Seaman and they agreed that it would be a good idea for *Punch* to publish some of the verses before they appeared in book form. Lucas suggested Ernest Shepard as the illustrator, an idea that did not inspire Milne with much enthusiasm at first, until Lucas persuaded him that it was at least worth a try. Shepard illustrated eleven of the verses that appeared in *Punch* from January to June 1924, and the results convinced Milne that Shepard would be the right illustrator for the book to be published by Methuen later that year. *When We Were Very Young* was received enthusiastically in America and England, reprinted four times that same year, and the public immediately clamored for more books about Christopher Robin.

In 1925 A. A. Milne purchased a country home in Sussex called Cotchford Farm, where he, his wife, and son could retreat from London for weekends and summer holidays. Situated in a valley, the house was surrounded by meadows and woods that reached out to a hilly countryside beyond. It was this countryside that inspired the next books on Christopher Robin and Winnie-the-

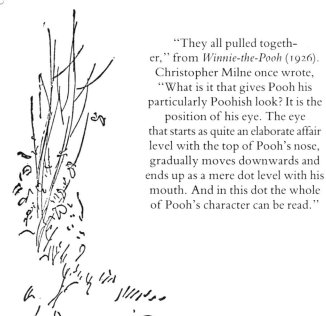

"They all pulled together," from *Winnie-the-Pooh* (1926). Christopher Milne once wrote, "What is it that gives Pooh his particularly Poohish look? It is the position of his eye. The eye that starts as quite an elaborate affair level with the top of Pooh's nose, gradually moves downwards and ends up as a mere dot level with his mouth. And in this dot the whole of Pooh's character can be read."

Pooh, an imaginary world created by an only child and his observing father. "It is difficult to be sure which came first," wrote Christopher Milne in his book, *Enchanted Places*. "Did I do something and did my father then write a story about it? Or was it the other way about, and did the story come first?

"Who Found the Tail? 'I,' said Pooh . . . Eeyore frisked about the forest, waving his tail so happily . . ." from *Winnie-the-Pooh* (1926).

Certainly my father was on the look-out for ideas; but so too was I. He wanted ideas for his stories, I wanted them for my games, and each looked towards the other for inspiration. But in the end it was all the same: the stories became part of our lives; we lived them, thought them, spoke them."

Crossing a bridge that came to be called "Poohsticks Bridge," Christopher Robin could enter Posingford Wood through a path that led to Ashdown Forest. "So if we wanted to go up to the Forest," recalled Christopher Milne,

we went on foot. So did others: only those who could walk to the Forest went there. This meant that when we got there we had the Forest almost entirely to ourselves. And this, in turn, made us feel that it was our *forest and so made it possible for an imaginary world —Pooh's world—to be born within the real world. Pooh could*

never have stumped a forest that was littered with picnic parties playing their transistor radios.

Anyone who has read the stories knows the Forest and doesn't need me to describe it. Pooh's forest and Ashdown Forest are identical. We came there often and since it was more of a walk than a ramble these were frequently family occasions, the four of us [Mr. and Mrs. Milne, Christopher, and Nanny, the governess] in single file threading the narrow paths that run through the heather.

At the top of the Forest a clump of pines called Gill's Lap provided the setting for scenes in the Pooh books. "And of course you can see it as Shepard drew it in *The House at Pooh Corner*. In the book it is Galleon's Lap but otherwise it is exactly as described, an enchanted spot before ever Pooh came along to add to its magic." Hundred Acre Wood, where Owl lived, was actually Five Hundred Acre Wood where Christopher Milne roamed with his Nanny.

Like the setting, the cast of characters was inspired by Christopher's real companions in the nursery: the teddy bear ("Pooh was the oldest,

only a year younger than I was, and my inseparable companion"), Eeyore ("perhaps in his younger days he had held his head higher, but by the time the stories came to be written his neck had gone like that and this had given him his gloomy disposition"), Piglet ("a present from a neighbor who lived over the way"), and Kanga and Roo ("presents from my parents"). Only Owl and Rabbit were invented.

Shepard took all this very seriously, as did Milne. His own deep connection to Septimus, his wooden horse from childhood, was a lifelong reminder of the child's power to transform reality into something magical. With his own children, Ernest Shepard had shared their world of make-believe, organizing plays and charades to be performed in costume by Mary and Graham. An upstairs cupboard contained an imaginary grotto with real

water and a mermaid. The Shepard children had their favorite toys, too: Growler was Graham's beloved teddy bear, and Puck was Mary's gnome, each endowed with unique character traits respected by the entire family. If the memory of Septimus provided a basis of understanding for Ernest Shepard, no doubt these early memories offered the same to Mary Shepard. Years later she, too, would become an illustrator of children's books and her Mary Poppins would become almost as famous as her father's Pooh had become.

Off to Cotchford Farm Ernest Shepard drove when Milne described the next book to him. Milne's instructions about the book were more

detailed than Shepard was accustomed to receiving from other authors, and he worked hard to achieve the accuracy Milne expected of him. He wandered through the countryside to sketch the details that Milne only barely described in the text and he had photographs taken of the toys and Christopher

Robin, accurately depicting both in his pen-and-ink drawings made from these references. The time spent at Cotchford Farm gave Shepard an understanding of Pooh's world as well as the rather lonesome world of an only child whose sole playmates were inventions of his imagination. This sympathy was transmuted in his sensitive drawings of the boy. "Yet if Christopher Robin seems a rather odd little boy," wrote the subject years later,

in one respect he is now less odd than he once was. Today his long hair and curious clothes are very much in fashion. But at the time, when other little boys had short hair, shirts, and ties, they were decidedly unusual. Was this Shepard's idea, or my father's—or whose?

First let me say that it had nothing to do with Shepard. It is true that he used his imagination when he drew the animals, but me he drew from life. I did indeed look just like that.

The image of the chief character in the books—

Winnie-the-Pooh himself—was based on an actual toy bear, but not the one treasured by Christopher Robin. Instead, Shepard depicted the teddy bear called Growler who belonged to Graham. "A magnificent bear—I've never seen his like," said Shepard. "He was passed on to my granddaughter, Minette, a little worse for wear, but still the best bear in the world. Minette took him to Canada during the War, and poor Growler came to an untimely end, worried to bits by a Scottie dog in a Montreal garden."

Winnie-the-Pooh was published by Methuen in 1926, *Now We Are Six* published in 1927, and *House at Pooh Corner* in 1928, completing a remarkable quartet that demonstrates the finest example of a successful collaboration between author and illustrator. Yet their intimate connection to these loving books did not mean the two men were close friends. According to Shepard, "It was difficult to get beyond the facade. Each time I went down to see him I had to start all over again." To the naturally friendly Shepard, Milne seemed aloof, cordial but formal. The "facade" was present even in Milne's words of praise, expressed in verse for the first American edition of *Pooh*, a certain ambivalence that could be interpreted as jealousy:

When I am gone
Let Shepard decorate my tomb
And put (if there is room)
Two pictures on the stone:
Piglet, from page a hundred and eleven
And Pooh and Piglet walking (157)...
And Peter, thinking that they are my own
will welcome me to heaven.

It was in some ways a painful success, more so

"By-and-by they came to an enchanted place on the very top of the Forest called Gilleons Lap, which is sixty-something trees in a circle," from *The House at Pooh Corner* (1928).

for Milne, who declared that it was "easier in England to make a reputation than to lose one." From then on, A.A. Milne was unable to shake his identity as the creator of Christopher Robin, and no future efforts in writing for grownups ever achieved the attention he had received from the no-more-than-70,000 words he wrote for children.

While Milne endeavored to lose his identity as a children's writer, Shepard continued his association with the Pooh books for the rest of his life. He was continually asked to create new illustrations and variations on the old ones, prints and watercolors in full color, new editions, and dust jackets. After each publication Shepard exhibited the drawings he had prepared for the book and managed to sell

Very Young, for example, Shepard was asked by E. V. Lucas to illustrate his *Playtime and Company*, a book that contains some of Shepard's finest drawings, but has been altogether forgotten. While Shepard was surely aware that the Pooh books represented a tough act to follow, he was pleased by the amount of new work—both Pooh-related and otherwise—that was now coming to him, and he was probably oblivious to the disguised barb underlying A. A. Milne's introduction to Shepard's anthology of *Punch* cartoons in a volume called *Fun and Fancy*:

. . . When an author produces a book entirely on his own, no artist is asked to write an Introduction, whereas the book of Shepard cannot make its charming bow to the world unless Milne, or somebody respectable, has agreed to chaperone it. Mr. E.H. Shepard, of all people, needs no introduction in my hands. Anybody who has heard of me has certainly heard of Shepard.

As it happened, Ernest Shepard received an assignment that nearly eclipsed the Pooh books in his career. In 1931 he was invited to create the illustrations for the ever-popular *Wind in the Willows* by Kenneth Grahame. "I was more excited when they offered me that than Pooh," he exclaimed. The book had already been through three illustrators (Paul Branson, Nancy Burnhart, and Wyndham Payne), but Grahame felt these illustrators had done little more than render his characters "puppets." Arthur Rackham had been invited to illustrate *Wind in the Willows*, but he turned down the idea. (Rackham did eventually illustrate the book, after Grahame's death, and it turned out to be the last book Rackham ever illustrated.) In fact, Shepard was not at all sure the text should ever

some for £5 or £10, for in spite of his regular *Punch* income and the success of the Pooh books, money was short. Shepard found himself particularly strapped when his wife Florence died suddenly in 1927, leaving him with two children and a new home to be cared for. His personal grief and financial worries were never expressed in the drawings executed during this period, however. Every assignment was welcome, and Kipper worked harder than ever.

Although Shepard continued to produce some of his best work after the Pooh books were published, his later efforts tend to be overshadowed by the dazzling popularity of these little books. Immediately following the publication of *When We Were* have been pictured in the first place. "There are certain books," Shepard wrote in 1954, "that should never be illustrated . . . and I had felt that *Wind in the Willows* was one of these. Perhaps if it had not already been done, I should not have given way to the desire to do it myself, but it so happened that when the opportunity was offered me, I seized upon it gladly."

Shepard had learned his lesson with the Pooh books, for which he had received a not-very-large

From *Wind in the Willows* (1931).

From *Wind in the Willows* (1931).

flat fee, and he agreed to illustrate *Wind in the Willows* only if he was paid one-third of the royalty share, terms that were acceptable to Grahame. Before beginning, Shepard went to Berkshire to visit the elderly author. According to Shepard, the interview was memorable.

Not sure about this new illustrator of his book, he listened patiently while I told him what I hoped to do. Then he said, "I love these little people, be kind to them." Just that; but sitting forward in his chair, resting upon his arms, his fine handsome head turned aside, looking like some ancient Viking, warming, he told me of the river nearby, of the meadows where Mole broke ground that spring morning, of the banks where Rat had his house, of the pools where Otter hid, and of the Wild Wood way up on the hill above the river, a fearsome place but for the sanctuary of Badger's home, and of Toad Hall. He would like, he said, to go with me to show me the river bank that he knew so well, ". . . but now I cannot walk so far and you must find your way alone."

That afternoon Shepard sketched the river bank, the meadows, and Wild Wood, just as Grahame

From *Wind in the Willows* (1931).

"I've lost all my money, and lost my way," from *Wind in the Willows* (1931).

From *Wind in the Willows* (1931).

had described them. Shepard met the author only once again. "I went to his home and was able to show him some of the results of my work. Though critical, he seemed pleased and, chuckling, said, 'I'm glad you've made them real.' We seemed to share a secret pleasure in knowing that the pictures were of the river spots where the little people lived." Grahame died before the drawings were finished, but Shepard knew that the old man was pleased. In the end, the illustrations for *Wind in the Willows* were Shepard's own favorites as well.

Shepard maintained his intense pace of work, illustrating fourteen books in the 1930s, as well as dust jackets and frontispieces for others, and his weekly contributions to *Punch*. In 1932 E. V. Knox (dubbed "Evoe") succeeded Owen Seaman as editor of *Punch* and in 1937 married Ernest Shepard's daughter, Mary. At the outbreak of World War Two, Shepard launched into a series of *Punch* cartoons attacking Hitler and other warmongers, but his zeal for political subjects waned as he entered

the post-War period. Although he was a great admirer of John Tenniel, he had no appetite for the biting stiletto pen of his model. "I'm not a nature-born caricaturist," he remarked. "If there was anything particularly horrible I could do it. I think my drawings of Hitler and Himmler are as good as anyone's because I let myself go. But it was not so easy in the Atlee regime."

Toward the end of the War, shortly after his son Graham was killed at sea, Shepard married again at the age of sixty-five. Commissions were slow in coming. It was not until 1949 that he illustrated another book (*Bertie's Escapade* by Kenneth Grahame) and when Malcolm Muggeridge—who became editor of *Punch* in 1953—decided to replace Shepard with a cartoonist displaying more contemporary flair, the elderly illustrator might well have abandoned his profession to retire into the twilight years. On the contrary, after he was "sacked from *Punch*" (as he liked to describe it), Shepard turned his attention to new assignments with renewed vigor, illustrating nine books between 1954 and 1955. He traveled, gave lectures, and even launched a career as a writer with two autobiographies, *Drawn from Memory* and *Drawn from Life*, followed by two children's books he wrote and illustrated (*Ben and Brock* and *Betsy and Joe*).

Shepard continued this pace as long as he was able, even into his nineties. It seems only natural that his last venture would be to prepare colored editions of *Winnie-the-Pooh* and *House at Pooh Corner*. Working over line drawings Methuen had printed on watercolor paper, Shepard was eager to complete the entire set before time ran out. He colored 240 drawings in less than four months. Garish colors applied to the line work with a shaky hand, these colored drawings are nevertheless the marvelous efforts of a ninety-three-year-old man determined to complete his final assignment. When the illustrator died, three years later, preparations were well underway for the fiftieth-anniversary celebration of Winnie-the-Pooh's first appearance. Ernest Shepard would have been proud to see the turnout.

"I think we all ought to play Poohsticks,"
from *The House at Pooh Corner* (1928).

"As I was going to St. Ives," from *Mother Goose, The Old Nursery Rhymes*
(1913). Rackham has placed his self-portrait at lower left.

Arthur Rackham

From *Cinderella* (1919).

HE WAS NOT A WRITER. Instead he created pictures for books written by others. Several books had already been illustrated by artists before him—*Alice in Wonderland, The Fairy Tales of the Brothers Grimm, Aesop's Fables, Mother Goose,* for example—and others seemed almost unillustratable—*A Midsummer Night's Dream, Siegfried and the Twilight of the Gods* —but it didn't matter. Arthur Rackham took possession of whatever he illustrated; his images were the product of a vision so totally and completely his own that they existed almost independently of the words surrounding them. The words were simply suggestions for a visual rendition by the illustrator. "For his illustrations to be worth anything, he must be regarded as a partner [to the author] not as a servant," asserted Arthur Rackham when asked to present his concept of the artist's contribution to the text. ". . . An illustration may legitimately give the artist's view of the author's ideas; or it may give his view, his independent view of the author's sub-

ject. But it must be the artist's view; any attempt to coerce him into a mere tool in the author's hands can only result in the most dismal failure."

Arthur Rackham's imagery was every bit as memorable as the prose he illustrated, as clearly discerned as the author's voice he accompanied. Rackham's gift, and his fame, derived from an extraordinary, poetic imagination that produced a world of fantasy never before seen. His world was gossamer, ethereal, and mysterious, populated with gnomes, dwarfs, fairies, goblins, and elves, with sinuous root tendrils, mushrooms, ferns, and massive trees that transformed into humans. The pictures seem other-worldly, magically evoked by a wand passing over the pages. One might imagine that the artist emerged from some distant forest, where sunlight and shadow weave their eternal magic through the web of gnarled branches. Perhaps the artist was even a wizard!

On the contrary. It seems difficult to accept that

Arthur Rackham was, in fact, the most *unlikely* wizard or magician. He was British through and through—a cockney, actually—a kindly, mild-mannered gentleman, who enjoyed a game of tennis and the company of good friends. He wasn't even eccentric. The only connection between the man and his pictures seemed to be his face, his "wide and elfish grin," as the writer R.H. Ward described him. But that's not surprising: Rackham frequently used himself as a model for his paintings. It was, after all, more practical, and Rackham was a practical man.

The fantastic nature of Rackham's artistry has attracted a number of romantic biographers who suggest that a distant ancestor may have transmitted magical powers to the illustrator, that a certain John Rackham—a pirate hanged in Jamaica in 1720—might offer the glorious link. Such an explanation is better left to the rapturous zealots who belong to the still-active Rackham cult. It is always painful to acknowledge the discrepancy that exists between the creation and the creator when the contrast is so great.

Arthur Rackham's father, Alfred Thomas, was a civil servant, the chief clerk in the office of the Admiralty Marshal and Serjeant of Mace of the High Court of Justice, and the Rackham family was distinctly middle class. Born in 1867, Arthur was the fourth of twelve children, and the only child to demonstrate any interest in drawing. It was unthinkable, of course, that he would recklessly dedicate himself to art. As Randolph Caldecott had done a quarter of a century before, Arthur Rackham became a clerk in 1885, and relegated all artistic activities to his leisure hours away from the office. He did not, however, waver in his determina-

tion to become an artist one day. A four-month trip made to Australia for his health had given him the time and subject matter to convince him that his real ambitions lay at the easel. With unfaltering industry and discipline, Rackham applied himself to his position as a clerk in the Westminster Fire Office from nine to five and as an art student at Lambeth School of Art in the evenings. For eight years he worked at the insurance office—experience that no doubt sharpened his skills for financial management that he exercised to good advantage throughout his life—and in 1891 he began to sell his drawings to illustrated papers in London, *Scraps*, *Illustrated Bits*, and *The Pall Mall Gazette*. Only when he had satisfied himself that he could make a living from illustrations, did he leave the insurance office to become a full-time artist on the newly started *The Westminster Budget*. Here he contributed "Sketches from Life," drawings of public personalities in London.

Rackham was a cautious man, and his gifts in illustration were extremely slow in developing. The work he produced during this period was serviceable, but undistinguished, and temperamentally he was uncomfortable with the rigors of reportage. But he continued to work for *The Westminster Budget* until he was certain he could support himself otherwise. When asked years later to describe the worst time of his life, Rackham pointed to this period. "That really was a very thin time indeed for me, and may be considered the worst time I ever had. The kind of work that was in demand to the exclusion of almost all else was such as I had no liking for and very little aptitude. It was also clear that the camera was going to supplant the artist in illustrated journalism, and

Tom Thumb from *Grimm's Fairy Tales* (1909). During
his years as a news artist Rackham developed the skill of handling
pen and ink, and all his later work revealed this early training.

"New Lamps for Old," original watercolor illustration for *The Arthur Rackham Fairy Book* (1933).

my prospects were not encouraging.''

While his talents as a journalist were far from outstanding, the work he performed required skills that came to good use in later years. The assignments demanded a variety of treatments, a facility in line, and the ability to observe and portray details accurately and swiftly. This period of apprenticeship was long, but it made up for the minimal amount of formal training he had received in art school.

It was not until he was twenty-seven that Rackham was given an assignment to illustrate a book (a travelog to the United States called *To the Other Side*), and it was still another three years before his own personal style emerged. The training period had been long and arduous, the improvement slow, but it was worth the effort. Within a decade he would be the most widely sought-after illustrator of fantasy.

Rackham felt secure in leaving *The Westminster Budget* in 1896 and by the end of the 1890s had illustrated nine books, most notably *The Ingoldsby Legends* and Charles and Mary Lamb's *Tales from Shakespeare*. He was regarded as a dependable illustrator with genuine signs of promise for the future.

The real turning point in Rackham's life came in 1900. That year he met his future wife Edyth Starkie, a portrait painter of great talent, as spirited as he was down-to-earth, as romantic as he was rational. She encouraged him to follow his natural bent for fantasy and offered intelligent criticism which he took with great respect. This was also the year he was invited to illustrate *The Fairy Tales of the Brothers Grimm*, for which he prepared ninety-nine black-and-white drawings and one color

frontispiece. The book was immediately successful, and continued to sell well for many years to come. Two new editions were called for within the next ten years, until the publication of the best-known edition in 1909, containing forty colored pictures and fifty-five black-and-white-drawings. "In many ways," Rackham said, "I have more affection for the Grimm drawings than the other sets. (I think it is partly one's childhood affection for the stories.) It was the first book I did that began to bring success. . . ."

"Then all at once the door sprang open, and in stepped a little Mannikin," from "Rumpelstiltskin" in *Grimm's Fairy Tales* (1909).

Developments in printing had opened a great opportunity for an artist of Rackham's talent. Within the previous decade, the quality of color reproduction had improved greatly, thanks to the introduction of a process involving the photographic separation—by means of filters—of a full-color painting into three primary colors, yellow, red, and blue. When superimposed over a black plate, these colors re-created the illusion of the full-color original. The system had its limitations.

"Round the fire an indescribably ridiculous little man
was leaping, hopping on one leg, and singing," from "Rumpelstiltskin" in *Grimm's Fairy Tales* (1909).

Only a highly-glazed art paper could retain the colored inks sufficiently to simulate the original, paper that was far too heavy to be bound with the lighter-weight sheets of text paper. This shortcoming, however, was turned to advantage by the publishers. The heavier sheets were pasted on (or "tipped in" to) the pages of text stock after the book was printed. Such an operation was performed by hand, adding to the cost of production, but enhancing the appearance of the page which resulted in unusual decorative book designs. These developments gave rise to the gift book, and Rack-

ham was among the first and was surely the most prominent illustrator to benefit from this phenomenon in publishing.

In 1905 Rackham was invited to create fifty-one watercolors for such a gift book, *Rip Van Winkle*, the book that launched his long association with the publisher William Heinemann and established him finally as the leading decorative illustrator of the Edwardian period. By now he had captured the hearts of children and the sharp eye of collectors as well. In conjunction with the publishing of the book, the original drawings and paintings were

Detail of "The Fairies have their tiffs with the Birds,"
original watercolor illustration for *Peter Pan in Kensington Gardens* (1906).

exhibited at the prestigious Leicester Galleries where all but eight were sold. Simultaneously, a deluxe limited edition of 250 copies of the book, signed by Rackham, was issued by Heinemann, and sold out before the end of the exhibition. Foreign editions appeared in French and German almost immediately.

The excitement surrounding the publication of *Rip Van Winkle* attracted many new admirers, among whom was J.M. Barrie, the author of a play called *Peter Pan* that had just been successfully produced in London. Barrie urged Rackham to

illustrate his first story about Peter Pan, *The Little White Bird*, and Rackham agreed to prepare fifty illustrations for the publication in 1906. With Rackham's illustrations, the book was published as *Peter Pan in Kensington Gardens* and received much acclaim throughout the world. The success of the originals sold at the Leicester Galleries and the limited edition of 500 sold through the publisher continued to propel Rackham into the realm of the rarefied. Now he could select his books at will and cast his images on whatever prose appealed to him. When he chose to illustrate *Alice in Wonder-*

land, however, some felt he had gone too far.

In 1906, the copyright for the Tenniel edition of *Alice's Adventures in Wonderland* expired, and several publishers rushed to issue new editions of the popular book. When Rackham agreed to illustrate *Alice* for Heinemann, he fell under attack by critics who felt that the classic Tenniel illustrations were sacrosanct and that any attempt at retelling the Carroll story with new images represented sheer hubris on the part of the illustrator. One critic decried Rackham for taking the assignment, calling it "a piece of exceedingly bad taste, to say nothing of its unfairness." Not defiant by nature, Rackham nevertheless took on the challenge and proceeded with the illustrations for Heinemann.

Unrestricted by the limitations of reproduction that had hampered Tenniel forty years before, Rackham was able to execute subtleties of color and line that resulted in a set of illustrations so remarkably different from the Tenniel work that the controversy grew more intense when the book appeared in 1906. While one group of readers responded with dismay, others applauded the fresh images with enthusiasm. One supporter wrote to Rackham that his "delightful Alice is alive and makes by contrast Tenniel's Alice look like a stiff wooden puppet." Although *Alice in Wonderland* was extremely successful (it is still in print), Rackham was too shaken by the criticism to accept the offer to illustrate *Through the Looking Glass* as a companion volume.

The controversy created by *Alice in Wonderland* was a disruption in an otherwise stable and constant routine Rackham enjoyed. The income he received from his royalties and the sale of his originals was invested wisely and he was sufficiently prosperous to purchase an attractive home in Hampstead that contained two comfortable studios in which he and his wife could paint undisturbed. By nature he was a quiet man, with a simple, almost austere sense of values. He did not smoke, ate simply (roast beef was his favorite), and his only indulgence was an evening glass of Marsala wine. His navy blue suit, stiff white collar, and blue-and-white polka-dotted bow tie were his daily costume, even if he could well afford an extensive wardrobe. Rackham enjoyed contact with his colleagues, attending weekly Friday night meetings of the Langham Sketching Club, and as an active member of the Art Workers Guild, he followed his distinguished predecessors Walter Crane and William Morris by accepting the Master Chair.

The simplicity of Rackham's routine continued when he, his wife, and daughter Barbara moved farther out of London in 1920. He kept physically active by playing tennis regularly and became a familiar figure at the local tennis club. A fellow member reported that Rackham "would come to the club looking rather wizened and very like one of his own dwarf drawings, and would play tennis—he was an average club player—for about three hours without stopping. After about six sets, he would leave with only the briefest of farewells to the other members. He took, as far as I can remember, practically no part in the club's social activities, but was always extremely popular, and greatly admired for his fantastic energy and enthusiasm."

The marvelously fanciful images produced from Rackham's imagination were created very methodically. After all, from the outset his work had improved only because he had been so diligent,

"'Preposterous!' cried Solomon in a rage,"
from *Peter Pan in Kensington Gardens* (1906).

"They all crowded round it panting and asking, 'But who has won?'." from *Alice's Adventures in Wonderland* (1907). By daring to depict what John Tenniel had made sacrosanct, the mild-mannered Rackham unwittingly provoked controversy among the critics.

and this careful and disciplined approach to illustration never diminished with the years. He had developed a sure sense of line, a quality that dominated even his color work, which explains his fascination with the contours of sinuous tree roots, branches, and wrinkles. With the technical advances that had improved the methods of transferring the artist's line to the printing plate—no intermediaries in between to distort the original intention—Rackham developed a fluid, delicate and sensitive line that reproduced faithfully and he used it to good advantage.

Rackham would begin the process by carefully sketching the broad outlines of the composition with a soft pencil, rendering on cardboard or on a textured drawing paper that had been mounted on cardboard. First he blocked in the masses, then he worked in the detail. The size of his illustration was normally twice that of the intended reproduction, at least until he discovered that larger originals sold more effectively than the smaller, and so he created larger work. In some cases he would make more than one preparatory sketch, establishing precisely what he had conceived in his mind's eye. Into the general mass of pencil drawing he would place the lines in pen and india ink, removing the pencil marks below after he had completed the inking.

For a color illustration, Rackham would begin in the same manner, creating a drawing in pen and ink, perhaps applying a light wash of color to the entire surface of the paper first to unify the later applications of color, much the way the old masters laid on an imprimatura before applying their oils. In another respect his procedure resembled that of the old masters: he applied successive layers of transparent watercolor, just as the painters of the sixteenth century applied glazes of oil paint. Only occasionally would Rackham work with opaque watercolors, preferring instead the mysterious gossamer quality achieved by the several transparent veils of pigment. This method necessitated the use of a restricted palette of colors (too many hues over one another would result in muddied, rather than brilliant colors), with an occasional application of pure, bright color for accents. The restricted palette worked well on Rackham's behalf in another way also: the three- and four-color process of reproduction of the day did not lend itself to the translation of many variations in hue.

Rackham was extremely particular about the faithful reproduction of his watercolors and would alter color in his original if he suspected it would not translate well in reproduction. He frequently expressed his despair about faulty reproduction when he marked the color proofs sent him for approval. In exasperation he once wrote, "Try to get the Suffragettes to knife the man who invented four-color and every living man who won't swear not to use it again."

For as much as his images depicted a world of fantasy, the subjects themselves derived from real-world models used over and over again in his pictures: the tree in his garden, portraits of friends and family, and renditions of his own image reflected in the mirror. He kept a collection of costumes and props which he used regularly, and he relied heavily on living models. One model recalled that "a young girl might equally well serve him as the Vicar of Wakefield or an evil old witch. I remember one who even acted as a dismembered corpse."

"Hey! Diddle, Diddle!" from *Mother Goose, The Old Nursery Rhymes* (1913).

To get the broken plates just right for Alice's tea party in Wonderland, he used as props some dishes he broke himself, and he seated Alice in his own favorite wing chair surrounded by the family china. His model for Alice was a local girl, Doris Dommett, selected from a number of applicants, and her recollections demonstrate his concern for every detail: "I was so pleased he copied my print frock exactly, because it was one my mother had allowed me to design myself. The woolen stockings I wore were knitted by my old French nannie Prudence. They were so thick to keep out the cold, and how they tickled!"

This leap from the real (even mundane) to the fantastic was one Rackham made naturally, a leap he knew children made with him. Like Walter Crane before him, Arthur Rackham maintained that imagination, when stimulated, elevated the child's intelligence, a view clearly expressed in an entry he composed for an American encyclopedia, *The Junior Book of Authors*:

I can only say that I firmly believe in the greatest stimulating and educative power of imaginative, fantastic, and playful pictures and writings for children in their most impressionable years—a view that most unfortunately, I consider, has its opponents in these matter of fact days. Children will make no mistakes in the way of confusing the imaginative and symbolic with the actual. Nor are they at all blind to decorative or arbitrarily designed treatment in art, any more than they are to poetic or rhythmic form in literature.

By sharing his extraordinary imagination, Rackham continued to be stimulated himself, and he took on greater and greater challenges in his assignments. He illustrated Shakespeare's *A Midsum-*

"Suddenly the branches twined round her and turned into two arms," original watercolor illustration for *Little Brother and Little Sister* (1917). With his sinuous line and Nordic sensibilities, Rackham frequently transformed animals, trees, and flowers into fantastic creatures.

From *Cinderella* (1919). While Rackham's delicate linework was ideally suited for the wrinkles and roots so often seen in his ambitious work, these modest silhouettes also demonstrate his extraordinary sense of line.

mer Night's Dream, Swift's *Gulliver's Travels*, Richard Wagner's *Siegfried and the Twilight of the Gods*, books whose texts demand the most unusually imaginative images. Rackham worked steadily through World War One, although he worked under the strain of unhappy events in his personal life: when his wife became seriously ill, he sent her and his daughter to live apart from him where they would be safely distant from the 1914–1918 air raids.

Being forty-seven years old, Rackham was not able to serve in combat during the war, but he joined the Hampstead Volunteers. Rackham's commanding officer observed the middle-aged recruit: "I was then (1915) Sergeant Major of the Company, and it was great fun to see him endeavouring to do the 'Army Drill.' He found difficulty in 'forming fours,' and at rifle drill was a scream. But he was a good recruit, and did his best to please and to learn."

The quality of book production understandably declined during the War years, but even after the War the market for fine quality books failed to recover. Although Rackham continued to create some of his best work, including *Little Brother and*

Little Sister and remarkable silhouetted illustrations for *Cinderella* and *The Sleeping Beauty*, and although his income in 1920 was greater than it had ever been, the zeal for fairies and fantasy had been shattered by the grim experiences of the War. The sales from the 1919 Rackham exhibition held at the Leicester Galleries were disappointing, and it was the last such exhibition held there for many years. Rackham's popularity seemed to shift instead from England to the United States. From across the Atlantic the artist was besieged with fan letters and collectors' inquiries and the sales of his books surpassed those in England. Rackham exhibitions held at New York's Scott & Fowles Gallery in 1919, 1920, and 1922 were highly profitable.

Rackham was received like royalty when he finally sailed off to meet his public in America in 1927. During his visit he met with publishers, arranged exhibitions, and talked with his fans. After this trip, his American audience became paramount in the planning of his books. In spite of his enormous popularity, however, the deluxe picture book was becoming a thing of the past, and he lamented this development upon his return

A·LEGEND·OF
SLEEPY·HOLLOW

BY·WASHINGTON·IRVING
ILLUSTRATED·BY
ARTHUR·RACKHAM

Book jacket, original watercolor for *The Legend of Sleepy Hollow* (1928).
After World War One the primary market for Rackham's lavishly illustrated books
shifted from England to the United States.

from the States:

. . . I need not say what a difference the war has made. The market is now divided up among stacks of cheaply produced and relatively inexpensive books. The "trades" have so settled it—not without great consideration. And the difficulty of bringing out a rather better book is so great as to be all but prohibitive. I recently went over to the States to see for myself exactly what the conditions were there. And found them much the same. I might tell you of one experience. One of the great firms of New York agreed, after much deliberation, to do a book for me: but on hearing that other illustrations of mine were arranged to appear the same season, they at once withdrew their offer. As a matter of fact, the better class books do not sell half the number that they did before the war, and there is not as much profit to be made out of each book as there was, so neither publishers nor illustrators are having much of a time. The only men of my craft who are flourishing are portrait painters, and advertisement designers—branches that I only occasionally enter. . . .

The movement away from the lavish and expensively produced deluxe editions came at a difficult time for Rackham. His wife, never fully recovered from her illnesses contracted during the War, had become an invalid, requiring extensive nursing care, and she represented a constant preoccupation from which he escaped only while he was in his London studio. His fame was now so widespread that he never wanted for work, but he paid the price celebrated artists frequently must pay; his admirers wanted his work to remain as it was, reacting with skepticism to any attempt on his part to change. During a period in the 1920s, for example, he subdued the linear quality in his illustrations, softening the effect of his images with his color blended and suffused, rather than partitioned by sharply defined lines. His experiments with new forms of expression appeared in *Irish Fairy Tales* (1920) and *The Tempest* (1926), but his public responded less enthusiastically to these new efforts and the artist felt obliged to return to his earlier formulas. His work of the 1930s, while it remained ever popular, revealed signs of the artist's boredom.

The United States continued to be a strong market for Rackham's illustrations and the American publishers loyally continued to issue deluxe editions of his titles. In 1936, George Macy, representing the American Limited Editions Club, called on Rackham in England to discuss future assignments for the illustrator. Macy described Rackham as a character out of one of his own drawings, "his head seemed always cocked to one side, bright and eager and smiling and cheerful; his cheeks were pink and bright; his eyes bright blue and clear; his emotions used his face as a field to play on." As they chatted casually about books Rackham might like to do, Macy lightly tossed out a suggestion, "What about *Wind in the Willows*?" Macy was taken with Rackham's response: "Immediately a wave of emotion crossed his face; he gulped, started to say something, turned his back on me and went to the door for a few minutes." Rackham explained that the author of *Wind in the Willows*, Kenneth Grahame, had asked him to illustrate the book nearly thirty years before and that other commitments had prevented him from accepting the offer, a decision Rackham had always regretted. Now he was deeply moved to be given a second opportunity to illustrate the book.

The challenges presented by this commission

"Stand away from the window, please, madam; you're obstructing the
other passengers!" original watercolor illustration for *The Wind in the Willows* (1940).
Using an altogether different approach from that taken by Ernest Shepard
five years earlier, Rackham completed his career with the famous tale by Kenneth Grahame.

"'Onion-sauce! Onion-sauce!' (Mole mocks the Rabbits)," original watercolor
illustration for *The Wind in the Willows* (1940).

inspired Rackham to plunge ahead with unflagging enthusiasm, despite the stress of his wife's continuing illness and his own declining health. To trace the original and authentic locations of the scenes from the book, Rackham corresponded with Grahame's widow, and he strolled with her along the river banks and through the woods described in *Wind in the Willows*. After undergoing surgery for cancer, Rackham knew he was fighting for time as he pressed forward on the illustrations. Through the summer of 1939, he labored on the drawings until he finally completed the last, a scene in which Mole and Rat are loading the rowboat for a picnic. When presented the drawing for approval, Rackham's daughter pointed out to her father that the oars were missing from the boat. No amount of reassurance could prevent Rackham from returning to the drawing to correct the omission. After rendering the oars with great effort, the ailing illustrator sank back in his bed and sighed, "Thank goodness, that is the last one." He died a few weeks later, and *Wind in the Willows*, one of his crowning achievements, was published the following year.

From *Jack the Giant-Killer*.

"The Chamberlain goes in search of the Nightingale," from
"The Nightingale" in *Stories from Hans Andersen* (1911).

Edmund Dulac

From *The Sleeping Beauty and Other Fairy Tales* (1910).

As illustrators of deluxe gift books during the first two decades of the twentieth century, both Arthur Rackham and Edmund Dulac inherited what the industrial age had made possible the generation before. Never before had the climate been so ideal for the creation of exquisitely manufactured luxury items. The industrial revolution had produced the technical means of reproducing colorful paintings and an acquisitive market to which these stunning objects could be sold. Children's books were now items of beauty to be collected by adults, emblems of affluence and good taste. In the period between 1905 and World War One, gift book publishing was big business.

Because Arthur Rackham and Edmund Dulac were the most eminent illustrators of gift books, their names are often linked, just as Walter Crane, Kate Greenaway, and Randolph Caldecott had been linked twenty-five years earlier for their contributions to the burgeoning market in children's

books. Like their three predecessors, Dulac and Rackham also had much in common. Rival publishers competed for their services and the two artists exhibited original paintings at the same gallery with equal success. Even the stories they illustrated were similar, appealing to the prevailing ardor for stories about fairies and fantasy. In spite of what they shared, however, Dulac and Rackham differed greatly in technique, temperament, and sensibility.

Although the two illustrators painted in watercolor, for example, Dulac was a colorist fascinated above all with pigment and pattern, while Rackham's passion was for line. For subject matter Rackham seemed to reach more deeply into Nordic and Teutonic mythology, his brush inspired by images of dark forests inhabited with gnomes and goblins. Dulac, on the other hand, was intrigued by Eastern traditions, his imagination fired by brightly jeweled patterns that radiated in sparkling color.

Although they both illustrated many of the same stories, Rackham's style seemed more suited to Richard Wagner and to the Brothers Grimm, while Dulac was more in tune with *The Rubáiyát of Omar Khayyám* and *The Arabian Nights*. Not surprisingly, Arthur Rackham was firmly rooted by breeding and conviction in northern traditions—an Englishman, through and through—while Edmund Dulac was an expatriated Frenchman, drawn toward mysticism and the occult, with a fascination for the exotic.

Before he reached the age of thirty Dulac was among the most highly sought-after illustrators in the world, but the journey to success took several twists and turns, and brought him a considerable distance from where he started. From the beginning, he seemed out of place with his native French heritage. Dulac was born in 1882 as Edmond (spelled with an "o") in Toulouse where his *petit-bourgeois* parents kept a modestly comfortable home. The boy's interest in painting derived from his father, a traveling salesman who restored and traded in paintings during leisure hours and created a watercolor of his own now and then. Although Edmond liked to paint and draw from a very early age, it was not until he was fifteen that his efforts began to outrank those of his peers at school. Because it was unthinkable that Edmond should make a career as an artist, his parents allowed him to study art in the evenings at the nearby École des Beaux Arts only if he agreed to study law during the day at Toulouse University. He endured this program for two full years, submitting designs to various magazines in the hope that he might be rescued from his plight as a law student. To his delight, the designs were received warmly by

publications in Toulouse and in Paris and when he won a significant prize at the École for his painting, he abandoned the insufferable law studies to attend art school full time.

During this period, Dulac lived in the same house with a teacher who gave him English lessons in exchange for having a portrait painted. Already inspired by the designs of William Morris, Walter Crane, and particularly Aubrey Beardsley, Dulac became a passionate Anglophile. He changed the spelling of his name to favor the English (Edmund with a "u") and took to wearing white gloves, spats, and tight trousers, and carrying a cane in imitation of the current English fashions. At school he was dubbed, *"l'anglais."*

Dulac's hard work as an art student earned him several awards during his three-year course of studies at the École des Beaux Arts and finally a scholarship to study at the prestigious Académie Julian in Paris. With great expectations, Dulac ventured to Paris to study at the famous school where the great designer Alphonse Mucha had studied and where Kay Nielsen would eventually enroll. But the program was a disappointment. Tediously copying master paintings and plaster casts did little to stimulate the impatient young artist and he felt exceedingly lonely in Paris. Returning to Toulouse in an unhappy state of mind, Dulac met and hastily married an American woman thirteen years his senior, a union that terminated almost as quickly as it had begun. At twenty-one, alone again and living with his parents, Edmund Dulac seemed very far from achieving his goals.

Dulac yearned to go to England, but decided to launch his career in the more familiar city of Paris instead. Once he found himself back in the city he

Original watercolor illustration for the frontispiece
of *The Princess Badoura* (1913). Unlike Arthur Rackham who
demonstrated Nordic preferences, Edmund Dulac
had a particular affinity for Eastern traditions.

had abandoned less than two years earlier, however, the restless young man decided to move on, to satisfy his yearnings by taking a daring leap to London in search of assignments. It was either good fortune or demonstrable talent that earned him a major assignment within weeks of his arrival in London: the publisher J. M. Dent commissioned him to prepare sixty watercolors for the complete set of novels written by the Brontë sisters. His first assignment was *Jane Eyre*, to be published in 1905. That the neophyte Frenchman completed twelve watercolors depicting a thoroughly British subject (and did so within a period of only three months) was evidence of Dulac's eagerness to succeed. The illustrations for the Brontë novels may have been timid, not unlike much of what was currently being published, but they were cordially received by the critics and Dulac felt sufficiently encouraged to remain in England.

As a result of the favorable reception to the Brontë novels, Dulac was invited to contribute to the *Pall Mall Gazette*, a monthly magazine to which Arthur Rackham had contributed many drawings. Here Dulac felt free to experiment with his designs, overcoming the timidity of his first assignments. Joining the London Sketch Club also gave him the opportunity to develop the worthwhile skill for humorous drawing. By 1906 Edmund Dulac was confident and capable, ready to take on a major challenge.

As it happened, the time was ideal for a man of Dulac's particular talent for watercolor. Only the year before, Arthur Rackham had achieved great success with his watercolor illustrations prepared for a gift book entitled *Rip Van Winkle*. Simulta-

neously with the publication of this book, Leicester Galleries had exhibited Rackham's original illustrations and nearly all were sold. A second Rackham exhibition and publication, *Peter Pan in Kensington Gardens*, promised to be even more successful. In the hope that Leicester Galleries might consider taking on another artist of merit, Dulac presented his portfolio to the directors. The gallery was extremely impressed with his work and made an unusual offer: they would assume responsibility for publishing a book with Dulac's illustrations and the artist would provide fifty watercolors, including their copyright, to the gallery in exchange for a flat fee. Dulac happily agreed to illustrate the stories from *The Arabian Nights*.

Meanwhile, there were two London publishers competing for the gift book market—William Heinemann and Hodder & Stoughton. When Arthur Rackham eventually decided to sign on with Heinemann, Hodder & Stoughton immediately set out to find a suitable rival, and was thrilled with the candidate proposed by Leicester Galleries. *The Arabian Nights*, they agreed, would be an ideal gift book for the following Christmas, 1907, and the publishers felt confident that their book with illustrations by Edmund Dulac would stand up well against Rackham's next production, *Alice's Adventures in Wonderland*.

As it turned out *The Arabian Nights* could not have been a better choice. To Dulac, it provided a vehicle for depicting the exotic subjects he preferred. Since art school he had been fascinated by the East and by Arabic languages, intrigued by the designs of the written Arabic characters. (Dulac's keen interest in exotic languages through the years compelled him to study Chinese, Hebrew, Persian, and

"This way and that she led him," original watercolor illustration for
Stories from the Arabian Nights (1907).

even Malagasy!) The nocturnal scenes in *The Arabian Nights* also enabled him to experiment with rich shadings of blues—ultramarine, Prussian blue, indigo, violets, and purples—permitting him to create magical, translucent textures, starry nights sparkling with saturated watercolor pigments.

The watercolors were to be reproduced in three colors—yellow, red, blue—inks which would be overlaid onto a black key plate. For this process, Dulac's suffused watercolor technique was well-suited. In reproduction the initial ink drawing was essentially covered by three successive layers of printing inks, transforming the ink line into one that was no longer truly black, and happily muting

it at the same time. The softness of Dulac's illustrations was, therefore, enhanced by the reproduction process itself, and contributed to Dulac's reputation as a supreme colorist.

Leicester Galleries displayed the Dulac watercolors for *The Arabian Nights* in the autumn of 1907, at the same time the book was released. With unanimous praise the book was received by the critics and every picture sold even before the exhibition was opened to the general public. In light of this overwhelming success, Leicester Galleries promptly signed a contract with Dulac for one book a year, the subject to be chosen jointly between them and in consultation with Hodder & Stoughton. Al-

"Taking her hand he led her to the apartment of the Queen Pirouze,"
original watercolor illustration for *Stories from the Arabian Nights* (1907).

"The Doctors" or "It was in vain that all the best in the country were
summoned into consultation," original watercolor illustration for *Stories from the
Arabian Nights* (1907).

though it was an unorthodox arrangement—Dulac was accountable to the gallery, rather than to the publisher—these terms permitted the artist to concentrate his creative energies on painting, unencumbered with the technical problems of production and printing.

Having had the good sense to commission this young, relatively unknown illustrator, Leicester Galleries reaped the rewards of their foresight during the years that followed. Dulac would come to regret the flat-fee arrangement—he received no royalties from the sale of the gift books published by Hodder & Stoughton—but within five years he was one of the most highly paid illustrators of his time. Each year, until World War One erupted, Dulac created watercolors for a book and an exhibition at the gallery, preparing from a maximum of fifty watercolors (*Arabian Nights*) to a minimum of ten (*Princess Badoura*). Dulac's gift book for 1908 was *Tempest*; for 1909, *The Rubáiyát of Omar Khayyám*; for 1910, *The Sleeping Beauty and Other Fairy Tales*; for 1911, *Stories from Hans Andersen*; for 1912, *Bells and Other Poems* by Edgar Allan Poe; for 1913, *Princess Badoura*; for 1914, *Sinbad the Sailor and Other Stories from The Arabian Nights*.

These gift books, representing Dulac's classic contributions to the illustration of children's stories, demonstrate the evolution of the artist's style. From the outset, Dulac's penwork was used primarily to define figures and objects, while color was employed to create atmosphere and modeling. Unlike his contemporaries Arthur Rackham and Kay Nielsen, Dulac's drawing was secondary to color and as his work developed he became increasingly absorbed in matters of pattern and texture rather than contour. Always intrigued by Eastern cultures, Dulac was particularly fascinated with Persian miniatures and incorporated many Persian elements into his own work. Dulac's palette became brighter, resembling the enamel-like colors of the Persian miniatures as he turned to tangerine and carmine hues placed against large pastel color areas created by the addition of Chinese white to his watercolor pigments.

Like his palette, Dulac's composition also evolved as a result of his close study of the Persian miniatures: flat planes arranged in patterns, simplified shapes placed on a jeweled surface. With his extended color range, Dulac now took even greater delight in creating rich patterns on robes and draperies. In the later books, he liberated himself from the conventional perspective of Western art, concerned instead with juxtaposing shapes and color in pleasing patterns. He no longer directed the eye into a perspective view. Instead, he employed a high vantage point, manipulating perspective from above and below as he saw fit, so that the eye must scan the entire picture plane to receive all the visual information presented. Depth was reduced by tilting floors forward and by eliminating any differences in color or size between objects in the background and those in the foreground.

Dulac became critical of Western traditions in painting. He admired the first-century Syrian wall decorations that had been recently unearthed by archaeologists because the decorations were free of any conventional perspective, and he decried the Hellenistic and Renaissance devices of converging lines, receding planes, and light and dark modeling that were designed to produce the illusion of a third dimension. "The end result of objective imitative art," he asserted in an article written for

"I have hardly closed my eyes the whole night!" from "The Princess and
the Pea" in *Stories from Hans Andersen* (1911). The marvelous rendition of these patterns
and textures represents an artist's tour de force.

"He lifted it with a trembling hand and shouted with a trembling voice: 'Gold! Gold!'"
from "The Wind's Tale" in *Stories from Hans Andersen* (1911). Advancements in printing technology
made it possible to reproduce Dulac's subtle coloration with reasonable fidelity.

"'It is gold, it is gold!' they cried,"
original watercolor illustration for "The Snow Queen"
from *Stories from Hans Andersen* (1911).

the magazine *Discovery*, "is nothing less than coloured photography." Being too literal, objective art was simply a show of technical bravura, leaving nothing to the imagination. He argued that subjective art was more desirable because the viewer was stimulated to exercise imaginative powers, extracting what Dulac termed "the eternal" from what is "now."

Although his style evolved over the years, Dulac's methods of preparing his illustrations remained the same. It was an unusual technique that worked well for him because of his concern with pictorial arrangement. He began by using tracing papers to develop his first rough sketch. "An idea for the composition is roughed out on a sheet of tracing paper with a B pencil," Dulac explained when asked how he prepared his watercolors,

and another and another, the paper being turned over from time to time to see whether the design does not look better from the other side. One could go on like that for ever, but one of the designs has to be chosen—it is generally the first. The figures are drawn to the required size separately; a dozen rough sketches or so for each, this time with a BB pencil and traced over again until clean lines emerge from out of chaos. The background comes last and is dealt with in the same way. The process so far is secret. No one is allowed to witness its laborious steps and the wastepaper basket in the summer and the stove in winter take care that no evidence of it shall remain. The clean tracings are then superimposed and twisted about until some form of satisfactory arrangement is obtained.

Using bits and pieces of tracing paper in this way, Dulac actually composed his pictures as if he were playing with cutouts. He would, in fact, re-use these tracings on other paintings, a tree or

"Scene in a Moslem cemetery: a man leading a woman by the hand,"
original unpublished watercolor illustration for an unidentified book, probably intended for *Sinbad the Sailor, and Other Stories from the Arabian Nights* (1914).

"The room of fruits prepared for Abu-l-Hasan," from *Sinbad the Sailor, and Other Stories from the Arabian Nights* (1914).

"The Princess burns the Efrite to death," original watercolor
illustration for "The Story of the Three Calendars" in *Sinbad the
Sailor, and Other Stories from the Arabian Nights* (1914).

figure appearing elsewhere in a later work. A
meticulous craftsman, Dulac may have sacrificed
spontaneity with this method, but he left nothing
to chance, which suited his well-ordered temperament. After he had made these rather elaborate
preparations, he moved onto the painting phase,
working always on his favorite English handmade
paper (his choice, Whatman, is no longer available).
His report:

*Now appears the Whatman board, hot pressed, the
figures and background are rubbed upon it in their proper
order and grouping and drawn over carefully with the H
pencil. All is ready for the final ceremony. The jars are
cleaned and filled with fresh water, the brushes washed
and the china pots uncovered. The Whatman board with
its design is then hydropathetically treated with a few
pigments, not more than a blue, green, two yellows, a*
*crimson, a red, two reddish browns, raw amber, and
Chinese white; lots and lots of Chinese white.*

His materials for this entire operation consisted
simply of pencils, sheets (and so many sheets!) of
tracing paper, erasers, some putty, watercolors and
brushes, and his hot-pressed Whatman paper.
Among the most useful tools was the specially
long nail he grew on the little finger of his right
hand to assist him in scratching out passages here
and there. With only occasional exception, these
were the methods he employed throughout his
artistic life.

From the time he arrived in London as a twenty-
two-year-old Frenchman until World War One,
Edmund Dulac was set on a course that finally
seemed suited to his ambition. He was legally
divorced from his American wife in 1908, married

Elsa Arnalice Bignardi in 1911, and became a naturalized British citizen in 1912. Dulac's circle of friends widened to include eminent artists, writers, musicians, and designers, and he was able to pursue his intense curiosity about a wide variety of subjects: he was a student of Far Eastern music, a collector of Oriental paintings, a gourmet cook, a skilled hand book-binder, a marksman, and he designed all the furniture and equipment in his studio. He enjoyed dressing up for charades performed at the London Sketch Club, and for these occasions he designed his own costumes and demonstrated great skill in makeup, talents he would later apply to designing for major theatrical productions. In keeping with Dulac's great interest in the occult, although he tended to poke fun at spiritualism, he did attend seances periodically and, in later years, relied heavily on astrology and Tarot cards to help him make personal decisions. In the end, it was fortunate that Dulac was a man of such dimension, because he would find it necessary to draw upon these resources, reaching beyond his experience as an illustrator of children's books for practical and emotional sustenance in the difficult years ahead.

In 1914 Leicester Galleries offered Dulac a three-year contract to produce annually a set of illustrations for books to be published in 1915, 1916, and 1917. For nearly £1,000 per set (a sizable sum), Dulac would prepare twenty-five illustrations and additional decorations for books whose titles would be agreed upon by the two parties in consultation with Hodder & Stoughton. The generosity of the terms expressed optimism about the future of gift book publishing, but the outbreak of war shattered these hopeful plans. Restrictions on paper and production curtailed a good deal of publishers'

commercial activities, and preference was given instead to publishing designed to promote the war effort. To raise funds, for example, prominent personalities had begun to sponsor the publication of books, the proceeds from which would be sent to a cause selected by the sponsor. Contributing to these inexpensive gift books were famous writers and artists. In this capacity, Dulac offered his services, creating illustrations for three such sponsored books published by Hodder & Stoughton: *Princess Mary's Gift Book, King Albert's Book,* and *Edmund Dulac's Picture-book for the French Red Cross.*

With his income severely reduced during the War, Dulac fell into a state of despair and anxiety. Leicester Galleries came to his relief in 1915 by commissioning him to prepare a set of illustrations for a book of fairy tales. Published in 1916, *Edmund Dulac's Fairy Book—Fairy Tales of the Allied Nations,* represented a real tour de force for the illustrator. For each fairy tale, Dulac adapted his style to that of each country included—Japan, Serbia, Italy, Belgium, France, England, and Russia—demonstrating his profound empathy with a variety of different ages and cultures.

The War years continued to be extremely difficult for Dulac. He had a serious accident, almost losing the sight in one eye when his cat, in play, scratched the right cornea. The blackouts each night in London, the constant threats of bombing raids over their home, proved too great a strain for his wife and she suffered from frequent anxiety attacks and depression. There were a few respites from these tense years. Dulac was given the opportunity to design costumes and sets for Thomas Beecham's production of a stage version of Bach's cantata, *Phoebus and Pan* in 1915 and in 1916 he collaborated

"Drawing his sword he rushed at the monster," original watercolor
illustration for *Tanglewood Tales* (1918). Dulac's lifelong interest in the East and his
increasing fascination with mysticism more obviously influenced his later
illustrations. A close study of Persian miniatures resulted in simplified shapes
placed on a jewel-like surface.

"They were constantly at war with the Cranes," original watercolor illustration
for *Tanglewood Tales* (1918).

with his good friend, the poet W.B. Yeats, in a production of chamber plays called *At the Hawk's Well*, designing costumes, props, and makeup, and even composing the music for Yeats' plays. In 1916 the New York art gallery of Scott & Fowles exhibited Dulac's work (they later exhibited Arthur Rackham as well) and Hodder & Stoughton commissioned him to prepare Hawthorne's *Tanglewood Tales* for publication. For this project, Dulac made fourteen watercolors, completed in 1917, although publication was delayed until 1918 because of paper restrictions. This was the last of the Edmund Dulac–Hodder & Stoughton gift books. An era of publishing had come to an end.

When Arthur Rackham encountered the same diminishing demand for deluxe picture books in England, he planned his books for the more receptive American market, continuing to produce illustrated books—many of them for children—nearly every year for the rest of his life. Edmund Dulac turned his talents to other forms of design instead. Except for one or two books in the 1920s (most notably *Treasure Island*, which was his favorite), Dulac no longer illustrated stories that might be read by children. He illustrated adult fiction, including poetry written by his friend W.B. Yeats or novels by his lover and companion Helen Beauclerk (Dulac and his wife Elsa had separated in 1923).

The major source of his income (which was sporadic at best) derived from portrait commissions, humorous caricatures, and above all his regular contributions to the magazine *American Weekly*. The major sources of his *interest*, however, derived from designing postage stamps, as well as his designs of costumes and stages for the theater. He also applied his remarkable skills to designing playing cards, banknotes, coins and medals, and found this fascinating as well. He even designed furniture for a smoking lounge in the Canadian Pacific ocean liner *The Empress Britain*! Nor were all his activities restricted to design. Dulac composed music and became actively engaged in a movement to help obtain recognition for the cinema as an art form.

Until his death in 1953, Edmund Dulac remained vital and active, an intellectual with boundless curiosity about all cultures, expressed in all forms: writing, pictures, music, costumes. His curiosity extended even beyond earthly phenomena, as he grew increasingly interested in spiritualism. Dulac's pictures for children's stories were created within only a few years of his productive life, but they continue to delight children even today. In the end, the efforts of Edmund Dulac to transcend geographic and spiritual limits brought forth a legacy for children that remains eternal.

"This good Fairy placed her own baby in a cradle of roses and gave command to the zephyrs to carry him to the tower," from "Felicia or The Pot of Pinks," in *In Powder and Crinoline* (1913). With this book, Nielsen became the third of the great gift book illustrators, following Arthur Rackham and Edmund Dulac.

Kay Nielsen

From *East of the Sun and West of the Moon* (1914).

WHEN KAY NIELSEN ARRIVED in England in 1912, Arthur Rackham and Edmund Dulac were already famous illustrators. Although their pictures had first been published only a few years earlier, the meteoric success of Rackham and Dulac occurred precisely at the time when the vogue for the deluxe gift book was at its height. Kay Nielsen became the third great illustrator of the gift book, and was acknowledged then as an artist whose talent equaled that of Rackham and Dulac. Indeed, if he had only begun his career five years earlier he might have surpassed any illustrator of his day. But he was not so fortunate.

Kay Nielsen's reputation as an illustrator of children's books was based on only four books of fairy tales, two published before World War One, and two published afterward, when the fashion for fairies, fantasy, and extravagant books had all but vanished. While Arthur Rackham's reputation was sufficiently secure to transcend the passing vogue,

Kay Nielsen had not been visible long enough to withstand the vicissitudes of public taste. He abandoned England and even illustration, and by 1957 when he died, Kay Nielsen's name was almost totally forgotten. Through the years, Nielsen's books have been cherished by those who were lucky enough to encounter them, and recently interest in the illustrator has dramatically revived. Long after the publication of those four books of fairy tales, Kay Nielsen has rejoined his peers as one of the greatest illustrators of children's books.

What little is known about Kay Nielsen derives from information published now and then in catalogs and anthologies. From these, the facts are easily assembled, but the soul behind the facts is more elusive. He was not an opinionated man—on this his friends all agreed—so that the hopeful biographer is hard-pressed to locate journals and documents quoting Nielsen's ideas about the world, about his painting, or about art in general. He remained detached from the upheavals of politics, eschewed publicity, and applied his most fervent energies to his work, creating an imaginary world remote from any particular time or place. Removal from the "real world" may have been a pattern he adopted from his parents, whose professional domain must have crossed frequently into the world of fantasy.

The home in Copenhagen, Denmark, where Kay (pronounced "Kigh") Nielsen was born in 1886, abounded in creative energy. Both parents were distinguished by their eminent positions in the Danish theater: his mother, Oda Larssen, was a noted actress and singer, the leading lady of the Royal Theater, and his father, Professor Martinius Nielsen (who had been a classical actor himself), became Managing Director of the Dagmartheater in Copenhagen. Throughout his childhood, Kay Nielsen was surrounded by prominent writers, playwrights, actors, and artists (Ibsen, Bjornsen, Lie, Grieg, to name only a few) whose passion for theater and literature was intense. "They brought me up in a tense atmosphere of art," Nielsen said of his family many years later.

The Nielsens were a prosperous Danish family with cosmopolitan ideas, and the boy was encouraged to develop his talents from the outset. While stories were read aloud to him, he eagerly drew the characters as he imagined them, a pastime that earned him the name, "Little Philosopher of the Pencil." "Anything I heard about," he said, "I tried to put in situations on paper. I heard much and saw much concerning art, but I never really intended to be an artist myself."

At the age of twelve, Kay Nielsen was taken out of school to study with a private tutor. He in-

tended to follow in the steps of his grand uncle, Rasmus Nielsen, who had become a celebrated physician. By the time Kay Nielsen was seventeen, however, he abandoned any notion of a career in medicine and decided after all to study art in Paris. Living in Montparnasse, Nielsen studied art from 1904 to 1912, first at the Académie Julian, where Edmund Dulac had studied briefly, then at another independent art school, Colarossi's.

As a student in Paris, Kay Nielsen developed conventional skills of painting and drawing— copying the masters and working from plaster casts, exercises Edmund Dulac had so reluctantly performed a few years earlier. At the same time, Nielsen was stimulated by the current trends in contemporary art. Art Nouveau was then the fashion, and the decorative linework of Aubrey Beardsley in particular inspired the young student. Oriental art, which had captivated these contemporary artists and designers, had already begun to intrigue Kay Nielsen when he was a boy. "I loved the Chinese drawings and carvings in my mother's room, brought home from China by her father," Nielsen recalled. Now Nielsen was fascinated by the Japanese woodcuts of Hokusai, Hiroshige, and Utamaro, widely circulated in Paris, and he adopted many of their ideas in his own work: asymmetrical composition, large vacant areas, sinuous linework, and a flattened perspective. This affinity for Oriental art continued throughout his life and was revealed in all his later work.

When he wasn't following the routine of the classroom, painting and drawing from nature, Nielsen created pictures out of his imagination. During his leisure hours, he illustrated poetry and stories by Heine, Verlaine, and Hans Andersen,

"List, ah, list to the zephyr in the grove! Where beneath the happy
boughs Flora builds her summerhouse: Whist, ah, whist! while the cushat tells his
love." from "Felicia or The Pot of Pinks" in *In Powder and Crinoline* (1913).
Expressing many of the qualities of a *fin de siècle* artist, Nielsen's earliest work
reveals a strong influence of art nouveau.

"And there on a throne all covered with black sat the
Iron King," from "Minon-Minette" in *In Powder and Crinoline* (1913).

" 'Don't drink!' cried out the little Princess, springing
to her feet; 'I would rather marry a gardener!' " from "The Twelve
Dancing Princesses" in *In Powder and Crinoline* (1913).

From "The Three Princesses of Whiteland" in *East of the Sun and West of the Moon* (1914).

most of them in black and white, and he created a series of drawings called *The Book of Death*, illustrating the story of Pierrot's ardor for a lovely young maiden. Never issued in book form, these drawings were sent to England in 1910 and displayed in an exhibition held by London's Dowdeswell Galleries in 1912. It was Nielsen's good fortune to be reviewed with enthusiasm by the most prominent British critic, Sir Claude Phillips, whose appreciation of the young artist's work appeared shortly thereafter and attracted much attention.

As dealers for the gift book illustrators, Leicester Galleries lost no time in approaching Kay Nielsen with a business proposal similar to the arrangement they had so successfully enjoyed for five years with Edmund Dulac. They commissioned Nielsen to prepare twenty-four watercolors for a book of old fairy tales told by Sir Arthur Quiller-Couch, called *In Powder and Crinoline*. The book was issued in a deluxe and trade edition in 1913 by Dulac's publisher, Hodder & Stoughton, and later published in America as *Twelve Dancing Princesses*. Leicester Galleries held an exhibition of the watercolors and was sufficiently pleased with the results to make arrangements for the next book.

Nielsen's second book, published in the following year, became his most famous: *East of the Sun and West of the Moon*, a collection of fifteen old tales from Norway. Twenty-five watercolors were published in the first edition, demonstrating Nielsen's extraordinary prowess as an illustrator. In these elegant paintings, he combined qualities of Oriental design with those unique features of his native Scandinavia: the melancholic mystery of a bleak Nordic twilight seemed to cast a magical spell on the images themselves. If it were not for the

"And this time she whisked off the wig; and there lay the lad, so lovely,
and white and red, just as the Princess had seen him in the morning sun," from "The
Widow's Son" in *East of the Sun and West of the Moon* (1914).

"You'll come to three Princesses, whom you will see standing in the earth
up to their necks, with only their heads out," from "The Three Princesses of Whiteland"
in *East of the Sun and West of the Moon* (1914).

"Then he coaxed her down and took her home," from "The Lassie and her
Godmother" in *East of the Sun and West of the Moon* (1914).

"So the man gave him a pair of snow shoes" from "The Three
Princesses of Whiteland" in *East of the Sun and West of the Moon* (1914).

"The Unicorn drove her horn into the tree," from "The Brave Little Tailor" in *Fleur-De-Neige et D'Autres Contes de Grimm*.

outbreak of war that year, there is no doubt that Nielsen would have continued to produce many more of these remarkable paintings for children, to establish him as a great master of the Northern fairy tale.

Nielsen's career was abruptly interrupted by the war. His income might have vanished completely if it were not for the recognition he had received so quickly in America. Scott & Fowles Gallery (which had been successful with an Edmund Dulac show the year before) exhibited the watercolors of Kay Nielsen in 1917. The catalog for the exhibition, written by Martin Birnbaum, suggested that Nielsen was unique among his peers: "The unapproachable greatness of Aubrey Beardsley, the splendour

of Dulac, of the distinct personal charm of Rackham, did not interfere with his success in any way, for all the critics realized then that Nielsen's talents were original and of a very unusual kind. The incisive line was his own, and his fairyland less sombre than Rackham's. The extremely delicate and transparent colour left the drawing to take its part as a graceful woven pattern more clearly than in a drawing by Dulac."

These were not good times for an illustrator of Nielsen's bent, however. The public was far too preoccupied with the travesties of the war to indulge in tales of fantasy. As the war ended, Nielsen decided to return to Copenhagen where he found himself inevitably drawn back into the

"Scheherazade Telling the Tales," original watercolor illustration for the unpublished *A Thousand and One Nights* (1918–22). Like Edmund Dulac, Nielsen was intrigued by Eastern traditions.

familiar environment of the theater. There he became a close friend of Johannes Poulsen, an actor and producer. Their common interests resulted in a professional collaboration that remained productive for many years to come. Together they produced a spectacular version of *Aladdin* for the Royal Theater, Nielsen designing the sets and costumes. Their success with this production was followed by others produced in the early 1920s, *The Tempest, Midsummer Night's Dream*, and *Scaramouche* by Sibelius. The talents for fantasy that Nielsen might have directed to the printed page were now given to theater.

In an attempt to reinvigorate the market for gift books after the war, Hodder & Stoughton resumed the publishing of Kay Nielsen's books, though on a more modest scale. In 1924 they published a work that Nielsen had begun in 1912, *Hans Andersen's Fairy Tales*, including sixteen stories illustrated with twelve watercolors. Nielsen returned to London, and in 1925 his final book for Hodder & Stoughton, *Hansel and Gretel*, appeared with twelve color plates. Leicester Galleries exhibited Nielsen's illustrations simultaneously with the publication of each book.

In spite of the efforts made by publisher and gallery, the market for Nielsen's books failed to recover, and the artist returned to Copenhagen to resume his work in the theater with Poulsen, designing sets and costumes for *The Poet's Dream* and Ostrovsky's *The Storm*. In 1926 he married Ulla Pless-Schmidt who, by all accounts, remained devoted to Nielsen for the duration of their thirty-five years together, in spite of the difficult times they encountered.

In 1930 Nielsen again returned to London for

"A Brother and a Sister," original watercolor illustration for the unpublished *A Thousand and One Nights* (1918–22).
The jewel-like colors and patterns were more pronounced in Nielsen's later work, a feature that combined naturally with his strong sense of line so evident in his
earlier illustrations.

"The Daughter of the King of the Ebony Islands,"
original watercolor illustration for the unpublished *A Thousand
and One Nights* (1918–22). Arriving too late to enjoy
a full career as an illustrator of fine gift books—as Arthur
Rackham had—Kay Nielsen turned to theatrical
design, and eventually fell into obscurity.

the publication of his last book, *Red Magic*, a collection of fairy tales from around the world. Published by Jonathan Cape, the book was a modest edition, containing eight color plates and fifty black-and-white illustrations. The book exhibited little of Nielsen's powers as an illustrator and received only slight attention. With the exception of the watercolors he prepared for an ambitious project of *A Thousand and One Nights*—a series of twenty paintings that was considered too costly to reproduce at the time—Nielsen never illustrated another book. The future, it seemed, would be brighter in the theater.

At the invitation of the Festival Association of the Hollywood Bowl, Kay Nielsen and Johannes Poulsen traveled to America in 1936 to mount a production of Max Reinhardt's *Everyman*. There, in 1938, Poulsen died suddenly, and Nielsen decided to remain on without him. He began to work for Walt Disney, designing the "Bald Mountain" sequence for the film, *Fantasia*, but the arrangement did not last. Nielsen, who was proud and obstinate, didn't care for the dogmatic Disney and what began as a leave of absence from the studio eventually resulted in a permanently severed relationship.

The most difficult years for Nielsen lay ahead. No work was forthcoming and despite the generosity of their many friends and neighbors, who gave them food, and even an automobile, the Nielsens were destitute. They even tried their hand at raising chickens, failing to earn an income from this enterprise, and they returned to Denmark for work, but met with little success there. They finally decided to settle permanently in Los Angeles where work was unavailable but at least the sun was always shining, they said. Three mural commissions obtained more by luck than by intention kept them afloat for some months, and they sold off some of their valued works of art to raise funds. Only pride and good humor seemed to sustain them, and of these there was no shortage, their friends reported.

Nielsen's condition of poverty was known only to a circle of good friends in California. He had been forgotten by his public, and when he died in 1957 the newspapers barely took notice. Ulla Nielsen survived her husband by only a year. To her loving friends the Monhoffs she gave Nielsen's entire set of unpublished gouaches for *A Thousand and One Nights*. Hoping to establish a memorial to Kay Nielsen, the Monhoffs searched for a museum to house the collection, with no success. No museum, not even in Denmark, expressed interest in the paintings. It is our good fortune that these friends never abandoned hope; they remained confident that one day Nielsen's gifts would again be appreciated, which is precisely what happened. In 1977 the paintings were published for the first time by Peacock/Bantam Books, and the proceeds earned from the publication were applied to a fund for the benefit of promising artists, a fund established by the Monhoffs and administered by the Los Angeles County Museum of Art. Kay Nielsen is no longer an illustrator buried by changing fashions. He has returned to an adoring public, home at last.

Frontispiece from *Yankee Doodle* (1881). Despite efforts to the contrary,
American printers were unsuccessful in duplicating the high quality achieved by
Edmund Evans in England. Pyle was asked by Dodd, Mead and Company
to make color drawings for this book as an experiment in color printing designed to
imitate the popular English children's books. The results were disappointing and Pyle's future children's books were prepared in black and white only.

Howard Pyle

From *Otto of the Silver Hand* (1888).

WHILE MANY ENGLISH ILLUSTRATORS of children's books were widely known in America during the nineteenth century, only rarely did the fame of an American reach English shores. Howard Pyle was one exception. Of the thirteen children's books he wrote and illustrated, eleven were published simultaneously in England to outstanding reviews. Walter Crane selected Howard Pyle as one of the only two Americans to be represented in *The Decorative Illustration of Books* and Crane would not miss the opportunity to meet the great American illustrator in person during a brief visit to the States in 1891. Although the illustrations of the two contemporaries were very different (Pyle thought Crane used "too many draperies, too many draperies"), they were both pioneers in a similar field. Pyle's creative output alone would have qualified him as a great American illustrator of children's literature. But his legacy was far greater than the hundreds of books and articles he wrote and illustrated at the

turn of the century. He was a natural teacher, the major force in what later came to be known as the Brandywine School. A compelling and vital man, Pyle was possessed with the idea of training—both spiritually and artistically—a younger generation of artists to conquer new, unexplored frontiers. If any person could be called the Father of American Illustration, it would be Howard Pyle, for no other American artist has left such a personal and enduring influence on its development during the twentieth century.

No doubt such exalted words would have embarrassed Pyle, whose Puritanism discouraged lavish praise. Pyle himself was more restrained, and such flourishes would have seemed indulgent. Howard Pyle was born on March 5, 1853, the eldest of four children in an established Quaker family. At the time, his birthplace—Wilmington, Delaware—was still a small town just beginning to develop into a city. From his earliest years, young Howard was an avid reader, his imagination fired by the books he devoured: Grimm's *German Fairy Tales, A Midsummer Night's Dream, The Arabian Nights* were only a few of the classic tales he read regularly in front of the open fireplace or out in the countryside.

These hours spent reading, combined with the Quaker's recognition of the need for reflection and contemplation, formed the substance of his inner life on which he drew in later years. His imagination was nourished by his surroundings as well. The countryside was a source of comfort and stimulated his curiosity regularly as he tramped the fields, hills, and meadows around Wilmington. Throughout his entire life this region was his haven, and would later be home to several other artists who would venture to the area just for the chance to be associated with him.

In spite of the boy's obvious intelligence, his parents observed that his performance in school was mediocre at best. He tended to be a daydreamer, sketching idly, roaming the countryside, and writing on imaginary subjects that had little relationship to his studies. Abandoning any hopes that he might go to college, the Pyles sent their sixteen-year-old son to the nearest art school, Van der Weilen's school in Philadelphia, where Howard's performance as a student improved remarkably. For nearly three years he commuted daily to Philadelphia and acquired the technical training which was assumed necessary for an artist who hoped to make his way in the world. By neglecting the faculty of the imagination, however, Van der Weilen was a disappointment to Pyle. Convinced that it takes more than mechanical skill to be a creative artist, Pyle was to become a very different kind of instructor than his first had been.

Pyle was determined to experiment with his drawing, no longer interested in the mechanical copying he had endured at art school. As he observed years later: "The hardest thing for a student to do after leaving an art school is to adapt the knowledge there gained to practical use—to do creative work, for the work in art school is imitative . . . . When I left art school I discovered, like many others, that I could not easily train myself to creative work, which was the only practical way of earning a livelihood in art."

And so Pyle returned home: "Being offered a position by my father in his leather business in Wilmington I availed myself of it and during my spare time created illustrations, stimulated my imagination, and worked assiduously on drawings I never submitted. My work was idle for several years while I experimented."

During this period he read voluminously and applied himself to his writing and drawing. Finally, in 1876, he sent an offering to *Scribner's Monthly*, which was accepted. Shortly afterward another acceptance came from *St. Nicholas*, the most enterprising children's magazine of the day. Elated with these triumphs and encouraged by the compliments of *Scribner's* editor, Howard Pyle left for New York City to make his way as an artist. He was twenty-three years old.

His decision to leave the protective environment of Wilmington to embark on a career in New York City was a true act of courage. The city was a ruthless and impatient judge of new talent, and only a young man with tremendous determination could withstand the anonymity and isolation thrust upon him in his foreign setting. For every triumph the young artist encountered a reversal, some

Robin Hood · meeteth · the · tall
Stranger · on · the · Bridge

From *The Merry Adventures of Robin Hood* (1883).

The·stout·bout·between·Little·Iohn·&· Arthvr·a·Bland:·

From *The Merry Adventures of Robin Hood* (1883). Creating the lengthy manuscript and drawings for his first major book, Pyle established habits of working that he maintained throughout his entire career.

disappointment that would shake his confidence until the next triumph restored it. By the end of his first year, he had sold a group of drawings to *St. Nicholas,* and made the rounds of the other publishers. Finally, he received a favorable response from Charles Parsons, the editor at the largest publishing company in the country, the House of Harper. In addition to being aggressive book publishers, Harper also published the periodicals *Harper's Monthly, Harper's Weekly, Young People,* and later *Harper's Bazaar.* Pyle's relationship with the House of Harper was continually challenging, and he continued this association with the company for years to come. Although Pyle was not a salaried staff member, he could watch the publishing process from original manuscript and drawing to the printed bound copy, and he could meet some of the finest artists in the business. The art department at the House of Harper formed a nucleus that represented the beginnings of professionalism in illustration, with a staff equipped to adapt to a changing and dynamic new publishing industry.

Here Pyle acquired a basic understanding of printing technology that would be indispensable to him in preparing his work for the best possible results on the printed page. Wood engraving was still the process used for reproduction at the time and Pyle was quick to learn that only as technology improved could an artist expand his powers of expression. In his lifetime, Howard Pyle was to witness these important technological developments in the printing industry, and along with them the increasing sophistication of the art they were capable of reproducing. Until 1887 all of Pyle's work was in line form—pen and ink—so that the engravers could reproduce his art effectively. When photo-mechanical halftones were introduced, Pyle would add tonal work to his artistic repertoire as well.

Pyle continued to live in New York for three years, an apprenticeship that established him as a professional. Always gregarious, Pyle had a large circle of friends, a close association with such notable artists as Edwin Abbey and Arthur B. Frost, among others—a professional among professionals. He was developing a following among his readers as well. He returned to writing occasionally, illustrated several of his own stories, and found no lack of opportunity to draw or write.

In 1879 his group of friends began to disperse —Frost returning to Philadelphia, Abbey to England —and Pyle decided to return to Wilmington. From that point on, Pyle's life continued in a direct and even course; he rarely left Wilmington again.

Pyle's return to Wilmington brought him back in touch with his earliest associations: his Quaker heritage, the gentle landscape, and the literature he had devoured as a boy. Leaving the urban stimulation of New York, returning to his childhood home, Pyle rediscovered his roots. Throughout the rest of his career as an illustrator, he would draw from these rich associations and he would stress their significance to his students.

Pyle was already a well-established illustrator for periodicals when he took on his first book. He had, of course, contributed an occasional illustration for books now and then, but his first real commission came in 1881 from Dodd, Mead & Co.: two small children's books called *Yankee Doodle* and *The Lady of Shalott*. For these slender volumes Pyle was asked to prepare color drawings which would be reproduced in flat colors, emulat-

From *The Merry Adventures of Robin Hood* (1883). Although he had never left the American shores, Pyle's rich imagination permitted him to depict European legends and fables that were admired even by his skeptical English colleagues.

From *The Merry Adventures of Robin Hood* (1883).

ing the printing of Edmund Evans whose books by Walter Crane, Randolph Caldecott, and Kate Greenaway were so popular in the United States. Unfortunately, these two books were experiments that failed: the American printers had not yet developed the technology or skills required for better quality production and they bore little resemblance to the charming Evans creations. This disappointment did not prevent Pyle from undertaking another book project almost immediately, this time limiting himself to black and white only, and writing the full text himself. The book was *The Merry Adventures of Robin Hood*.

The idea for Robin Hood had been in Pyle's mind for many years, a holdover from his childhood enjoyment of English folktales he had read. Eager to make this first venture a success, Pyle supervised the design and production closely; the high quality of paper, printing, and binding required that the book be sold at a price higher than anticipated, a fact that may have damaged early sales. It wasn't long however, before the book became a children's favorite, establishing Pyle as a major writer and illustrator for children.

To Pyle's delight, *Robin Hood* was released simultaneously in America and in England. Being published in England was flattering, and so were his reviews. William Morris even expressed his surprise that something so worthwhile could actually originate in America! That Pyle had never seen the

From *The Merry Adventures of Robin Hood* (1883). Pyle's student, N.C. Wyeth, would follow this model in portraying the passing of Robin Hood.

From *The Wonder Clock* (1888). While his
books continued to represent European traditions,
Pyle was determined to advance the standards
of American illustration to surpass what
was being done abroad.

English countryside did not deter him from depicting the English folktales convincingly in both text and illustrations.

While meeting his constant deadlines for magazines, Pyle continued to write and illustrate books and within three years created five more titles. Of these, his children's books *Pepper & Salt*, *The Wonder Clock*, and *Otto of the Silver Hand* represented his greatest artistic achievements in black and white. All are still in print.

While Howard Pyle's books focused primarily on the romance and daring of imaginary heroes and villains from Europe, Africa, and the Caribbean, Pyle's magazine stories and illustrations concentrated almost exclusively on the American scene. And so he expressed the two, equally passionate, sides of his character—one deeply tied to his American roots, the other bound by his devotion to the legends and fables, romance and valor connected with his boyhood readings.

If his subject matter indicated two entirely divergent tendencies, so did his style as an illustrator reveal the marked influence of two very different trends: a traditional, decorative approach on the one hand, which he used in his books, and an Impressionist's fascination with the transitory effects of movement and light on the other, which he more likely would use for his magazine illustrations. The decorative illustrations suited the Medieval flavor of the legends and epic tales presented in his books, and his light-handed illustrations were more contemporary in feeling.

Such extremes in other artists might have created unnerving conflicts, but for Pyle these contradictions could be reconciled. No doubt this was possible because of his expansive character, an

 **earskin slayeth ẙ Dragon but will not go with ẙ Princess to ẙ castle.**

From *The Wonder Clock* (1888).

**aving been thrice adjudged in the wrong, the poor man is left by the rich man blind upon the highway.**

From *The Wonder Clock* (1888).

intensity and energy that permitted him to put forth all aspects of his abundant and complex character without confusion. He had, for example, an extraordinary capacity for intense concentration so that his productivity never faltered, despite the varied nature of his commitments. Even after he married, became a father of six, and a dedicated teacher as well, Pyle continued to be an inexhaust-

ible artist and writer. One of his students —Thornton Oakley—was astonished to observe this scene on entering the Pyle house one summer day: "On the stairway landing I found my teacher at his easel, working on a canvas for his series 'Travels of the Soul,' his young children cavorting about his knees, a model posed nearby in costume to give him some detail of texture, Mrs. Pyle

The Swan carries the Prince
over the hills and far away.
HP.

From *The Wonder Clock* (1888).

sitting beside him reading aloud proofs from King Arthur for his correction, he making comments for her notation." It became well known that Pyle was able to paint and dictate a text to his secretary at the same time. Rumor had it that Pyle's mind worked in separated compartments that did not interfere with each other.

Nowhere was Pyle's extraordinary personality more evident than in his brilliant achievements as a teacher. As the publishing industry was becoming more demanding, art editors searched constantly for creative talents. Pyle was well aware of the shortage of gifted artists prepared to serve. He attributed this paucity to the outdated and medio-cre education the younger artists were receiving at the time, and he resolved to share his talents and experience with those who were eager to learn.

Pyle was critical of the current art programs because they tended to emphasize copying rather than imagination. Students were expected to draw from a model who posed stiffly before them in a position that could be held for the long, tedious hours of class. The results produced by the students tended to be as inert as the model. Pyle's own interest in the Impressionists, moreover, had convinced him that the constant and unvarying north light prevalent in these classroom studios tended to encourage a certain mechanical monotony in the students' work. The artist, according to Pyle, should learn to think beyond the model, to develop a vast storage of pictorial memories —awakened by the changing mysteries of light and atmosphere—upon which to draw.

Fortified with an almost missionary zeal, Pyle applied for a teaching post at the Pennsylvania Academy of the Fine Arts, and was refused (a decision the Academy was to sorely regret years later). He taught instead at Philadelphia's Drexel Institute of Art, Science and Industry. The small fee required for the class combined with Pyle's wide reputation meant that the enrollment immediately reached its maximum limit of thirty-nine.

From the outset Pyle found the contact with the students enormously rewarding. His magnetic personality quickly earned him a reputation as a fine instructor and, by the second year at Drexel, students from many miles away ventured to Philadelphia to study in his class. Drexel reorganized the curriculum of the art department, making illustration the most important course. Pyle agreed to increase his teaching from one half day to two full days a week, yet he never reduced his output

for the New York publishers, in spite of the extra demands on his time.

Pyle's teaching reflected his zest for experimentation. Unlike the traditional approach to teaching art—in which technical skill was stressed—Pyle's approach placed the greatest importance on developing a pictorial sense, building upon the student's latent imaginary powers. "My final aim in teaching," Pyle reported to his friend Edward Penfield, "will not be essentially the production of illustrators of books, but rather the production of painters of pictures. For I believe that the painters of true American Art are yet to be produced. Such men as Winslow Homer and [George] Fuller in figure painting, and a group of landscape painters headed by George Inness as yet are the only occupants of the field. To this end, I regard magazine and book illustration as a ground from which to produce painters."

One of Pyle's experiments was to result in the formation of his own school. Desiring a more total atmosphere for study, Pyle selected his most gifted students for a summer session in 1898 and again in 1899. With funds he managed to acquire from Drexel, Pyle awarded ten scholarships so that these students could study with him at Chadds Ford, ten miles from Wilmington along the Brandywine River. He worked with this small group, living from day to day in an outdoor environment that stimulated both teacher and students and seemed to enhance the impact of his words. Teaching under these conditions, Pyle decided, was the ideal method of inspiring the student to do his best work. Based on this conviction, Pyle resigned from Drexel in 1900 to establish his school. It became one of the earliest examples of experimen-

"Poor Brother John came forward and took the
boy's hand," from *Otto of the Silver Hand* (1888).

"Abbot Otto, of St. Michaelsburg, was a gentle, patient, pale-faced old man," from *Otto of the Silver Hand* (1888). The engraving process was appropriate for an artist drawn to the work of the Middle Ages. Like Walter Crane, Pyle adapted the Medieval influence to his own purposes.

tal education in America.

Pyle had grown impatient with the dilettantes he was obliged to instruct at Drexel, and was convinced that only the students' total commitment to work could produce superior artists. The forty-seven-year-old Pyle handpicked candidates for his experiment, and turned full attention to his new school. He financed the building of studios in Wilmington where the students lived and worked. In effect, this was actually more than a school: it was Howard Pyle's vision, a colony of dedicated students eager and willing to develop under the demanding yet loving tutelage of the master of American illustration.

Restricting the number of students to under twenty, Pyle was a stern admissions officer. The prospective student was expected to submit examples of his work and to have a personal interview with Pyle. If Pyle considered the applicant promising, he accepted the student on a trial basis. The student paid for his own room, board, and supplies, but there was no charge for tuition.

The student was expected to live a Spartan existence in order to develop all the disciplines necessary for good work. Winters were spent in Wilmington and summers in Chadds Ford. The students worked in their studios six days a week, from eight in the morning until five or six in the evening, and during the summers Pyle had them work outdoors, a revolutionary concept during a time when traditional art training permitted only indoor work.

He spelled out the course of instruction in a letter to Edward Penfield as follows:

The students who come to me will be supposed to have studied drawing and painting as taught in the schools.

*My first object shall be to teach them to paint the draped
and costumed model so that it shall possess the essentials
of a practical picture. To teach this requires considerable
knowledge not usually possessed by the artist-teachers in
the schools, and this knowledge I feel myself competent
to impart. I believe I am not devoid of a sense of color
and I trust that I will be able so to instruct the pupil as
to preserve whatever color talent he may possess.
My experience is that within a year of such teaching
the pupil will be sufficiently grounded in a practical
knowledge of painting to be able to embark upon illus-
trative work.*

Beyond these fundamentals, Pyle imparted his
notions of good picture-making. The commanding teacher possessed a great talent for communicat-
ing the fundamental qualities inherent in all superior
work, yet in tune with the individual qualities in
the student's character. As N.C. Wyeth described
his teacher, "Howard Pyle's extraordinary ability
as a teacher lay primarily in his penetration. He
could read beneath the crude lines on paper, detect
therein our real inclinations and impulses; in short,
unlock our personalities. This power was in no
wise a superficial method handed out to those who
might receive. We received in proportion to that
which was fundamentally within us."

In his weekly composition classes—during which
time Pyle reviewed the work of the students—he
conveyed to his students the importance of total
immersion, a kind of physical and mental projec-
tion *into* the picture until the artist senses that he
has actually *become* the object. Only in this manner,
Pyle emphasized, can the subject come to life in
the painting. "Pictures are the creations of the
imagination," he once said, "and not of technical
facility . . . I subordinate that technical training en-

"No one was within but old Ursela, who
sat crooning over a fire," from *Otto of the Silver Hand*
(1888). Deeply admiring of this book, Walter Crane
was eager to meet Howard Pyle during an American
tour in 1891. Though cordial, Pyle was less
enthusiastic about Crane's illustration.

tirely to the training of the imagination.''

But imagination was not stirred simply by standing before an easel. Pyle urged his students to meet all facets of experience with an equal degree of delight and intensity, in work as well as in play. After all, both mind and muscle needed release. And so Pyle organized picnics, swimming parties, musical performances, costume parties, bicycle, sleigh and buggy rides throughout the year.

These years of the Howard Pyle school probably represented the most joyous and productive period of the artist's life. Some of his former pupils had already become established professionals in the city, Violet Oakley and Jessie Willcox Smith, for example. Maxfield Parrish, who studied only briefly with Pyle at Drexel, had also moved on to great success. To the Wilmington school came N.C. Wyeth, Frank Schoonover, Harvey Dunn, illustrators who would rise to fame within the next decade. Pyle also extended his teaching further by lecturing in New York and in Chicago.

The small city of Wilmington had become an important center for American illustration, and before long no American publication was without some indication of Pyle's influence as a teacher. For years to come publishers would be eager to commission work from Pyle students. The "Pyle look" became evident in paintings that depicted cowboys and Indians, seafaring life, American history; it was apparent in illustrations of the classics and interpretations of the contemporary scene. Moreover, several of his students went on to become teachers themselves, passing along Pyle's principles to younger generations of artists. The so-called Brandywine School has continued to this day, still flourishing under the brush of the Wyeth fam-

ily—Andrew, Carolyn, Henriette, and Jamie—and evident in the work of other contemporary artists drawn to the beauty of the Brandywine region.

Even while his school was in full swing, there was no lessening in Pyle's own creative output. By now the publications were capable of reproducing oils and watercolors (primitive though it was, the photo-mechanical process of halftone reproduction had been introduced), and Pyle painted as long as the daylight sun poured into his studio. Although Pyle tended to relegate questions of technique to a secondary position, his own technical facility in oil painting was acute. He painted rapidly, with great ease, but avoided any self-conscious display of his skill—a restrained Puritan even here—seldom piling on the pigment in an impasto technique or revealing his dexterity with the brush in a showy manner. These hours standing at the easel (he called it "his only real exercise") were terminated as dusk drew near, when he would leave his studio and devote the balance of the day to his students and family, or resume his work on a manuscript. An average working day was ten or eleven hours.

On entering the first years of the twentieth century, however, Pyle encountered the sudden jolt of changing times. The publishing world, once so innocent and incorruptible, was undergoing profound changes which troubled Pyle. A new generation of artists had begun to capture the imagination of a vast American public—artists whose talents were eagerly sought by the magazines at any cost. The bitter competition for talent elevated fees to levels that would have been unimaginable just ten years before. Charles Dana Gibson had emerged as the new star, and with him

 xcalibur the Sword.

From *The Story of King Arthur and His Knights* (1903).
Pyle's later works demonstrate heightened artistic powers.

King Arthur of Britain.

From *The Story of King Arthur and His Knights* (1903).

came a new wave of sophisticated fashions and fancy imitators. Pyle sensed he was growing out of date, was repeating himself, had gone stale. Looking back, he had written and illustrated twenty-four of his own books, illustrated well over 100 other books, and every major magazine in America —*Century*, *Collier's*, *Harper's Monthly*, *Harper's Weekly*, *Harper's Young People*, *Ladies' Home Journal*, *St. Nicholas*, *Scribner's*—had printed hundreds of his stories and illustrations. What was left for him to do?

At this time he decided to take on the most monumental of all projects: writing and illustrating the King Arthur legends. Appearing at intervals between 1903 and 1910, four titles were published in the series: *The Story of King Arthur and His Knights*, *The Story of the Champions of the Round Table*, *The Story of Sir Launcelot and His Companions*, and *The Story of the Grail and the Passing of Arthur*. His principal source for the text was the version written by Sir Thomas Malory, which he had read as a child, but Pyle modified this extensively to

he Lady Guinevere

From *The Story of King Arthur and His Knights* (1903).

suit his purpose, drawing from many other accounts of the Arthurian legends, in order to create the classic tales children still read today.

But the challenge of the Arthur volumes alone was not enough to sustain his interest. Pyle still sought other outlets for his restless energy. No one quite believed it in 1906 when they heard that Howard Pyle had accepted a position as art director of the magazine *McClure's* for a salary of $36,000 a year. Just why he accepted this post—whether it was his anxiety over mounting expenses at home, or his

fear of losing the esteem of the American public—is not really known. It was an impossible arrangement from the start, and his term lasted only a few months. This was Pyle's only conspicuous failure in a long line of successes.

If Pyle had been uncertain about his creative powers before taking the position with *McClure's*, his failure as art director seriously shook his self-assurance even further. He was fifty-three years old, restless, consumed with self-doubt. His gifted students had moved on to their own professional

Uther-Pendragon.

From *The Story of the Champions of the Round Table* (1905).

triumphs and the newer generation of students coming to Wilmington failed to interest him.

Although he continued to receive a steady stream of assignments, he considered them mediocre and felt that this reflected the fatigue that was setting into his work. In a letter to the *Harper's* editor, Pyle wrote in 1907, "I am in great danger of grinding out conventional magazine illustrations for conventional magazine stories."

Pyle searched within himself for newer challenges, for greater pictorial possibilities, anxious to prove that his creative abilities had not dwindled with middle age. Mural decoration offered him just such a challenge. He happily accepted several commissions offered to him. Pyle discovered that the projects challenged all his faculties as he made adjustments to the scale and lighting that were so different from the conditions imposed on his studio work.

But Pyle's first efforts disappointed him. In a serious effort to master the art of mural decoration, Pyle decided to venture to Europe, where he could study the Italian masterpieces and learn what only the great muralists of the Renaissance could teach— an experience he was certain would renew his creative powers. In 1910 Pyle and his family sailed for Italy.

We will never know whether the Italian journey would have accomplished for Howard Pyle all that he had intended. While still on board the trans-Atlantic liner, only a week from his departure from New York, his health began to fail. Although good health returned to him a few weeks after his arrival in Italy, the illness hovered over him for the following months. Successive disappointments from his editors in New York, combined with his weakened physical state, must have contributed to his rapid decline. Less than a year after his arrival in Italy, Howard Pyle passed away. He was fifty-eight years old.

"Blind Pew," original oil painting for *Treasure Island* (1911).

N.C.Wyeth

From *Susanna and Sue* (1909).

IN 1902, WHEN HE WAS ADMITTED to Howard Pyle's school in Wilmington, Delaware, Newell Convers Wyeth knew he was among the privileged. It was, after all, the best school of illustration in America. Limiting the enrollment to twenty, Howard Pyle carefully handpicked his pupils, examining examples of the candidates' work and evaluating their character in a personal interview. Pyle was inspired by a mission to elevate the standards of American illustration, and his expectations were necessarily high. If ever American illustrators were to achieve the greatness of their European counterparts, the time was now while there were more opportunities than talent. In selecting N.C. Wyeth, Pyle chose wisely. The student continued Pyle's tradition—becoming the greatest American illustrator of children's classics—and Wyeth inspired the next generation of artists with his mentor's vision as well.

Wyeth came to Wilmington just three days

before his twentieth birthday, feeling grateful to his family in New England for their support. Always sensitive to the yearnings of her son, Henriette Zirngiebel Wyeth had understood the significance of young Convers' passion for drawing. She had urged her husband to allow their oldest boy to leave the school he disliked and instead study drafting at the Mechanic Arts School in Boston. When he graduated in 1899, N.C. Wyeth borrowed money from his reluctant father to continue studies at the Massachusetts Normal School and the Eric Pape School of Art in Boston. At the urging of his friend, Clifford Ashley, Wyeth summoned up the courage to apply to Howard Pyle's school where he could study with the man whose work he had admired since boyhood.

Dedicated to the notion that art and life were inextricably linked, Howard Pyle introduced Wyeth to a regimen that included both hard work and pleasant festivities. The student was expected to live a Spartan existence in order to develop the disciplines necessary for good work, spending winters in Wilmington and summers just ten miles away on the Brandywine River in the open country of Chadds Ford, Pennsylvania. "Pyle emphasized that hard work, constantly applied, and the living of the simple life were two things that would bring about my making," N.C. Wyeth recalled years later. In between long hours at the easel, parties were organized, picnics and swimming, and Wyeth was called upon to demonstrate his excellence in horsemanship by driving the other students through the countryside.

N.C. Wyeth's trial period at the Pyle school lasted only a few months before he was elevated to advanced standing; he progressed rapidly. He was naturally responsive to the rigors of long hours of concentration, and both his talents and exuberant personality won him the respect and affection of his colleagues and his master. Before long he was receiving commissions from the magazine publishers in New York and Philadelphia and sending money home to New England to repay his family for their support.

Early in his career he was attracted to the potential of illustrating the cowboys and Indians of the West. Understanding the value of first-hand knowledge, he made a three-and-one-half-month trip to the West in 1904, earning his way as he traveled by working on a ranch in Colorado and as a mail rider in New Mexico. During this trip he gathered costumes and props from the cowboys and from the Navajo Indians, the beginnings of a collection that was to grow through the years, material vital to the authenticity of his illustration. This trip to the West—and the second that followed two years later—made an indelible contribution to his reservoir of images and impressions, a rich supply from which he would draw again and again.

But N.C. Wyeth was too searching in nature to restrict himself exclusively to the Western scene. Unlike many of his contemporaries, Wyeth sought to expand his subject matter—and with that his own education—into many areas. And so he read voluminously, collected costumes and props of all periods, and went on to illustrate subjects as vastly different from each other as colonial America, biblical Judea, and medieval England.

As a professional illustrator, Wyeth furnished black-and-white drawings and oil paintings for magazines and for advertising, but the commercial work that most interested him was book illustration. His opportunity came in 1910 when the publishing company of Charles Scribner's invited him to illustrate *Treasure Island* by Robert Louis Stevenson, the first book scheduled for the Scribner's Illustrated Classic series. Three additional books by Stevenson followed in the series: *Kidnapped* (1913), *Black Arrow* (1916), and *David Balfour* (1924). Wyeth's association with Scribner's lasted many years: of the twenty-six classics Wyeth eventually illustrated, a total of sixteen were published by the same company. Wyeth's books for Scribner's were so popular that he inevitably received offers from other publishers to illustrate such epics as *Robin Hood*, *Rip Van Winkle*, and *Robinson Crusoe*. "The juvenile book field has opened very wide for me, offering splendid opportunities from a half dozen directions, so attractive in fact, that I am unable to further refuse such tempting propositions," Wyeth wrote in 1919.

Although Wyeth was attentive to historical details in his illustration and researched thoroughly the periods he was depicting in these books, history was not simply an accumulation of facts: history was *experience*. He found in history those very moments that corresponded to something true within him, an emotional truth. For him the past contained vital stories of romance, of triumphs and failures, of expectations and disappointments, but these experiences were not buried with the past; only the setting changed. All experience could be reawakened. "In my own life I try to live the life that I depict," Wyeth explained.

Some may wonder how I can live the life of the twelfth century, which most of my costumed romance represents. All I can say is that the elemental feelings of long ago are identical with our own. The costumes and accessories of the twelfth century may be different, but the sunlight on a bronzed face, the winds that blow across the marshlands, the moon illuminating the old hamlets of medieval England, the rainsoaked travelers of King Arthur's day passing across the moors are strictly contemporaneous in feeling. The farmer swinging a scythe uses the same muscles, experiences the same sensations as we do today. But you've got to do these things to understand them.

N.C. Wyeth learned from Howard Pyle the value of what could be termed "corporal identification" with his subject, an empathy in which the artist and subject would palpitate with the same life force, would actually become the same. He consciously worked to transform himself into his subject. As he explained the process:

My brothers and I were brought up on a farm, and from the time I could walk I was conscripted into doing every conceivable chore that there was to do about the place.

"The Siege of the Round-House," original oil painting for *Kidnapped* (1913).

"At the cards in Cluny's cage," original oil painting for *Kidnapped* (1913).

"In the fork like a mastheaded seaman, there stood a
man in a green tabard, spying far and wide," original oil painting
for *The Black Arrow* (1916).

"But be at rest the black arrow flieth nevermore,"
original oil painting for *The Black Arrow* (1916).

"He blew three deadly notes," original oil painting for *The Boy's King Arthur* (1917). N.C. Wyeth completed this illustration the very day his son Andrew was born.

This early training gave me a vivid appreciation of the part the body plays in action.

Now when I paint a figure on horseback, a man plowing, or a woman buffeted by the wind, I have an acute sense of the muscle strain, the feel of the hickory handle, or the protective bend of head and squint of eye that each pose involves. After painting action scenes I have ached for hours because of having put myself in the other fellow's shoes as I realized him on canvas.

It is no accident, therefore, that Wyeth's painting would be related to his own physical stature. His appearance was distinctive: at 6 feet 2 inches he was normally the tallest person in the room, and he weighed 210 pounds, more or less. (Periodically he would control his healthy appetite and reduce.) His broad chest was the most expansive section of his frame, which narrowed at the hips and was supported by surprisingly slight legs. His arms were also slender, and his hands were rather small for his size and extremely delicate. His body, therefore, was a kind of contradiction of extremes: small and large, delicate and massive, refined and rugged. He was graceful when he moved, an excellent dancer, yet was a rugged athlete in his younger days. He was assertive and commanding, yet his voice was surprisingly high for a man of his size. Several people observed that his entrance into a room would bring voices to a hush. Yet he was not overbearing. N.C. Wyeth was a man whose mere physical presence charged the room with energy, a kind of vitality one seldom encounters.

When he painted, Wyeth was continually in motion. Although in reproduction his illustrations would be reduced to page size—8 × 10″, per-haps—he preferred painting the original oil on a large surface—frequently 32 × 40″—with broad brushes and occasionally a palette knife. He applied his juicy pigment in assertive strokes to the canvas, a movement that involved his entire body, like a fencer striking out in a duel. He would then back away from the canvas to study the composition through squinting eyes, returning swiftly on the attack to make the necessary alterations and additions. He worked rapidly, frequently completing an illustration in one day, and rarely in more than three. The subjects were generally men—seldom women—massive and bulky like the artist himself. Heroic and violent action—dueling, buffalo hunting, bronco busting—was part of his vast repertoire of work, but it was not the essence of his power as an artist, for he created a total world within the confines of his canvas, an atmosphere, a mood that colored after the battle was over. Action itself was secondary: tension, expectation, melancholy, fear, or triumph—these were the moods children recalled long after the pages of the book were closed.

N.C. Wyeth's paintings were big in both scale and in vision. It was natural, in view of this preference for large scale, that N.C. would be attracted to a still larger format, so he gladly accepted commissions to paint murals, and he completed some forty murals and large decorations for institutions, banks, and public buildings. To accommodate the size of his mural work, he built an addition to his studio and outfitted the large wing with ladders and scaffolding, which he would climb up and down vigorously—again, he was always in motion.

Because corporal identification was closely linked to emotional empathy, it is not surprising that

intensity of feeling was a quality he valued in himself and nurtured in his family: it was the lifeblood of the artist, the prize for being alive. All experience—if intensely felt—was precious, and the artist could summon and express those feelings in limitless ways. Building experience upon experience, the artist creates an abundant repository of impressions upon which he can play over and over: the richer this reservoir, the more precious.

"How desperately I cling to memories!" he wrote in 1917.

They are shrines to which I constantly attend! They bring to me more vividly than by any other means of contemplation the significance of the eternal past, the eternal future—and our place between the two eternities. As I look back over my experiences, for the recent sharp and defined ones and follow them as they recede in the rapid perspective of only thirty-four years, it has the effect of precipitating my imagination down the countless ages of all experience!

And from this repository of images and associations N.C. Wyeth could transform a grove of trees in Chadds Ford into a Sherwood Forest, a sloping bank along the Brandywine River into a Civil War battle scene, a young woman into a bearded woodsman. From his imagination emerged the vivid characterization of Robin Hood, Bill Bones, Long John Silver, individuals as human as the artist's uncle or the postman who delivered the mail each day.

If so much richness lay just beyond the threshold of his home, there was no need to travel farther for inspiration. In fact, too much travel represented a hazard to the artist: the loss of his integrity. Like Henry David Thoreau, whose writings he admired,

"I stood like one thunderstruck," original
oil painting for *Robinson Crusoe* (1920).

Wyeth spurned travel, fearing the evil effects of fragmentation or, as he put it, "the profound risk of being adulterated by others." Remaining intimate with his environment was vital to creativity. "I have come to the *full* conclusion that a man can only paint that which he knows even more than intimately; he has got to know it spiritually. And to do that he has got to live around it, in it, and be a *part* of it.

"I feel so moved sometimes toward nature that I could almost throw myself face down into a ploughed furrow—*ploughed* furrow understand! I love it so."

If Wyeth's intensity of feeling was conveyed in his epic paintings, it was also transmitted to his

family. He shared his thoughts and feelings spontaneously with his wife Carol (whom he had married in 1906) and with his five children, Henriette, Carolyn, Nathaniel, Ann, and Andrew. It is no accident that each of the children would one day become distinguished in the pursuit of their careers: all were inspired by their father's passion for life and by his eloquently expressed spiritual longings. Wyeth never lost sight of the basic ingredients needed for a wholesome family setting, although he was certainly an unorthodox parent. The qualities that made him such an extraordinary father were those that he conveyed to the children who read his books—his life and his work

"The Passing of Robin Hood," original oil painting
for *Robin Hood* (1917).

"Deerslayer threw all his force into a desperate
effort," original oil painting for *The Deerslayer* (1925).

were always expressions of the total man.

Perhaps Wyeth's greatest gift as a father was his own childlike nature, his exuberant personality—"his charisma," some have called it. Wyeth's interest was swiftly ignited—by an abstract aesthetic theory, perhaps, or the child's first steps, or a budding bluebell on the Brandywine. These were miracles to him; he responded to them with a joyful outburst of enthusiasm. This spontaneous curiosity, this recurring state of wonder at even the simplest phenomenon, never diminished with the years. And nowhere was his delight in life more evident than where his children were concerned. Just moments after the birth of a new child, N.C. was alert to what was inherently unique in the infant, instantly sensitive to a certain revealing expression in the eyes or a decisive movement in the body. Preserving this individuality and even expanding the singular qualities in each child was to be his primary mission as a parent. He took a passionate interest in their training, beginning with the earliest years of walking through the countryside. "We make a great deal of these simple experiences," he wrote a year after the birth of his fifth child. "I believe them to be the real foundation of one of the most profound ethical ideas in regard to early training, to obtain the utmost of pleasure and inspiration for the simplest and homeliest events of the life about us."

From the depths of his soul, N.C. Wyeth understood Howard Pyle when the elder illustrator extolled the virtues of a simple life. A simple life meant that the artist would not be subjected to continual distractions from his work. But it meant more than that to N.C. His New England predecessors—writers such as Ralph Waldo Emerson

and Henry David Thoreau, whose works he devoured passionately—had written of the simple life in more profound terms. Like Thoreau, N.C. Wyeth saw in nature a cosmos, inexhaustible in its potential for beauty. He wrote, "I am beginning to think that people of today are divided into two classes: those that accept elemental Nature casually, as a mere accessory to the important business of *trivial living*; and those who sense the perfect amalgamation of elemental nature and human life, that *cosmic relationship* which if not felt leaves us superficial and at bottom *useless* to ourselves and to the world."

And to nature he returned time and time again as his source of inspiration. Yet it would be inaccurate to say that he regarded nature as his "subject matter," so hostile was he to the so-called landscape painters who tramped through the fields "like hunters with guns over their shoulders, to 'shoot landscape,' and nothing more." Just as Pyle had taught him to project himself into his subject, so had N.C. applied this to his painting of nature. As he wrote in 1921, "To paint a landscape wherever one is endeavoring to represent with passionate emotion the hot molten gold of sunlight, the heavy sultry distances and the burning breath of soft breezes, one returns home in the evening proud and happily sympathetic in sweaty clothes and burned arms and neck. To feel thus completes one's sense of identification and unity with nature."

And so the walks through the countryside became a family ritual: a team of explorers—N.C. and the children—out to discover the wonders of their land. The aroma of moist, spring blossoms, the mud that oozed between bare toes, the sunlight flickering on the water lilies . . . a morning's walk was an excursion into the world of the familiar and the unknown, the world of mushrooms and goblins, clouds and princes, reality and romance ever entwined within the woods of Chadds Ford, along the banks of the Brandywine River. A leaf falling from a tree was a magical event, and N.C.'s contagious enthusiasm intoxicated the children as they shared in the mystery of those rapturous moments, building upon those experiences the rich repository of associations N.C. found so vital to the development of the artist within.

Long before educational experimentation was fashionable, the Wyeths sent their young children to a nearby Montessori school, where classroom work was tailored to the individual child's particular interests and gifts. When they were too old to continue in the school, and experiences with public education proved unsatisfactory, Wyeth withdrew them from the formal classroom setting and hired tutors for individual work. "Every mother's son of us is born with that supreme gift of individual perception," he wrote, "but the sheeplike tendency of human society soon makes inroads on a child's unsophistications, and then popular education completes the dastardly work with its systematic formulas, and *away* goes the individual, hurling through space into that hateful oblivion of mediocrity." Each of the five Wyeth children received individual instruction, liberated from the "menace of all organized schools and colleges."

Wyeth's theory did not imply, however, that children should be liberated from study. On the contrary, the training of Wyeth's children was even more rigorous, because it was designed to awaken dormant talents, to amplify the gifts that set each child apart. Having a natural gift, after all, was

only the beginning: "All the 'natural' talents of youth cannot take the place of *disciplined training*. Beethoven was a prodigy as a boy pianist, but witness the infinite and painstaking training which followed his initial flowering. Without this exhaustive discipline we would not have had the Beethoven of the nine symphonies."

Henriette, Carolyn, and Andrew, by revealing their preference for art, worked with N.C. Wyeth in the studio for several hours each day. Ann, showing an early gift for music, studied piano with a tutor, then continued on to study composition. As a boy, Nathaniel exhibited his affinity for mechanical structure by building elaborate ship models. N.C. predicted that his son would create, "but not in art," and he was correct. Because his interest lay in the sciences, Nat went on to college to study engineering. He became a design engineer, one of the few in this country hired by a major corporation to design whatever new system might interest him.

N.C. Wyeth, like Howard Pyle, deplored dilettantism. It was better not to work at all than to dabble; work was a total commitment, regardless of the chosen field. This attitude made N.C. a formidable teacher. From the day his student first entered the studio, disciplined training began. Scornful of the leniency most art schools permitted, N.C. was a strict and exacting instructor. First, the basics: "It makes me weary to see how students insist upon avoiding the one thing that will fundamentalize their work throughout their lives—that vital necessity of knowing how to draw." Each student began with the basic geometric forms (cone, sphere, and so on) and would draw—until achieving near perfection—plaster casts, then still

"The flight across the lake," original oil painting for
The Last of the Mohicans (1919).

"Sally, Merrillee and Johnny," original oil painting
for *Drums* (1925).

life, then landscape exercises. Only through knowledge can creative interpretation begin, he maintained. "A thing done right is done with the authority of knowledge (coupled with temperament). One has difficulties only when one lacks the knowledge of *truth*, which includes the knowledge of craft as well as of nature—a clear vision is absolutely necessary before the creation of a piece of art is undertaken and the power to execute said piece of art with precision and fluidity is just as necessary."

The children advanced rapidly in their personal and creative development, ever under the watchful eye of their proud father. Henriette, Carolyn, and Andy were showing great promise in their painting, each embarking on a very different avenue of expression. By 1935 two more artists had joined the family by marriage, both of them painters who had studied with N.C. Wyeth: Peter Hurd and Henriette Wyeth were married in 1929, and John McCoy married Ann Wyeth in 1935.

"This watching of the unfolding of all the younger members of the family is a glorious episode of my life," N.C. wrote in 1939. ". . . I am asked interminably, 'Aren't you proud of it all?' Of course I am, beyond the expression of any words. But my answer is always restrained because I am still in the battle myself, in spirit at least, and I still have a fairly clear vision of what lies ahead to be done before a real mark is achieved."

N.C. Wyeth did not live long enough to enjoy the full measure of his children's attainments. Nor did he meet the third generation of artists to emerge in the family—George Weymouth (married to Ann, the daughter of Mr. and Mrs. John McCoy) and Jamie Wyeth (the son of Mr. and Mrs. Andrew Wyeth). On October 19, 1945—exactly forty-three years from the day N.C. first arrived in Wilmington, Delaware—he and his grandson Newell Convers II were driving just two miles from home. N.C. approached a railroad crossing, which was obstructed by foliage, and an oncoming train struck the car he was driving. N.C. and his four-year-old grandson both died only moments after the collision.

"I am the Witch of the North," from *The Wizard of Oz* (1900).

W. W. Denslow

From *The Wizard of Oz* (1900).

BORN WITHIN ONLY THREE YEARS and fifteen miles of each other, the two American illustrators Howard Pyle and W. W. Denslow might just as well have come from different planets. Howard Pyle's name is mentioned in every discussion of "The Golden Age of American Illustration" and included in every anthology of children's literature, while Denslow failed to appear in any until only recently. Even the overwhelming popularity of *The Wonderful Wizard of Oz*—for which Denslow created the original illustrations—failed to earn him a place on the shelves of classic stories for children, most librarians dismissing the book for its lack of literary quality.

Howard Pyle, as well as his student N. C. Wyeth, was truly American, but they both continued a time-honored tradition. Pyle was a gentleman, much like his counterparts abroad and his colleagues in New York and Philadelphia; he was somewhat austere, demonstrating a sincere respect

for discipline, thrift, and fairness. The epic tales Pyle favored for illustration often took place in European settings or on the high seas still dominated by the English. Even stories that may have been set in Colonial America were populated with heroic characters familiar to English readers.

William Wallace Denslow, on the other hand, represented a very different kind of American. A restless news artist, he rarely lived in one home for more than a few years and the robust city of Chicago, where he spent much of his professional life, was very different from the staid community of Pyle's Wilmington, Delaware. Nor was Denslow the Victorian-American that Pyle represented with such dignity. On the contrary, Denslow's traits were unlikely to win any friends among the establishment: he was a bohemian, married three times, and eventually returned to a serious drinking problem he had managed to overcome years earlier. Denslow was more like the American cowboys he admired when he spent some months as a cow-puncher in the West: a bit rough around the edges, combative, rugged, and rather too avaricious to sustain long-lasting collaborations that might have proved mutually rewarding over time. Indeed, his career became most promising when he joined forces with another talent, but his suspicious temperament deceived him into believing he would be better off on his own. "You can hardly tell who to trust," he wrote in his diary. "Those that pretend to be your friends you find later on are the ones that are giving you 'the cross'. . . . I shall believe no one and pretend to trust all and endeavor to carve out my salvation." It was this cynicism that earned him a nickname, "the Growler." "Denslow's sense of humor was upside down," wrote an observer. "Always grumbling about nothing, always carping, always censorious and laughing uproariously when he had secured his effects."

In recent years Denslow's contribution to the field of American illustration has been reassessed. His talent, like the texts he chose to illustrate, may have been imperfect, but were significant because they helped to transform an English tradition into something entirely American. Moreover, Denslow ushered the children's book from the nineteenth into the twentieth century, providing an ideal conclusion to a volume devoted to the great classic illustrators of children's books. With Denslow, we are left on the threshold of twentieth-century America, poised for entry into a new era of illustrated books for children.

While Denslow may have been better off illustrating words written by another hand, he was not the best judge of what text to illustrate. He did not, as his contemporaries were doing with great success,

choose to illustrate the classics—familiar and time-less stories which would have drawn greater attention to his talents as an illustrator—but preferred instead to illustrate the writing of contemporary authors. Even when he illustrated classic verses, such as the old nursery rhymes, he altered the writing as he saw fit, not always improving upon the traditional version. By making this choice, Denslow's talents were seen only in relation to the text he illustrated, generally inferior writing that dated rapidly and was soon forgotten. If he had maintained relations with the author of the Oz stories, his work might have at least remained *visible* to a wide public, even if the illustrations continued to be associated with a class of popular books not regarded seriously by critics of children's literature. Surely, the continued collaboration with L. Frank Baum could have been rewarding to both author and illustrator, but neither party was willing to make any diplomatic or financial concessions. After all, Baum had his pride too!

Lyman Frank Baum was every bit as American in temperament as W. W. Denslow, an entrepreneur and showman who applied his ingenuity to whatever would appeal to a wide marketplace. At seventeen Baum had already begun his career as a cub reporter in New York, and before he was twenty was running his own paper. Soon bored with newspaper work, he managed a chain of opera houses owned by his father, performed occasionally with traveling stock companies, and eventually turned his hand to writing for the stage. For his first successful musical comedy, *The Maid of Arran*, Baum actually wrote the book, music, and lyrics, produced and directed the New York production, and even played the romantic lead! The responsibilities of marriage and family prompted this enterprising young man to seek greater opportunities in the West. In the territory that would become the state of South Dakota, he operated a variety store called Baum's Bazaar, then ran a weekly newspaper in Aberdeen for two years. When the paper failed, he moved his family to Chicago where he took a job as a reporter for the *Chicago Post*, then became a traveling salesman for an importing firm, and finally founded his own magazine, a monthly periodical for window trimmers, called *Show Window*.

To entertain his four sons, Baum told stories based on his version of the Mother Goose Rhymes, which he wrote down and had published in 1897. (A moderately successful publication, *Mother Goose in Prose* was the first book illustrated by Maxfield Parrish.) Baum was unable to find a publisher for the next book, *By the Candelabra's Glare*, and was obliged to publish it himself, at his own expense. From his friends at the Chicago Press Club he acquired the illustrations, including a pair of pen-and-inks made by his good friend W. W. Denslow. (To repay the illustrator, Baum hired Denslow to draw a cover for a fall issue of *Shop Window* in 1895.) This second book was less successful than the first, but Baum was undaunted. He immediately proceeded to plan the next, a collection of nonsense rhymes for children, which would be illustrated entirely by W. W. Denslow.

Although they became friends through their association with the Chicago Press Club, Baum and Denslow rarely socialized in the same circles. Baum was warm-hearted, high-spirited, and optimistic, essentially ill-at-ease in the cynical company of the bohemian friends Denslow sought out. Baum felt more at home with the businessmen he met at the Chicago Athletic Club. A family man, happily married, Baum preferred to entertain the irascible illustrator in the warmth of his own home. While Baum puffed on his cigar and Denslow on his corncob pipe, the Baum children were

" . . . it's very tedious being perched
up here night and day to scare away crows."
from *The Wizard of Oz* (1900).

CAPTAIN
BING.

From *Father Goose, His Book* (1899).
Influenced by Walter Crane and his colleagues in
England, Denslow intended to create
the book as an object of beauty.

nearby, amused by the eccentric visitor whom one son described as "ferocious looking . . . with a heavy 'walrus' mustache . . . like a brigand."

By strange coincidence, Baum and Denslow were born in the same year (1856), actually within ten days of each other, but their lives had taken very different directions before these evening meetings in Baum's livingroom. Denslow had made comic drawings since he was a boy growing up in the East, convinced from the start that he would become an artist one day. He was only fourteen when his father died and he set out at once to begin his formal art training in New York City, studying at the Cooper Institute for the Advancement of Science and Art and at the National Academy of Design, also attending sessions at an art association

that came to be called the Salmagundi Club. Before he was twenty, he was already earning a living, albeit meager, as an illustrator for newspapers, and wandered from town to town for more than six years until he settled temporarily in Philadelphia. Here he married a Philadelphia girl, terminated that union after only one year, leaving her with a son he never acknowledged.

During this time, Denslow had developed a reputation for designing theatrical posters and show cards, work that led to assignments in New York City for a weekly magazine called *The Theatre*. Drawing scenes of theatrical performances for the publication gave him experience in costume, stage setting, and lighting, and his published work attracted the attention of the *Herald* in Chicago,

Captain Bing was a Pirate King
And sailed the broad seas o'er;
On many a lark he sailed his bark
Where none had sailed before,
And filled his hold so full of gold
That it would hold no more.

From *Father Goose, His Book* (1899).
Each element in the spread—words and images
reproduced a detail to be integrated
into a single, designed unit.

where he accepted a full-time position on the art staff. It was in Chicago that his problems with drinking began to interfere with his performance on the job, and several times he was fired then re-hired by the paper. Finally, in 1890, he took a cure for alcoholism and, sober but bitter, left Chicago to work for a newspaper in Denver. After two months in Colorado, Denslow resigned from his job over a disagreement with the editor, tried his hand at cowpunching for a few months, then moved farther west to resume work as a news illustrator. He remained in San Francisco for two years, finding the city "rank and rotten to the core," and returned in 1893 to Chicago (which he called "one immense cash register") just in time for the opening of the grand Columbian Exposition.

He was then thirty-seven years old, having wandered from one coast to the other, armed now with the required experience and talents to finally make a reputation for himself.

The *Herald* again hired the now-sober Denslow and he formed a partnership with an artist-friend, Charles Saalburg, which inevitably terminated shortly thereafter over disagreements involving money. Denslow's illustrations of the Exposition earned him a wide public and the *Herald* gave him the arena to present his comic style and strong facile line which he had been refining over the years. To his signature, "Den," he added a rebus in the form of a seahorse (or hippocampus), much the way Walter Crane had introduced the crane as his trademark. Soon Denslow was nicknamed

FATHER GOOSE

Old Mother Goose became
quite new,
And joined a Woman's Club;
She left poor Father Goose
at home
To care for Sis and Bub.

They called for stories by the score,
And laughed and cried to hear
All of the queer and merry songs
That in this book appear.

When Mother Goose at last returned
For her there was no use;
The goslings much preferred to hear
The tales of FATHER GOOSE.

From *Father Goose, His Book* (1899).

Have you seen little Sally
Dance the Ostrich Dance?
The dainty way she does it
Will surely you entrance.
With the left foot here,
And the right foot there,
And the ostrich feathers waving
In her golden hair:

She's surely very charming —
You'll see it at a glance —
When little Sally dances
In the Ostrich dance.

From *Father Goose, His Book* (1899).

"Hippocampus Den."

Denslow resigned from the *Herald* when the paper merged with the *Times* in 1895 and pursued work for the theater, designing posters and costumes. Denslow married a second time and, although he was doing well as a freelance illustrator, decided to move to the suburbs, stabilize his income, and take on full-time work designing book covers for Rand McNally and Company. Within two years, Denslow created more than one hundred cover designs, often turning out as many as one per day, several of which demonstrate some of the best graphic design being done in America at the time. In 1898, Denslow was accepting additional assignments from the mail order company of Montgomery Ward, and by the time he and Baum joined forces he had become one of the most expensive and desirable artists in the region.

Frank Baum and Wally Denslow were in their mid-forties when they sat in the livingroom planning their first book together. Both men had bumped around the country, trying their hands at a variety of trades, and both were ready to embark on a major project. Although Denslow had illustrated a half-dozen books already, he had not attempted a children's book, an endeavor that he had wanted to undertake for years. Since childhood, he recalled, "there was precious little printed then for a boy to laugh at, and I made up my mind that someday I'd furnish . . . [children] the laugh material." For his part, Frank Baum sought a venture that would establish him once and for all as a supreme writer of children's books, finally bringing him fame and fortune.

The collaboration seemed ideal. Unlike Lewis Carroll, who wanted his illustrator simply to render the literary idea precisely as he saw it, Frank Baum welcomed Denslow's contributions. Denslow illustrated verses that Baum had already written, and Baum wrote verses to Denslow's pictures. The project had sufficient promise for them to proceed with publication. They selected the title—*Father Goose, His Book*—filed for copyright, and agreed to share the royalties equally. Unable to secure a Chicago publisher, Baum and Denslow decided to publish it themselves, calling themselves The Picture Book Company. There was a dispute over the handling of the credits on the title page—Denslow feeling his name should be larger than Baum's because his name, being more familiar, would enhance the sales of the book—but the matter was resolved as Denslow eventually agreed to equal credit.

To avoid the cost of a typesetter, Denslow hired a young artist to letter the pages by hand, paying him only $50.00 for the entire job, but promising him credit in the book. They were well on their way when the Chicago publisher, George M. Hill, agreed to invest some money in the book, paying for the paper, binding, and distribution, if author and illustrator agreed to pay for everything else, including advertising posters.

Published in 1899, *Father Goose, His Book* was a *tour de force* of the day. In England, Edmund Evans had successfully printed inexpensive and attractive picture books for children as early as the 1860s, but in America no such equivalent existed. Howard Pyle had attempted two children's books in color (*Yankee Doodle* and *Lady of Shalott*) in 1881, but the results were so disappointing that the artist refused to do any more book work in color. W. W. Denslow had admired the books of Walter Crane, printed

From *Father Goose, His Book* (1899).

From *Father Goose, His Book* (1899).

255

From *Father Goose, His Book* (1899). Hand-lettered
and printed in yellow, gray, red, and black, this book instantly
established the popularity of the Denslow-Baum team.

by Edmund Evans, and he felt a kinship with the ideas of Crane and William Morris about the importance of design and craftsmanship. Denslow had, in fact, helped to foster the Arts and Crafts movement in America by designing several fine books for the Roycroft Press in New York, an emulation of William Morris' Kelmscott Press in England. Like Crane, Denslow was dedicated to the notion that a book should be an object of beauty, designed carefully from cover to cover, with attention to every detail, including endpapers, frontis and title page, typography and illustrations. To get every detail just right, Denslow spent six months "at hard labor" on *Father Goose*, a great deal of time for an artist who worked so rapidly. For each verse, Denslow integrated text and pictures to form an artistic whole. Color, although limited because of expense, was used nevertheless. Restricting himself to only yellow, gray, red, and

black, Denslow applied a black or red line to enclose the shapes of color, a device Crane also employed to enhance the effect, and he composed the colors so that each page unfolded a surprising new arrangement.

Father Goose was an immediate success when it was published: within three months it had been reprinted four times, a total of more than 75,000 copies. Baum was exuberant. No author could be more appreciative of an illustrator, sentiments he expressed when he inscribed a personal copy of *Father Goose* to Denslow:

Dear Den: Within my chiffonier
Are many drawers; yet I fear
No drawer there can hope to beat
The pictures that you drew so neat
For dear old "Father Goose: His Book"—
Unless I'm very much mistook.

There's better things (this goes to show)
In some old drawers that we know,
And even I shall draw in time
A check to pay me for my rhyme,
Which proves that both of us can draw—
You with your paw—I with my jaw.

Before the completion of *Father Goose*, Baum and Denslow were already making arrangements for *The Wonderful Wizard of Oz*, a book idea Baum had developed out of the stories he had told his youngsters over the years. (Baum had landed on the name "Oz" one evening when his children urged him to identify the name of the place where these extraordinary adventures occurred. Looking about for inspiration, Baum noticed a filing cabinet in the room with two drawers. A-N and O-Z. The second label gave its name to Oz.) It was not easy for Baum and Denslow to find a publisher (the book was "too different, too radical—out of the general line," Mrs. Baum recalled in a letter). George Hill agreed finally to risk publishing this unusual book, but only on the same financial basis as the one he enjoyed with *Father Goose*: Denslow and Baum would assume the expenses for the plates, cover, and advertising, while Hill would pay for paper, printing, binding, and distribution, and pay an advance against royalties of $500 to each man.

Baum and Denslow applied their talents to the new project with great enthusiasm. The challenge to Denslow was enormous. Not since *Alice's Adventures in Wonderland* had an artist been given an opportunity to work directly with an author in creating a world of pure fantasy. Together Denslow and Baum could invent a strange and wonderful

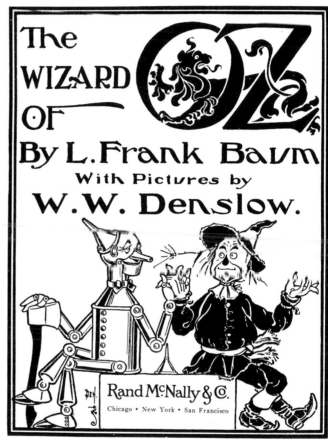

Title page for *The Wizard of Oz* (1900).
The matter of credits—whose name would be larger
—was an early dispute between Baum and
Denslow that foretold their future disagreements.

"Dorothy gazed thoughtfully at the Scarecrow."
from *The Wizard of Oz* (1900).

land populated by the most unusual creatures. Out of their discussions, Baum developed the story and Denslow the visual interpretations, a collaboration that seemed remarkably supportive. The Scarecrow and Tin Woodsman, for example, offered a particularly great challenge to Denslow. In an interview years later Denslow recalled, "I made twenty-five sketches of the two monkeys before I was satisfied with them. You may well believe that there was a great deal of evolution before I got that golf ball in the Scarecrow's ear or the funnel on the Tin Man's head. I experimented and tried out all sorts of straw waist-coats and sheet-iron cravats before I was satisfied."

To be convincing, every detail in the frontier of fantasy had to be worked out; not only the creatures themselves, but an unusual landscape out of which grew strange trees and flowers. Each section of the fairyland was designated a color—purple in the North, blue in the East, yellow in the West, red in the South, green in the center, each bordered in brown. As the setting changed, so changed the color, the appropriate tint applied as the characters moved through the pages of the book. Denslow's figures danced in and out of the woods, more than one hundred illustrations leading the reader through the pages. The artist was particularly painstaking in rendering these figures, as his friend Charles Waldron observed:

He would have a different sketch tacked on to different boards, with his box of colors handy at his right hand. . . . When one drawing became tiresome he would work on another. In order to get the right action . . . the figure might have as many as six different legs, four heads, and as many arms. When the right ones were selected . . . they would be drawn in with ink and the others erased.

In addition to the illustrations darting through the pages of text, Denslow prepared twenty-four full-page illustrations for reproduction in color. Here he was at his best, applying his diverse experience to a task that demanded all his ingenuity. Since his days spent wandering through Chinatown in San Francisco, Denslow had been intrigued by Oriental art and design. He, like many other contemporary artists in America and abroad, had

"Permit me to introduce to you her Majesty, the Queen." from *The Wizard of Oz* (1900).

been inspired by the Japanese woodcut—unusual configurations of flat color skillfully arranged on a two-dimensional surface. In his book covers and in his theatrical posters, Denslow had employed these techniques with great effect, but nowhere was he more inventive than in these twenty-four color illustrations prepared for *The Wizard*. Even his familiar seahorse, a device also inspired by Japanese tradition, was integrated into a carefully planned composition. "It is well to have a sign or totem," Denslow wrote to his friend, the photographer Alfred Stieglitz, "as my hippocampus has saved many a composition for me, and I hold him in reserve for that purpose." With careful attention given to each illustration, Denslow also integrated every detail into the design of the book as a whole, presenting to children what William Morris would have praised as an object of beauty.

If Denslow was determined to elevate the aesthetic standards of the American picture book, Frank Baum also had a mission: he would create a modern fairy tale that was truly American, a story that would "bear the stamp of our times and depict the progressive fairies of today." In so doing, Baum aimed to replace the rather gloomy stories of Aesop, Grimm, and Andersen with those "in which the wonderment and joy are retained and the heart-aches and nightmares left out." In his introduction to *The Wonderful Wizard of Oz*, Baum acknowledged that "the old-time fairy tale" had served its purpose, but "may now be classed as 'historical' in the children's library; for the time has come for a series of newer 'wonder tales' in which the stereotyped genie, dwarf and fairy are eliminated, together with all the horrible and bloodcurdling incidents devised by authors to

point a fearsome moral to each tale. Modern education includes morality," Baum asserted, "therefore, the modern child seeks only entertainment in its wonder-tales and gladly dispenses with all disagreeable incident."

Gone are the vast nordic forests; the fearsome goblins lurking in darkness. In plain Yankee language, Baum places Dorothy and her dog Toto in the prairie, whirled away by a Kansas cyclone to a utopia based very much on wholesome American ideals—a sunny world without poverty or illness; without snobbery or class-consciousness; a land of brotherhood and unselfishness. A modern American utopia must also possess the most advanced technology, of course, and so Oz would contain marvelous gadgetry, every bit as inventive as the horseless carriage recently introduced on the American scene. This is no English fairyland: Baum's Oz was as remote from Carroll's Wonderland as Chicago was from the City of London!

The Wonderful Wizard of Oz was published in the first year of the twentieth century. Reviews were flattering and sales were brisk (90,000 copies were sold within two years), but signs of friction between Denslow and Baum were already in evidence. As ambitious men, they resented having to share credit for their books. In public they each claimed full responsibility for *Father Goose*, and their success with *The Wizard* only intensified these feelings of rivalry. Denslow had already agreed to illustrate Baum's *Dot and Tot in Merryland*, but he decided to turn his attention first to a book of his own, which he called *Denslow's Mother Goose*, before collaborating again. Revealing his proprietary feelings about his own project, this audacious title also declared that he was *not* going to be

"You ought to be ashamed of yourself!" from *The Wizard of Oz* (1900).

"The Eyes looked at her thoughtfully."
from *The Wizard of Oz* (1900).

From *The Wizard of Oz* (1900).

inhibited by tradition. Although other illustrators might have regarded the time-honored rhymes as inviolate, Denslow changed the text wherever "the change would give a gentler and cleaner tone to the verse. . . . When I illustrate and edit childhood classics I don't hesitate to expurgate," he insisted. A 40,000 copy sale of the book convinced Denslow that he was right, and that his success depended on no one else. By the time Denslow was ready to turn his attention to *Dot and Tot in Merryland*, Frank Baum had come to the same conclusion, having convinced himself with a successful book of his own, *The Master Key*, that he was not dependent on any other talent either. Neither author nor illustrator seemed distressed, therefore, when *Dot and Tot* did not sell well; perhaps they were even relieved that their collaboration was no guarantee of success.

Baum and Denslow had already decided not to produce any more books together when plans were underway for the production of a musical extravaganza based on *The Wonderful Wizard of Oz*.

With their extensive experience in the theater, it was logical that they would have much to gain by working together on the production. After much bickering, they agreed that Baum would write the libretto, composer Paul Tietjens would write the music, and Denslow would design the costumes and sets. Heated arguments ensued throughout the entire process, about the division of earnings, about the script and staging, acrimony that continued almost until opening day. In spite of the contentious atmosphere surrounding the production, *The Wizard of Oz* opened on Broadway to great acclaim in 1903 and, running as it did for eight years, represented one of the most successful productions of its time. By then, of course, antagonism between Baum and Denslow was so acute that nothing could ever tempt them to collaborate again. They parted company forever.

When he wrote *The Wonderful Wizard of Oz*,

From *The Wizard of Oz* (1900).

Baum did not plan a sequel. Instead, he followed up the idea of a modern American fairy tale with another book: *Baum's American Fairy Tales: Stories of Astonishing Adventures of Boys and Girls with Fairies of their Native Land*. The overwhelming popularity of the Oz book overshadowed this later effort, however, and he eventually yielded to the demands of his readers by publishing a sequel to the first, which he called *The Marvelous Land of Oz* (later retitled *The Land of Oz*). For this book, Baum selected an illustrator named John R. Neill, a far more even-tempered artist than Denslow, and one who did not demand an equal share of the royalties. The success of volume two proved conclusively that Denslow was not an indispensable member of the Oz duet, and John R. Neill illustrated every volume that followed in the series.

Reluctantly, Baum continued to write more installments. In 1910, after completing five books, he tried in vain to abandon the series, terminating all communication with Oz in the final chapter of *The Emerald City of Oz*, but he was persuaded to resume the saga, and finally promised his readers, "as long as you care to read them I shall try to write them." And so he resigned himself to writing a new Oz book each year, completing thirteen sequels before he died in 1919. As it turned out, Baum was no more indispensable to Oz than Denslow: other writers successfully continued the series after his death—Ruth Plumly Thompson (who wrote eighteen), Rachel Cosgrove, and Jack Snow. Even the illustrator, John R. Neill, wrote three of his own.

With so many books earning royalties—including about sixty others written under seven different pseudonyms—Baum became a prosperous man.

He continued to be enterprising in forms of entertainment other than books as well. He purchased an island off the coast of California called Pedloe Island which he planned to convert into a miniature land of Oz for children, a "Disneyland" before its time. The plan never materialized. Moving to Hollywood in 1910 (where he lived in a home he named "Ozcot"), he produced a musical version of *The Tik Tok Man of Oz*, and eventually formed the Oz Film Manufacturing Company to produce motion pictures of the Oz stories. (He completed five.)

Meanwhile, the restless Denslow had moved to New York, divorcing his second wife and marrying for the third time. He occupied himself with a series of projects for children—including *Denslow's Night Before Christmas*; *Denslow's Picture Books*, a series of toy books based on the Crane tradition; and *Denslow's Scarecrow and the Tin Man* (for which he claimed the right because he was joint owner of the copyright to the Oz book). He tried his hand at theatrical projects and briefly created a comic strip called *Billy Bounce*. In 1903 Denslow purchased a mansion on an island in Bermuda, crowned himself King Denslow I, and for three or four months of the year reigned as monarch of his kingdom in the tropics. This prosperous period of his life was short-lived, however. By 1910, his work had become dated and was no longer in demand. He was replaced instead by younger artists whose work was more appropriate to the sophisticated methods of photo-reproduction. His poster style, so much in vogue in the 1890s, had fallen from repute. He was shunned by a new class of professional whose mandate was to judge the suitability of reading material for children: the librarian. "Such books as Denslow's Mother Goose," declared Anne Carroll Moore, who organized the children's division of the New York Public Library, "with a score of others of the comic poster order, should be banished from the sight of impressionable children."

Weary and pressed for funds, Denslow gave up his home in Bermuda and spent his last days working for $25.00 per week at an art agency in New York City. Having returned to drinking and separated from his third wife, he was alone and depressed when he died in 1915. Not even an obituary appeared in the newspapers for which he had worked so many years.

The Broadway success of *The Wizard of Oz* was only the first production of the original book. Two silent films were made, in 1910 and in 1925, to be succeeded by the 1939 film extravaganza starring Judy Garland. In the 1970s, *The Wiz*, a Broadway musical and later a film, placed Dorothy in Harlem rather than Kansas, bringing the story into a contemporary framework that would have delighted the modern Baum. But W. W. Denslow, the very first visitor to Oz, was forgotten. By the 1920s none of his books was in print any longer. When a new edition of *The Wizard of Oz* was printed shortly after 1920, the old worn plates were destroyed and heavy-handed copies of Denslow's illustrations replaced the originals. For the 1944 edition, a new illustrator was selected altogether. It would have been small consolation to the cantankerous illustrator that artists of the 1890s are once again enjoying favor and that today readers are seeking out the original Denslows. The facsimile editions of the original *Oz* currently being reissued would only have represented a bitter reminder of what he already knew to be true. "This world seems to be built on the joke principle," he maintained. "It always has been and I suspect it will always be. . . ."

"The good witch grants Dorothy's wish."
from *The Wizard of Oz* (1900).

Acknowledgments

Snuggled in my father's lap as I sleepily gazed at the pages before me, I was introduced to Winnie-the-Pooh and Piglet for the very first time. These are precious memories: the light-hearted stories and kindly pictures, my father's soft voice as he read aloud to me under the lamplight, the marvelous sense of well-being. My father died just before my twelfth birthday, but the recollection of these loving moments represents his enduring gift to me, and this book was surely inspired by those memories.

The others in my family have continued to share their love for books with me, and their contributions are felt throughout this entire volume: my mother, Dorothy Meyer, happily aided me with research on Edward Lear, and my brother, Karl Meyer, offered intelligent advice based on his own sound knowledge of the subject. Their support and enthusiasm emboldened me throughout the entire course of the writing, and to them I am most grateful.

When I first considered writing this book four years ago, I turned to Beverly Sanders for assistance in research. To her I extend my heartfelt thanks for her dedication in locating solid reference material, so much of which had been buried in dusty archives.

The bibliography here in this book testifies to the number of scholars already drawn to the subject of children's book illustration. Several of the illustrators in this volume have been favorites for some time—Beatrix Potter and Edward Lear, for example—but others have been relatively ignored. It is, therefore, to the earnest students of the more neglected subjects to whom I am particularly indebted, especially to Michael Patrick Hearn and Douglas Greene for their work on W. W. Denslow, to Rawle Knox for his book on Ernest Shepard, and to Rodney Engen for his fine biography of Kate Greenaway. Without them, these artists would undoubtedly have been deprived of the treatment they deserve.

From the outset we had decided that it was imperative to achieve the very best reproductions in order to present the illustrators to greatest advantage. Despite the advancements in color reproduction achieved during the nineteenth century, the subtle paintings of several illustrators included here demanded twentieth-century ingenuity. To obtain the finest reproduction quality, therefore, we made every effort to locate the original paintings of Kate Greenaway, Beatrix Potter, Arthur Rackham, Edmund Dulac, and N. C. Wyeth, a monumental task that was undertaken cheerfully by two professionals. I extend my thanks, first to Sybille Millard, who performed the initial picture research, and to Eric Himmel at Harry N. Abrams, Inc., who went well beyond the call of duty to track down a most impressive array of original art. Thanks are also given to several individuals who cordially gave assistance in acquiring pictures: Jean Gilmore at the Brandywine River Museum; Kenneth Lohf and Rudolph Ellenbogen at the Rare Book and Manuscript Library at Columbia University; Angeline Moscatt at the Donnell Library Center of the New York Public Library; Barbara Edwards; Jennifer Luithlen at Hodder & Stoughton, Limited; George T. McWhorter at the Rare Books and Special Collections of the University of Louisville Library; James Hamilton at the Mappin Art Gallery, Sheffield, England; Joseph T. Rankin at the Spencer Collection of the New York Public Library; Susan Coley at Frederick Warne (Publishers) Ltd.; and Colin White.

While I was lost in the nineteenth century, captured by the fantastic images of another time, Edith Pavese at Abrams supervised the events of the real world, providing pressure where required and reassurance where needed, and to her I am most grateful.

Assembling all the pieces, integrating them into a cohesive and sensitive visual delight, Patrick Cunningham at Abrams executed a design worthy of William Morris's highest praise.

And, to my dear friend and business partner, Marsha Melnick, I am ever thankful for her advice, her encouragement, and, most of all, for her good humor throughout the many months I spent at the typewriter.

S.E.M.

Bibliography

Allen, Douglas and Allen, Douglas, Jr. *N. C. Wyeth*. New York: Crown Publishers, 1972.

Anscombe, Isabelle and Gere, Charlotte. *Arts & Crafts in Britain and America*. New York: Rizzoli International Publications, Inc., 1978.

Ariès, Philippe. *Centuries of Childhood*. New York: Vintage Books, 1962.

Bader, Barbara. *American Picturebooks from Noah's Ark to The Beast Within*. New York: Macmillan Co., Inc., 1976.

Billington, Elizabeth T., ed. *The Randolph Caldecott Treasury*. London and New York: Frederick Warne & Co., 1978.

Blount, Margaret. *Animal Land*. New York: Avon Books, 1974.

Darton, F.J. Harvey. *Children's Books in England*. Cambridge: Cambridge University Press, 1958, 1982.

Davidson, Angus. *Edward Lear*. Port Washington, N.Y.: Kennikat Press, Inc., 1938, 1968.

De Maré, Eric. *The Victorian Woodblock Illustrators*. New York: The Sandstone Press, 1981.

Engen, Rodney K. *Kate Greenaway*. New York: Schocken Books, 1981.

——. *Randolph Caldecott*. London: Oresko Books, 1976.

——. *Walter Crane as a Book Illustrator*. New York: St. Martin's Press, 1975.

Gardner, Martin and Nye, Russel B. *The Wizard of Oz and Who He Was*. East Lansing: Michigan State University Press, 1957.

Gattegno, Jean. *Lewis Carroll*. New York: Thomas Y. Crowell, 1974.

Gettings, Fred. *Arthur Rackham*. New York: Macmillan Co., Inc., 1976.

Greene, Douglas G. and Hearn, Michael Patrick. *W.W. Denslow*. Clarke Historical Library, 1976.

Guiliano, Edward, ed. *Lewis Carroll Observed*. New York: Clarkson N. Potter, 1976.

Hudson, Derek. *Arthur Rackham*. New York: Charles Scribner's Sons, 1960.

——. *Lewis Carroll: An Illustrated Biography*. New York: New American Library, 1977.

Hürlimann, Bettina. *Three Centuries of Children's Books in Europe*. Cleveland and New York: The World Publishing Company, 1968.

Hutchins, Michael, ed. *Yours Pictorially*. New York and London: Frederick Warne & Co., Ltd., 1976.

King, Arthur and Stuart, A.F. *The House of Warne*. London and New York: Frederick Warne & Co., Ltd., 1965.

Knox, Rawle, ed. *The Work of E.H. Shepard*. New York: Schocken Books, 1980.

Lane, Margaret. *The Magic Years of Beatrix Potter*. London and New York: Frederick Warne & Co., Ltd., 1978.

——. *The Tale of Beatrix Potter*. London and New York: Frederick Warne & Co., Ltd., 1946.

Lanes, Selma G. *Down the Rabbit Hole*. New York: Atheneum, 1972.

Larkin, David, ed. *Dulac*. New York: Peacock Press/Bantam, 1975.

——. *Kay Nielsen*. New York: Peacock Press/Bantam, 1975.

Lehmann, John. *Edward Lear and His World*. New York: Charles Scribner's Sons, 1977.

Linder, Enid and Leslie, eds. *The Art of Beatrix Potter*. London and New York: Frederick Warne & Co., 1955.

Linder, Leslie. *A History of the Writings of Beatrix Potter*. London and New York: Frederick Warne & Co., 1971.

——, ed. *The Journal of Beatrix Potter*. London and New York: Frederick Warne & Co., Ltd., 1966.

McLean, Ruari, ed. *The Reminiscences of Edmund Evans*. Oxford: Oxford University Press, 1967.

Mahoney, B.E. et al. *Illustrators of Children's Books, 1744–1945*. Hornbook, 1965.

Meyer, Susan E. *America's Great Illustrators*. New York: Harry N. Abrams, 1978.

Milne, A.A. *It's Too Late Now*. New York: E.P. Dutton, 1939.

Milne, Christopher. *The Enchanted Places*. New York: E.P. Dutton & Co., 1975.

Muir, Percy. *Victorian Illustrated Books*. New York: Praeger Publishers, 1971.

Noakes, Vivien. *Edward Lear*. London: Collins, 1968.

Ovendon, Graham and Davis, John. *The Illustrators of Alice in Wonderland*. New York: St. Martin's Press, 1979.

Pierpont Morgan Library. *Early Children's Books and Their Illustration*. Toronto: Oxford University Press, 1975.

Pitz, Henry C. *Howard Pyle*. New York: Clarkson Potter, 1975.

——. *Illustrating Children's Books*. New York: Watson-Guptill Publications, 1963.

Price, R.G.G. *A History of Punch*. London: Collins, 1957.

Pudney, John. *Lewis Carroll and His World*. New York: Charles Scribner's Sons, 1976.

Reid, Forrest. *Illustrators of the Eighteen Sixties*. New York: Dover, 1975.

Sale, Roger. *Fairy Tales and After*. Cambridge and London: Harvard University Press, 1978.

Sarzano, Frances. *Sir John Tenniel*. New York: Pellegrini & Cudahy, 1936.

Shepard, Ernest H. *Drawn from Life*. London: Methuen & Co. Ltd., 1961.

——. *Drawn from Memory*. Philadelphia: Lippincott Company, 1957.

Spencer, Isobel. *Walter Crane*. New York: Macmillan Publishing Co., Inc., 1975.

Spielmann, M.H. *History of Punch*. London: Cassell, 1895.

Spielmann, M.H. and Layard, G.S. *Kate Greenaway*. London and New York: Benjamin Blom, 1905, 1968.

Whalley, Joyce Irene. *Cobwebs to Catch Flies*. Berkeley and Los Angeles: University of California Press, 1975.

White, Colin. *Edmund Dulac*. New York: Charles Scribner's Sons, 1976.

Wyeth, Betsy James, ed. *The Wyeths: The Intimate Correspondence of N.C. Wyeth*. Boston: Gambit, 1971.

Index

Credits